EASY
MEALS
— IN —
MINUTES

COOKING AT HOME HAS NEVER BEEN EASIER

DELICIOUS RECIPES WITH EVERYDAY
INGREDIENTS FOR QUICK-FIX MEALS

Cookbook Resources, LLC.
Highland Village, Texas

Easy Meals-in-Minutes
Cooking at Home Has Never Been Easier
Delicious Recipes with Everyday Ingredients for Quick-fix Meals

Printed March 2013

International Standard Book Number: 978-1-59769-199-4

Library of Congress Control Number:

Library of Congress Cataloging-in-Publication Data

Cover and design by Rasor Design

Illustrations by Nancy Griffith and Nancy Bohanan

Edited, Designed, Published and Manufactured in the United States of America by
Cookbook Resources, LLC
541 Doubletree Drive
Highland Village, Texas 75077

Toll free 866-229-2665

www.cookbookresources.com

cookbook resources LLC
Bringing Family and Friends to the Table

EASY MEALS-IN-MINUTES

"What's for Dinner?" is an age-old question we hear almost every day, which should let us know how important it is to the people who ask the question. When we think we're too busy, we stop at McDonald's, the pizza place or other fast food drive-through to pick up our meal or we call for delivery on the phone.

In the same amount of time you spend driving to the drive-through window or waiting for delivery, you can use the simple recipes in *Easy Meals-in-Minutes* to create a meal for your family that is better for them and makes them happier!

Most people, especially kids, don't show how much they appreciate the efforts of the cook, but they feel it and they know it. It may not surface until they are away from home for the first time or until the first year of marriage and a new life, but they will always remember family meals.

Everyone remembers family meals and the kitchen table! Memories are made there, people become families and kids get their starts to secure futures.

We all have enough time to cook at least one meal a day for the well-being and nourishment of our families and friends. We nourish our bodies and just as importantly we nourish our souls and feel blessed.

Easy Meals-in-Minutes makes any cook's job easier, more rewarding and more satisfying! Try it and enjoy the blessings of family and friends around the table.

—*The Editors*

CONTENTS

Get quick starts for snacks and even use snacks for meals.

Add a little fun to everyday drinks.

Get a fast, easy start for a good day.

Use simple solutions to make life easier.

Comforting, hearty meals make everyone feel at home.

Put great-tasting, healthy freshness on your table.

CONTENTS

FAMILY MEALS

More statistical studies are finding that family meals play a significant role in childhood development. Children who eat with their families four or more nights per week are healthier, make better grades in school, score higher on aptitude tests and are less likely to have problems with drugs.

Maybe the little things, like having a meal at the table, are more important than we realize. Maybe these little things are the things we never forget… our memories and family traditions.

DEDICATION

Cookbook Resources' mission is

Bringing Family and Friends to the Table.

We recognize the importance of shared meals as a means of building family bonds with memories and traditions that will last a lifetime. At mealtimes we share more than food. We share ourselves.

This cookbook is dedicated with gratitude and respect to all those who show their love by making home-cooked meals and bringing family and friends to the table.

GREAT MEMORIES BEGIN WITH GREAT FOOD.

APPETIZERS

**Get quick starts for snacks
and even use snacks for meals.**

Aᴘᴘᴇᴛɪᴢᴇʀꜱ Cᴏɴᴛᴇɴᴛꜱ

BLACK BEAN SALSA

1 (15 ounce) can black beans, drained
4 - 6 green onions with tops, diced
½ - ¾ cup snipped fresh cilantro leaves
1 - 2 cloves garlic, minced
1 tablespoon oil
1 teaspoon fresh lime juice

☐ Mix all ingredients and refrigerate before serving. Serves 4.

CONFETTI DIP

1 (15 ounce) can whole kernel corn, drained
1 (15 ounce) can kidney or pinto beans, drained
⅓ cup Italian salad dressing
1 (16 ounce) jar salsa

☐ Combine all ingredients. Refrigerate several hours before serving. Serve with chips.

Vegetables like carrots, celery and potatoes that have become limp can regain much of their crispness if soaked in ice water for at least 1 hour.

FRESH TOMATO SALSA

4 medium tomatoes
2 - 4 green onions with tops
1 - 2 jalapeno peppers
½ cup fresh cilantro
Juice of 1 small lime
1 teaspoon sugar

☐ Dice tomatoes and onions in large bowl to save juices. Wear gloves to remove stems and seeds from jalapenos and dry with paper towels. Dice jalapenos and add to tomatoes.

☐ Add all other ingredients plus 1 teaspoon salt. Refrigerate for about 15 to 20 minutes.

☐ Remove from refrigerator and taste. If tomatoes are too tart, add a little sugar to sweeten. Refrigerate for about 30 minutes more to blend flavors and serve. Makes 1½ cups.

Family meals help children learn the basics of good nutrition and how to take care of themselves. Family meals don't have to big deals, but can be simple meals with basic nutrition. Children learn how to strive for good health and about being responsible for themselves. Family meals provide a time for family traditions and family memories to grow.

BEAN DIP

1 (15 ounce) can Mexican chili beans
½ teaspoon ground cumin
½ teaspoon chili powder
¼ teaspoon dried oregano

☐ Drain beans and set aside 2 tablespoons liquid. Combine beans, the set aside liquid, cumin, chili powder and oregano in food processor. Pulse several times until beans are partially chopped.

☐ Pour mixture into small saucepan and cook over low heat, stirring constantly until thoroughly hot. Serves 4 to 6.

SPEEDY BROCCOLI-CHEESE DIP

1 (10 ounce) can broccoli-cheese soup
1 (10 ounce) package frozen, chopped broccoli, thawed
½ cup sour cream
2 teaspoons of dijon-style mustard

☐ In saucepan, combine soup, broccoli, sour cream, ½ teaspoon salt and mustard and mix well. Heat and serve hot. Serves 4.

BROCCOLI DIP

¾ cup (1½ sticks) butter
2 cups thinly sliced celery
1 onion, finely chopped
3 tablespoons flour
1 (10 ounce) can cream of chicken soup
1 (10 ounce) box chopped broccoli, thawed
1 (5 ounce) garlic cheese roll, cut in chunks
Wheat crackers or corn chips

☐ Melt butter in skillet and saute celery and onion, but do not brown; stir in flour.

☐ Spoon into small slow cooker, stir in remaining ingredients and mix well.

☐ Cover and cook on LOW for 2 to 3 hours and stir several times.

☐ Serve with veggies, crackers or chips. Serves 6 to 8.

Dark green and deep yellow vegetables such as spinach, broccoli, carrots and sweet potatoes have the highest nutritional value.

VEGGIE DIP

1 (10 ounce) package frozen, chopped spinach, thawed, well drained
1 (16 ounce) carton sour cream
1 (1 ounce) packet dry vegetable soup mix
1 bunch fresh green onions with tops, chopped
¾ cup chopped pecans, optional

☐ Squeeze spinach between paper towels to completely remove excess moisture.

☐ Combine spinach, sour cream, soup mix and green onions in bowl.

☐ Refrigerate for several hours before serving. Add chopped pecans if you want a little crunch. Serves 6 to 8.

SASSY ONION DIP

Plain and simple, but great!

1 (8 ounce) package cream cheese, softened
1 (8 ounce) carton sour cream
½ cup chili sauce
1 (1 ounce) packet onion soup mix
1 tablespoon lemon juice
Raw vegetables

☐ Beat cream cheese in bowl until fluffy. Add sour cream, chili sauce, soup mix and lemon juice and mix well.

☐ Cover and refrigerate. Serve with strips of raw zucchini, celery, carrots, etc. Serves 8.

ROASTED RED PEPPER-ARTICHOKE DIP

1 (14 ounce) can artichoke hearts, drained, chopped
1 cup mayonnaise
1½ cups shredded mozzarella cheese
½ cup roasted red peppers, drained, chopped

☐ Preheat oven to 350°.

☐ Combine all ingredients in bowl and place in sprayed 8-inch baking dish. Bake for 25 minutes or until thoroughly hot. Serves 4 to 6.

PEPPER POT-BEAN DIP

1 (15 ounce) can refried beans
1 (16 ounce) package cubed Mexican Velveeta® cheese
½ cup (1 stick) butter
1 teaspoon garlic powder

☐ Combine all ingredients in large double boiler. Heat on low, stirring often, until cheese and butter melt. Serve hot in chafing dish. Makes 1½ pints.

AVOCADO OLÉ

3 large ripe avocados, mashed
1 tablespoon fresh lemon juice
1 (1 ounce) packet onion soup mix
1 (8 ounce) carton sour cream

☐ Mix avocados with lemon juice in bowl and blend in soup mix and sour cream. Makes 1 pint.

INDIAN CORN DIP

1 pound lean ground beef
1 onion, finely chopped
1 (15 ounce) can whole kernel corn, drained
1 (16 ounce) jar salsa
1 (1 pound) package cubed Velveeta® cheese
Tortilla chips

☐ Brown and cook beef in skillet on low heat for about 10 minutes and drain.

☐ Transfer to slow cooker and add onion, corn, salsa and cheese; mix well.

☐ Cover and cook on LOW for 1 hour, remove lid and stir. Serve with tortilla chips and veggie sticks. Serves 6 to 8.

HAMBURGER DIP

Men love this meaty, spicy dip.

1 pound lean ground beef
1 tablespoon dried minced onion
1 teaspoon dried oregano leaves
1 tablespoon chili powder
1 teaspoon sugar
1 (10 ounce) can diced tomatoes and green chilies
¼ cup chili sauce
1 (16 ounce) package cubed Mexican Velveeta® cheese
Chips or crackers

☐ Brown ground beef in large skillet, drain and transfer to sprayed slow cooker.

☐ Add remaining ingredients plus ½ cup to 1 cup water and stir well.

☐ Cover and cook on LOW for 1 hour 30 minutes to 2 hours. Stir once or twice during cooking time. Add a little salt, if desired. Serve hot with chips or crackers. Serves 8 to 10.

Preliminary research indicates that 8 to 10 glasses of water a day could significantly ease back and joint pain for up to 80% of sufferers.

CHICKEN-ENCHILADA DIP

2 pounds boneless, skinless chicken thighs, cubed
1 (10 ounce) can enchilada sauce
1 (7 ounce) can diced green chilies, drained
1 small onion, finely chopped
1 large red bell pepper, seeded, finely chopped
2 (8 ounce) packages cream cheese, cubed
1 (16 ounce) package shredded American cheese
Tortilla chips

☐ Place chicken thighs, enchilada sauce, green chilies, onion and bell pepper in sprayed slow cooker.

☐ Cover and cook on LOW for 4 to 6 hours. Stir in cream cheese and American cheese and cook an additional 30 minutes until cheese is melted. Stir several times during cooking. Serve with tortilla chips. Serves 8 to 10.

ARTICHOKE-BACON DIP

1 (14 ounce) jar marinated artichoke hearts, drained, chopped
1 cup mayonnaise
2 teaspoons Worcestershire sauce
5 slices bacon, cooked crisp, crumbled

☐ Preheat oven to 350°.

☐ Combine all ingredients in large bowl. Pour into sprayed 8-inch baking dish. Bake for 12 minutes. Makes 1½ cups.

CHEESY BACON DIP

2 (8 ounce) packages cream cheese, softened
1 (8 ounce) package shredded colby Jack cheese
2 tablespoons mustard
2 teaspoons Worcestershire sauce
4 fresh green onions with tops, sliced
1 pound bacon, cooked, crumbled
Rye or pumpernickel bread

☐ Cut cream cheese into cubes and place in 4 to 5-quart slow cooker.

☐ Add colby Jack cheese, mustard, white Worcestershire, green onions and ¼ teaspoon salt.

☐ Cover and cook on LOW for 1 hour and stir to melt cheese.

☐ Stir in crumbled bacon. Serve with small-size rye bread or toasted pumpernickel bread. Serves 6 to 8.

Raised flower beds or large containers make perfect small gardens for apartment or townhome dwellers or those with small yards. Grow your own tomatoes, peppers, onions or lettuce for the best flavor and best price. Fresh herbs are also great for container gardening. You'll feel a real sense of pride when you eat healthy produce you grow yourself.

PEPPERONI DIP

1 (6 ounce) package pepperoni
1 bunch fresh green onions, thinly sliced
½ red bell pepper, finely chopped
1 medium tomato, finely chopped
1 (14 ounce) jar pizza sauce
1½ cups shredded mozzarella cheese
1 (8 ounce) package cream cheese, cubed
Wheat crackers or tortilla chips

☐ Chop pepperoni into small pieces and place in small slow cooker.

☐ Add onion, bell pepper, tomato and pizza sauce and stir well.

☐ Cover and cook on LOW for 2 hours 30 minutes to 3 hours 30 minutes.

☐ Add mozzarella and cream cheese and stir until they melt.

☐ Serve with wheat crackers or tortilla chips. Serves 4 to 6.

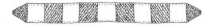

The next best thing to your own garden is a farmers' market. Find one near you and also look for farms where you can pick your own produce. Not only will kids like picking their own foods, but you'll save money and improve the quality of food you put on the table.

FIVE-LAYER DIP

1 (15 ounce) can refried beans
1 (8 ounce) carton sour cream
1 (1 ounce) packet ranch dressing mix
1 cup diced tomatoes, drained
1 (4 ounce) can diced green chilies, drained
½ cup shredded cheddar cheese
½ cup shredded Monterey Jack cheese
1 (2 ounce) can chopped black olives, drained
Chips

☐ Spread beans on 10-inch serving platter or 9-inch glass pie pan.

☐ Combine and mix sour cream and dressing mix in bowl and spread over beans.

☐ In separate bowl, combine tomatoes and green chilies and spread over sour cream.

☐ Next, sprinkle both cheeses over tomatoes and green chilies. Last, sprinkle olives over top. Refrigerate. Serve with chips. Serves 6 to 8.

SPICY HAM DIP

2 (8 ounce) packages cream cheese, softened
2 (6 ounce) cans deviled ham
1 heaping tablespoon horseradish
¼ cup minced onion

☐ Beat cream cheese in bowl until creamy. Add remaining ingredients. Refrigerate. Makes 1½ pints.

UNBELIEVABLE CRAB DIP

1 (6 ounce) can white crabmeat, drained, flaked
1 (8 ounce) package cream cheese, softened
½ cup (1 stick) butter, sliced
2 tablespoons white cooking wine

☐ Combine crabmeat, cream cheese, butter and wine in small, sprayed slow cooker.

☐ Cover and cook on LOW for 1 hour and gently stir to combine all ingredients. Serve from cooker with chips or crackers. Serves 4 to 6.

EASY TUNA DIP

1 (6 ounce) can tuna, drained
1 (1 ounce) packet Italian salad dressing mix
1 (8 ounce) carton sour cream
2 green onions with tops, chopped

☐ Combine all ingredients in bowl and mix well. Refrigerate for several hours before serving. Makes 1½ cups.

The Atlanta bluefin tuna can live to up to 50 years, grow as long as 15 feet and weigh more than 1000 pounds. Almost all tuna species have been overfished and are threatened.

BREEZY PINEAPPLE ISLAND SPREAD

2 (8 ounce) packages cream cheese, softened
1 (8 ounce) carton sour cream
1 (8 ounce) can crushed pineapple, drained
½ cup finely chopped pecans

☐ Beat cream cheese and sour cream in bowl until creamy. Fold in pineapple and pecans and mix well. Refrigerate. Makes 1½ pints.

WALNUT-CHEESE SPREAD

¾ cup chopped walnuts
1 (16 ounce) package shredded cheddar cheese
3 green onions with tops, chopped
½ - ¾ cup mayonnaise
½ teaspoon liquid smoke
Crackers

☐ Preheat oven to 250°.

☐ Roast walnuts for 10 minutes.

☐ Combine all ingredients in bowl and refrigerate overnight. Spread on assorted crackers. Serves 8.

DELUXE PIMENTO CHEESE SPREAD

1 (16 ounce) package shredded sharp cheddar cheese
2 (4 ounce) jars diced pimentos, drained
1 cup salsa
¼ teaspoon freshly ground black pepper
3 tablespoons mayonnaise

☐ Combine cheese, pimentos and salsa in large bowl and mix well. Add pepper and mayonnaise and blend well.

☐ Refrigerate. Spread on wheat crackers or use to make sandwiches. Serves 6.

PARTY CHEESE FINGERS

12 slices whole wheat bread
2½ cups shredded sharp cheddar cheese
⅓ cup chili sauce
¾ cup mayonnaise
½ cup chopped olives
½ cup chopped pecans
1 (2 ounce) jar chopped pimentos, drained
¼ teaspoon garlic powder

☐ Trim crusts off bread.

☐ Combine all remaining ingredients in bowl and mix well.

☐ Spread mixture on 6 slices of bread and top with remaining bread slices. Cut each sandwich into 3 strips and refrigerate. Serves 8 to 10.

Smoked Oyster Spread

1 (8 ounce) package cream cheese, softened
3 tablespoons mayonnaise
1 (3.5 ounce) can smoked oysters, chopped
½ teaspoon onion salt
2 tablespoons grated parmesan cheese
Crackers

☐ Beat cream cheese and mayonnaise in bowl until creamy. Add oysters, onion salt and cheese. Mix well and spread on crackers. Serves 6.

Easy Cheese Fondue

The soup keeps this from getting stringy.

1 cup dry white wine
2 cloves garlic, minced
1 (16 ounce) package shredded Swiss cheese
¼ cup flour
1 (10 ounce) can condensed cheddar cheese soup
French bread, cubed

☐ In fondue pot, mix wine and garlic and cook over medium heat until garlic is tender. Add cheese and melt, stirring constantly.

☐ Add flour and condensed soup, continue stirring and cooking until well blended with other ingredients. Makes about 4 cups.

SPINACH-CHEESE SQUARES

¼ cup (½ stick) butter
1 cup flour
3 eggs
1 cup milk
1 teaspoon baking powder
1 teaspoon dry mustard
1 (10 ounce) package frozen spinach, thawed, drained*
1 (8 ounce) package shredded mozzarella cheese
1 (8 ounce) package shredded cheddar cheese

☐ Preheat oven to 350°.

☐ Melt butter in 9 x 13-inch baking dish in oven.

☐ Combine flour, eggs, milk, 1 teaspoon salt, baking powder and mustard in bowl and mix well. Add spinach and cheeses and mix well. Pour into pan and bake for 30 minutes.

☐ When set, cut into squares and serve warm. Serves 8.

*TIP: Squeeze spinach between paper towels to completely remove excess moisture.

Freezer Tip:

Don't freeze items with a lot of dairy products in them. Items like milk, cream, cream cheese and mayonnaise don't freeze well and will curdle or separate when they are thawed out or reheated.

CHEESY VEGETABLE SQUARES

1 (8 ounce) package refrigerated crescent rolls
1 (8 ounce) package cream cheese, softened
½ cup mayonnaise
1 (1.4 ounce) packet ranch salad dressing mix
1 cup broccoli slaw
1½ cups shredded cheddar cheese

☐ Preheat oven to 350°.

☐ Press crescent roll dough into 9 x 13-inch baking dish and press perforations to seal. Bake for 12 minutes or until dough is golden brown; cool.

☐ Beat cream cheese, mayonnaise and ranch dressing mix in bowl; spread over crust. Sprinkle with broccoli slaw and top with cheese; gently press into cream cheese mixture.

☐ Cover and refrigerate at least 3 hours. Cut into squares to serve. Serves 6.

QUICK CHEESY BROCCOLI QUESADILLAS

1 (8 ounce) package shredded cheddar cheese
1 (10 ounce) package frozen chopped broccoli, thawed, drained
⅓ cup salsa
8 (6 inch) flour tortillas

☐ In bowl, combine cheese, chopped broccoli and salsa and mix well. Spoon about ¼ cup cheese-broccoli mixture onto 4 tortillas. Top each with remaining tortillas.

☐ Spray non-stick skillet with cooking spray. Carefully place each quesadilla on skillet and cook over medium for 3 to 5 minutes per side, or until tortillas are light brown. Cut into wedges and serve immediately. Serves 4.

TEX-MEX NACHOS

About 35 tortilla chips
1 (8 ounce) package shredded Monterey Jack cheese
2 tablespoons sliced jalapeno peppers
⅛ teaspoon chili powder
Bean Dip (recipe on page 11)

☐ Arrange chips in 9 x 13-inch baking dish and sprinkle with cheese. Top with jalapeno peppers and sprinkle with chili powder.

☐ Broil until cheese melts. Serve with Bean Dip. Serves 4 to 6.

GRILLED TOMATO-BASIL FLATBREAD

Extra-virgin olive oil
1 (11 ounce) package flatbread
2 large tomatoes, seeded, diced, drained
1 bunch green onions with tops
¼ cup basil
1 cup shredded mozzarella cheese

☐ Spread light coating of olive oil on both sides of flatbread. Spread tomatoes, onions and basil on top of each flatbread. Cover with cheese.

☐ Place over low heat on grill and cook until cheese melts. Cut into pieces or serve whole. Serves 4.

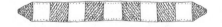

GARLIC-STUFFED MUSHROOMS

1 tablespoon extra virgin olive oil
2 tablespoons butter
¾ cup Italian breadcrumbs
3 cloves garlic, peeled, minced
¼ teaspoon oregano
Seasoned salt
Cracked black pepper
18 large white mushrooms, stems removed

☐ Preheat oven to 400°.

☐ Heat olive oil and butter in skillet over medium heat. Add breadcrumbs, stir to coat and cook about 5 minutes.

☐ Add garlic, oregano, seasoned salt and fresh ground black pepper and saute until garlic is translucent.

☐ Stuff each mushroom with breadcrumb mixture and place in sprayed 9 x 13-inch baking pan. Bake for 20 minutes or until mushrooms are tender. Serve hot or at room temperature. Serves 8 to 10.

SHORTCUT BRUSCHETTA

1 (16 ounce) loaf Italian bread
Butter
1 (15 once) can Italian-style diced tomatoes, drained
2 - 3 cloves garlic, peeled, minced
3 - 4 tablespoons minced plus several whole leaves fresh basil
1 tablespoon extra virgin olive oil
1 teaspoon balsamic vinegar

☐ Preheat oven to 300°.

☐ Slice bread in thick pieces, butter one side and lay, buttered side up on sprayed baking sheet. Bake until slices are crispy.

☐ Combine tomatoes, garlic, minced basil, olive oil, balsamic vinegar, and a dash each of salt and pepper. Stir to mix well.

☐ Place several tablespoons tomato mixture on each bread slice just before serving. Garnish with whole basil leaves. Serves 6 to 8.

Each man, woman and child in the United States eats about 80 tomatoes annually in the form of fresh, processed, chopped, or stewed tomatoes as well as ketchup, sauces, juices and hundreds of consumer products that use tomatoes.

EASY BAKED MOZZARELLA STICKS

1 egg
1 cup Italian-seasoned breadcrumbs
1 (12 ounce) package mozzarella string cheese
½ cup marinara sauce

☐ Preheat oven to 350°.

☐ Beat egg until foamy in small bowl.

☐ In small skillet, cook breadcrumbs over medium heat until light brown, about 5 minutes. Place in shallow bowl.

☐ Dip cheese in egg, then coat completely with breadcrumbs. Place on sprayed, foil-lined baking sheet. Bake for 5 to 6 minutes or until hot. Serve with warmed marinara sauce. Serves 6 to 8.

Cutting up vegetables:

Mince – cut into tiny, irregular pieces about ⅛ inch or less.

Dice – cut into small, uniform pieces about ⅛ to ¼ inch.

Chop – cut into small, irregular pieces about ¼ inch.

Cube – cut into large, uniform pieces, about ½ inch.

GILROY'S BEST BAKED GARLIC

2 large heads elephant garlic or 4 - 6 regular heads garlic
½ cup chicken stock
½ cup white wine
2 tablespoons unsalted butter, melted
Italian bread, sliced

☐ Preheat oven to 300°.

☐ Cut about ½-inch off top of garlic to expose cloves, remove papery skin and discard. Place in small baking dish and pour chicken stock and wine to almost cover garlic.

☐ Pour melted butter into heads and sprinkle with a little salt and pepper. Bake until tender.

☐ Remove garlic, break into cloves and squeeze garlic from each. Spread on Italian bread and serve with sauce from baking dish for dipping. Makes 1 cup.

Equivalent measurements for garlic:

1 bulb garlic = 6 to 8 cloves

2 small cloves garlic = 1 teaspoon minced garlic

2 medium cloves garlic = 1½ teaspoon minced garlic

1 large clove garlic = 1½ to 2 teaspoons minced garlic

1 clove elephant garlic = 2 cloves regular garlic

SWEET AND SOUR MEATBALL BITES

1 (10 ounce) jar sweet and sour sauce
⅓ cup packed brown sugar
¼ cup soy sauce
1 teaspoon garlic powder
1 (28 ounce) package frozen cooked meatballs, thawed
1 (20 ounce) can pineapple chunks, drained

☐ Combine all ingredients in sprayed slow cooker and mix well. Cover and cook on LOW for 5 to 6 hours; stir occasionally. Serves 6.

TIP: This can be served as an appetizer or served over seasoned spaghetti.

ENGLISH MUFFIN PIZZAS

English muffins, halved
Canned or bottled pizza sauce
Sliced salami or pepperoni
Shredded mozzarella or cheddar cheese

☐ Split muffins in half. Spread muffin with canned pizza sauce. Add salami or pepperoni.

☐ Top with cheese and place under broiler until cheese melts and begins to bubble.

TIP: If you want to go all out, add a combination from the following ingredients: cooked chopped onion, cooked chopped green pepper, sliced jalapeno peppers, and/or chopped green or black olives.

SPICY FRANKS

1 cup packed brown sugar
1 cup chili sauce
1 tablespoon red wine vinegar
2 teaspoons soy sauce
2 teaspoons dijon-style mustard
2 (12 ounce) packages frankfurters

☐ Combine brown sugar, chili sauce, vinegar, soy sauce and mustard in small, sprayed slow cooker and mix well. Cut frankfurters diagonally in 1-inch pieces. Stir in frankfurters.

☐ Cover and cook on LOW for 1 to 2 hours.

☐ Serve from cooker using cocktail picks. Serves 4.

CHEESE WEDGES

1 (10 ounce) package refrigerated biscuits
¼ cup (½ stick) butter, melted
⅓ cup shredded cheddar cheese

☐ Preheat oven to 400°.

☐ Cut each biscuit into 4 wedges. Roll in melted butter, then cheese. Place in sprayed baking pan.

☐ Bake for 10 minutes. Makes 40 wedges.

QUICK-AND-EASY SAUSAGE BALLS

1 pound hot pork sausage
1 (16 ounce) package shredded cheddar cheese
3 cups biscuit mix
⅓ cup milk

☐ Preheat oven to 375°.

☐ Combine all ingredients in bowl and form into small balls. If dough is a little too sticky, add a tablespoon more biscuit mix.

☐ Bake for 13 to 15 minutes. Makes 20 to 28 balls.

MINI REUBENS

½ cup Thousand Island dressing
24 slices party rye bread
½ pound deli thinly sliced corned beef
1⅓ cups chopped sauerkraut, well drained
1 (12 ounce) package Swiss cheese slices

☐ Preheat oven to 375°.

☐ Spread dressing on each slice of bread. Place 1 slice corned beef on bread and top with sauerkraut. Cut cheese same size as bread and place over sauerkraut.

☐ Place open-face sandwiches on baking sheet. Bake for 10 minutes or until cheese melts. Serves 12 to 15.

CHEESE SQUARES

1 (16 ounce) package cubed Velveeta® cheese
1 cup finely chopped nuts
3 - 5 teaspoons hot sauce
Crackers

☐ Melt cheese in top of double boiler over hot water. Stir in nuts and hot sauce and mix well.

☐ Pour into sprayed 9 x 13-inch pan and refrigerate until firm.

☐ Cut into squares and serve with crackers. Makes 3 cups.

BACON-OYSTER BITES

1 (5 ounce) can smoked oysters, drained, chopped
⅔ cup herb-seasoned stuffing mix, crushed
8 slices bacon, halved, partially cooked

☐ Combine oysters, stuffing mix and ¼ cup water in bowl. Add another teaspoon water if mixture seems too dry.

☐ Form into balls with about 1 tablespoon mixture for each. Wrap half slice bacon around each and secure with toothpick.

☐ Cook on sprayed, preheated grill over medium fire until grill marks show, about 5 to 8 minutes. Turn and repeat. Cook until bacon is crisp. Serves 6 to 8.

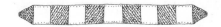

CRAB BITES

This recipe is a scrumptious dish. Serve as hors d'oeuvres or luncheon sandwich.

1 (7 ounce) can crab
1 cup (2 sticks) butter, softened
1 (5 ounce) jar sharp Old English cheese
½ teaspoon garlic salt or seasoned salt
2 tablespoons mayonnaise
2 dashes Worcestershire sauce
6 English muffins, split

☐ Preheat oven to 400°.

☐ Combine crab, butter, cheese, garlic salt, mayonnaise and Worcestershire sauce into paste in bowl. Spread on muffins.

☐ Bake for 10 to 15 minutes or until brown. Each muffin may be cut into 8 bite-size pieces or left whole as an open-face sandwich. Serves 6 to 8.

If you don't have a garlic press, put a clove between two pieces of wax paper and press the bottom of a glass to flatten the clove. You can also use a rubber mallet or flat side of a large knife. Mashing or pressing garlic releases more flavor than slicing or mincing.

TUNA MELT SNACK

1 (10 ounce) package frozen spinach, drained
2 (6 ounce) cans white tuna in water, drained, flaked
¾ cup mayonnaise
1½ cups shredded mozzarella cheese, divided

☐ Preheat oven to 350°.

☐ Squeeze spinach between paper towels to completely remove excess moisture.

☐ Combine spinach, tuna, mayonnaise and 1 cup cheese in large bowl and mix well.
Spoon into sprayed pie pan and bake for 15 minutes.

☐ Remove from oven and sprinkle remaining cheese over top. Bake for additional
5 minutes. Makes 1½ pints.

*Fish like salmon, tuna and mackerel are considered
fatty fish, but are still thought of as healthy and
nutritional. It is thought that eating fish helps to
prevent heart disease and even aids in preventing
diseases like Alzheimer's and strokes.*

RASPBERRY-GLAZED WINGS

¾ cup seedless raspberry jam
¼ cup cider vinegar
¼ cup soy sauce
1 teaspoon garlic powder
16 whole chicken wings

☐ Preheat oven to 350°.

☐ Combine jam, vinegar, soy sauce, garlic powder and 1 teaspoon pepper in saucepan. Bring to a boil; boil for 1 minute.

☐ Cut chicken wings into 3 sections and discard wing tips. Place wings in large bowl, add raspberry mixture and toss to coat. Cover and refrigerate for 4 hours.

☐ Line 10 x 15-inch baking pan with sprayed foil. Use slotted spoon to place wings in pan and reserve marinade.

☐ Bake for 30 minutes and turn once. Cook reserved marinade for 10 minutes, brush over wings and bake for an additional 25 minutes. Serves 6 to 8.

Buffalo wings are usually credited to the Anchor Bar in Buffalo, New York in 1964. Instead of using chicken wings for stock, Teressa Bellisimo, the owner's wife, deep-fried chicken wings and tossed them in a spicy, hot cayenne sauce. Today buffalo wings are a must for football and sports parties.

HONEY-SPICED WINGS

1½ cups flour
18 - 20 chicken wings
¼ cup (½ stick) butter
¾ cup honey
⅔ cup chili sauce

☐ Preheat oven to 325°. Combine flour and a little salt in shallow bowl and dredge chicken in flour. Melt butter in large skillet and brown wings a few at a time over medium heat.

☐ Place in sprayed 9 x 13-inch baking pan. In small bowl, combine honey and chili sauce, mix well and pour over each wing. Cover and bake for 45 minutes. Serves 8 to 10.

CHICKEN LICKERS

2 white onions, sliced
12 chicken livers
4 strips bacon
⅓ cup sherry

☐ Preheat oven to 350°.

☐ Place onion slices in shallow pan. Top each onion slice with chicken liver and one-third strip bacon. Pour sherry over all.

☐ Bake for about 45 minutes or until bacon is crisp. Baste occasionally with pan drippings. Serves 6 to 10.

PARTY MIX

1 (12 ounce) box Corn Chex®
1 (12 ounce) box Wheat Chex®
1 (12 ounce) box Crispix®
2 cups thin pretzels
2 (12 ounce) cans mixed nuts
1 cup (2 sticks) butter
2 tablespoons garlic powder
2 tablespoons hot sauce
2 tablespoons Worcestershire sauce
2 teaspoons cayenne pepper

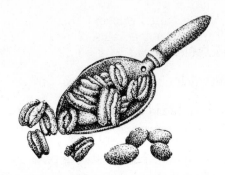

☐ Preheat oven to 250°.

☐ Combine cereals, pretzels and nuts in large roasting pan.

☐ Melt butter in saucepan. Add garlic powder, hot sauce, Worcestershire sauce, cayenne pepper and 2 teaspoons salt; mix well. Pour over cereal mixture and stir.

☐ Bake for 2 hours, stirring every 30 to 45 minutes.

☐ Store in airtight containers. Serves 10 to 14.

CHEESE FONDUE

1 (16 ounce) package cubed Velveeta® cheese
1 (10 ounce) can cheddar cheese soup
1 (6 - 8 inch) round loaf bread

☐ In saucepan, melt cheese with soup. Stir constantly to prevent scorching.

☐ Cut center from bread to form bowl. Cut removed bread into cubes.

☐ Pour cheese fondue into bread bowl and surround bread bowl with bread cubes. Use cubes to dip into fondue. (You can also eat the bread bowl.) Makes 3 cups.

CREAMY ORANGE DIP

1 (6 ounce) can frozen orange juice concentrate, thawed
1 (3.4 ounce) package vanilla instant pudding mix
1 cup milk
¼ cup sour cream
Fresh fruit

☐ Combine orange juice, pudding mix and milk in bowl. Stir with whisk until mixture blends and is smooth.

☐ Stir in sour cream. Cover and refrigerate for at least 2 hours. Serve with fruit. Makes 1 pint.

GINGER FRUIT DIP

1 (3 ounce) package cream cheese, softened
1 (7 ounce) jar marshmallow creme
½ cup mayonnaise
1 teaspoon ground ginger
1 teaspoon grated orange peel
Fresh fruit

☐ Beat cream cheese in bowl on medium speed until smooth. Add marshmallow creme, mayonnaise, ginger and orange peel. Stir until smooth.

☐ Cut fresh fruit into sticks or bite-size pieces and serve with dip. Serves 8.

KAHLUA FRUIT DIP

1 (8 ounce) package cream cheese, softened
1 (8 ounce) carton frozen whipped topping, thawed
⅔ cup packed brown sugar
⅓ cup Kahlua® liqueur
1 (8 ounce) carton sour cream
Fresh fruit

☐ Beat cream cheese in bowl until creamy and fold in whipped topping. Add brown sugar, Kahlua® and sour cream and mix well.

☐ Refrigerate for 24 hours before serving with fresh fruit. Serves 8.

BEVERAGES

**Add a little fun to
everyday drinks.**

BEVERAGES CONTENTS

Do all the good you can,
By all the means you can,
In all the ways you can,
In all the places you can,
At all the times you can,
To all the people you can,
As long as ever you can.

—John Wesley: "John Wesley's Rule"

FRESH LEMONADE

14 - 16 lemons
1½ - 2 cups sugar

☐ Squeeze lemons into large pitcher with 3 quarts cold water. Add sugar and stir well. Serve over cracked ice. Store in refrigerator. Serves 12.

LEMONADE TEA

2 family-size tea bags
½ cup sugar
1 (12 ounce) can frozen lemonade concentrate
1 quart ginger ale, chilled

☐ Steep tea in 3 quarts steaming water and mix with sugar and lemonade. Refrigerate. Add ginger ale just before serving. Serves 8 to 12.

VICTORIAN ICED TEA

4 individual tea bags
¼ cup sugar
1 (12 ounce) can frozen cranberry-raspberry juice concentrate, thawed

☐ Place tea bags in teapot and add 4 cups boiling water. Cover and steep for 5 minutes. Remove and discard tea bags. Add sugar and mix. Refrigerate tea.

☐ Just before serving, combine cranberry-raspberry concentrate and cold water according to concentrate directions in 2½-quart pitcher.

☐ Stir in tea and serve with ice cubes. Makes 2½ quarts.

INSTANT CHAI TEA MIX

2½ cups sugar
2 cups powdered non-dairy creamer
1½ cups unsweetened instant tea
1 cup nonfat dry milk powder
2 teaspoons ground cinnamon
2 teaspoons ground ginger
1 teaspoon ground cardamom
1 teaspoon ground cloves
Vanilla

☐ Combine all ingredients except vanilla in blender or food processor and process until all ingredients mix evenly. Store in airtight jar.

☐ When ready to serve, pour boiling water into mugs and add ½ to 1 teaspoon vanilla plus 2 heaping tablespoons of chai tea mix for each mug. Serve hot. Makes 3 cups of mix.

HOT CRANBERRY CIDER

1½ quarts cranberry juice
1 (12 ounce) can frozen orange juice concentrate, thawed
½ teaspoon cinnamon

☐ Combine cranberry juice, orange juice and 1½ orange juice cans of water in large saucepan. Bring to a boil to blend flavors. Add cinnamon and stir well. Serve hot. Serves 8 to 10.

INSTANT COCOA MIX

1 (8 quart) box dry milk powder
1 (12 ounce) jar non-dairy creamer
1 (16 ounce) can instant chocolate-flavored drink mix, divided
1¼ cups powdered sugar

☐ Combine all ingredients and store in airtight container. To serve, use ¼ cup cocoa mix per 1 cup of hot water. Makes 2 gallons (about 32 cups).

HARVESTTIME COFFEE

1 cup instant coffee granules
4 teaspoons grated lemon peel
4 teaspoons ground cinnamon
1 teaspoon ground cloves

☐ Combine all ingredients in small jar and cover tightly.

☐ For each serving, spoon 2 teaspoons coffee mix into coffee cup and stir in ¾ cup boiling water. Makes 28 cups coffee.

PRALINE COFFEE

3 cups hot brewed coffee
¾ cup half-and-half cream
¾ cup packed light brown sugar
2 tablespoons butter
¾ cup praline liqueur
Whipped cream

☐ Cook coffee, half-and-half cream, brown sugar and butter in large saucepan over medium heat, stirring constantly, until well blended. Do not boil.

☐ Stir in liqueur. Serve in individual mugs topped with whipped cream. Serves 5 to 6.

SPANISH COFFEE

1 tablespoon sugar
4 cups hot, brewed coffee
¾ cup Kahlua® liqueur
Sweetened whipped cream or frozen whipped topping, thawed

▢ Stir sugar into hot coffee and add Kahlua®. Pour into 4 serving cups. Top with whipped cream. Serves 4.

ICY CARAMEL COFFEE

1½ cups brewed coffee, room temperature
½ cup milk
½ cup sugar
2 tablespoons caramel syrup
1 teaspoon chocolate syrup
A few drops vanilla

▢ Mix coffee, milk, sugar, caramel syrup, chocolate syrup, vanilla and a pinch of salt in blender container. Add about 2 to 3 cups ice cubes and blend until creamy. Serves 2 to 3.

Coffee is one of the most popular beverages in the world. It is grown in more than 70 countries worldwide and comes from the seeds of the coffea plant.

SMOOTH MOCHA MUDSLIDE

2 cups cafe mocha liquid coffee creamer
2 tablespoons French roast instant coffee granules
2 cups vanilla ice cream or frozen yogurt

☐ Mix creamer and coffee granules in blender. Add ice cream and about 4 cubes ice and blend until smooth. Serve cold. Serves 3 to 4.

CAPPUCCINO PUNCH

¼ cup instant coffee granules
¾ cup sugar
3 pints milk
1 (1 pint) carton half-and-half cream
1 quart chocolate ice cream, softened
1 quart vanilla ice cream, softened

☐ Combine coffee granules and sugar in bowl and stir in 1 cup boiling water. Cover and refrigerate. When ready to serve, pour chilled coffee mixture into 1-gallon punch bowl.

☐ Stir in milk and half-and-half cream. Add scoops of both ice creams and stir until most of ice cream melts. Serves 16 to 22.

BEST TROPICAL PUNCH

1 (46 ounce) can pineapple juice
1 (46 ounce) can apricot nectar
3 (6 ounce) cans frozen limeade concentrate, thawed
3 quarts ginger ale, chilled

☐ Combine pineapple juice, apricot nectar and limeade in container and refrigerate. When ready to serve, add ginger ale. Makes 1 gallon.

PINA COLADA PUNCH

1 (46 ounce) can pineapple juice, chilled
1 (20 ounce) can crushed pineapple with juice
1 (15 ounce) can cream of coconut
1 (32 ounce) bottle lemon-lime carbonated drink, chilled

☐ Combine all ingredients in punch bowl. Serve over ice cubes. Makes 1 gallon.

Whole fruit is more filling than fruit juices and has more fiber.

SPARKLING WINE PUNCH

6 oranges with peels, thinly sliced
1 cup sugar
2 (750 ml) bottles dry white wine
3 (750 ml) bottles sparkling wine, chilled

☐ Place orange slices in large plastic or glass container and sprinkle with sugar. Add white wine, cover and refrigerate for at least 8 hours. When ready to serve, stir in sparkling wine. Makes 1 gallon.

CHAMPAGNE PUNCH

1 (750 ml) bottle champagne, chilled
1 (32 ounce) bottle ginger ale, chilled
1 (6 ounce) can frozen orange juice concentrate
Orange slices

☐ Mix champagne, ginger ale and orange juice in punch bowl. Refrigerate. To serve, garnish with orange slices. Makes 1½ quarts.

Punches can be a mixture of two or more ingredients and are usually served in a large punch bowl. Punches may or may not have alcohol as an ingredient.

BASIC SMOOTHIE

BASE: 1 cup fresh or frozen fruit(s) and/or vegetable(s)
LIQUID: 1 cup liquid (milk, soymilk, juices, almond milk, coffee, tea, coconut milk, water)

☐ Blend all ingredients. Makes 1 smoothie.

TIP: *The thickness of smoothies will vary depending on the type of fruits/vegetables used, and whether you use fresh or frozen fruits/vegetables. If your smoothie is too runny, you can either add more of your base (fruits or vegetables) or a thickening addition. If your smoothie is too thick, just add more liquid.*

ADDITIONS TO BASIC SMOOTHIE:

THICKENING ADDITIONS: yogurt, silken tofu, avocado, canned pumpkin, non-fat powdered milk, ice cream, frozen yogurt, sorbet, sherbet, ice

FLAVOR ADDITIONS: honey, stevia, flavor extracts, cocoa powder, peanut butter

HEALTHY ADDITIONS: protein powder, wheat germ, flaxseed

TIP: *Use this basic recipe for smoothies to create your own "super-duper" drink. Don't get hung up on measurements or strict guidelines. The most important thing about smoothies is that they are good ways to get kids to eat vegetables. Any vegetable added to fruit smoothies will be covered up by the fruit flavors. Kids will never know you added spinach or any other vegetable!*

FOUR-FRUIT MEDLEY STARTER

1½ cups orange juice
1 ripe banana, peeled, thickly sliced
1 ripe peach, sliced
1 cup frozen strawberries

☐ Pour orange juice into blender and add banana, peach, strawberries and 1 cup ice cubes. Blend on high speed until creamy. Serves 2 to 4.

EARLY MORNING STARTER

1½ cups low-fat milk
1 banana, peeled, sliced
½ cup frozen blueberries
½ cup frozen unsweetened strawberries
2 teaspoons peanut butter
1 tablespoon honey

☐ Place all ingredients into blender and process until smooth. Serve immediately. Makes 2 smoothies.

TIP: For slushier smoothies, place banana slices in plastic wrap and freeze before making smoothies.

ICE POP BREAKFAST

½ cup low-fat milk
½ cup orange juice
1 (6 ounce) carton low-fat vanilla yogurt
1 all-fruit flavored ice pop (stick removed)
1 banana, peeled, sliced
⅓ cup instant oatmeal

☐ Combine all ingredients in blender and process until smooth. Makes 1 to 2 smoothies.

TIP: For slushier smoothies, place banana slices in plastic wrap and freeze before making smoothies. You can also add ½ cup ice cubes to blender.

CARROT CAKE SNACK-A-ROO

1 cup pineapple-coconut juice or orange juice, chilled
1 (6 ounce) carton low-fat vanilla yogurt
¾ cup baby carrots
½ cup frozen pineapple chunks
1 tablespoon shredded sweetened coconut, optional
1 - 2 tablespoons honey
1 whole graham cracker, optional
¼ cup sliced almonds, optional

☐ Place all ingredients in blender, except almonds, and process until smooth. Pour into glass and sprinkle almonds on top. Makes 2 smoothies.

TIP: Add a dash of cinnamon and pumpkin pie spice.

TIP: For a slushier smoothie, add ½ cup ice cubes.

TANGY VEGGIE FUSION

1 (16 ounce) can tomato juice, chilled
¼ cup fresh lemon juice (about 2 lemons)
1 medium cucumber, peeled, quartered
½ red bell pepper, seeded, quartered
1 rib celery, sliced
3 green onions with tops, divided
2 tablespoons Worcestershire sauce

☐ Place all ingredients, except green onions, in blender and add a dash of salt and pepper.

☐ Add 1 green onion and several ice cubes and process until desired consistency. Garnish each glass with green onion. Makes 2 smoothies.

DON'T TELL THE KIDS SMOOTHIE

They will never know you put spinach in their smoothie!

1 cup orange juice, chilled
4 florets broccoli
1 cup stemmed spinach
4 - 6 baby carrots
1 orange, peeled, separated
1 apple, cored, quartered

☐ Place all ingredients in blender with several ice cubes and process until creamy. Makes 2 smoothies.

BREAKFAST

**Get a fast, easy start
for a good day.**

BREAKFAST CONTENTS

ANGEL BISCUITS

3 packages yeast
5 cups flour
⅓ cup sugar
1 cup shortening
2 cups buttermilk*

☐ Dissolve yeast in ⅓ cup warm water in bowl and set aside. In separate bowl, combine flour and sugar and cut in shortening. Add buttermilk and yeast and stir. Refrigerate.

☐ On floured board or wax paper, pat out dough. Cut out biscuits with biscuit cutter and place on sprayed baking pan. Let rise in warm place for 2 to 3 hours.

☐ When ready to bake, preheat oven to 425°. Bake for 12 minutes or until brown. Dough should last about 10 days in plastic container in refrigerator. Makes 24 to 30 biscuits.

*TIP: To make buttermilk, mix 1 cup milk with 1 tablespoon lemon juice or vinegar and let milk stand for about 10 minutes.

Mixing flour and water is one of the oldest prepared foods. Additional ingredients such as salt, grains and leavening agents make bread a staple in today's cultures.

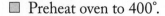

EASY DATE BISCUITS

1 cup chopped dates
2 cups biscuit mix
½ cup shredded American cheese
¾ cup milk

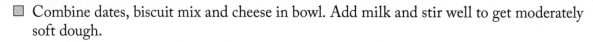

☐ Preheat oven to 400°.

☐ Combine dates, biscuit mix and cheese in bowl. Add milk and stir well to get moderately soft dough.

☐ Drop teaspoonfuls of dough onto sprayed baking sheet. Bake for 12 to 15 minutes. Serve hot. Makes 8 to 12 biscuits.

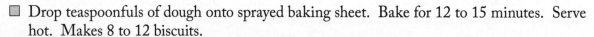

MAPLE SYRUP BISCUITS

2¼ cups biscuit mix
⅔ cup milk
1½ cups maple syrup

☐ Preheat oven to 425°.

☐ Combine biscuit mix and milk. Stir just until moist. On floured surface, roll dough into ½-inch thickness. Cut with 2-inch biscuit cutter or small glass.

☐ Pour syrup into 7 x 11-inch baking dish. Place biscuits on top of syrup.

☐ Bake for 13 to 15 minutes or until biscuits are golden brown. Serve warm and with butter. Makes 10 to 12 biscuits.

BISCUITS AND SAUSAGE GRAVY

This is about as down-home as you can get and it is every bit as good as you can imagine.

3 cups biscuit mix
4 cups milk, divided
½ pound pork sausage
2 tablespoons butter
⅓ cup flour
3¼ cups milk

☐ Preheat oven to 400°. Combine biscuit mix and ¾ cup milk in bowl and stir. Roll dough on floured wax paper to ¾ inch thickness and cut with biscuit cutter. Place on sprayed baking sheet. Bake for 12 to 15 minutes or until golden.

☐ For gravy, brown sausage in skillet, drain and reserve pan drippings in skillet. Set sausage aside. Add butter to drippings and melt. Add flour and cook 1 minute, stirring constantly.

☐ Gradually add remaining 3¼ cups milk and cook over medium heat, stirring constantly until mixture thickens. Stir in ½ teaspoon each of salt and pepper and sausage. Cook until heated, stirring constantly. Serve sausage gravy over cooked biscuits. Serves 8.

Biscuits and country gravy were popularized in the South when soft dough biscuits were drenched in a white gravy made with sausage or bacon drippings. The dish gained widespread popularity in the South when people needed a cheap, hearty breakfast before going to work in the fields.

BASIC PANCAKES

2 cups flour
1 tablespoon sugar
1 tablespoon baking powder
2 eggs
1½ cups milk
Vegetable oil
Maple syrup
½ cup melted butter

☐ Combine flour, sugar, baking powder and ¼ teaspoon salt in large mixing bowl.

☐ In separate bowl, beat eggs and milk. Pour egg mixture into flour mixture and stir until smooth. If batter is too thick, add a little milk. There will be a few lumps in batter.

☐ Heat griddle to medium heat and coat lightly with oil. Pour batter on griddle to equal desired size of pancake (an ice cream scoop works great to deliver uniform amounts of batter onto skillet).

☐ After bubbles form on top and edges brown, gently flip pancake to cook other side. Serve immediately with warm syrup and melted butter. Serves 4.

BLUEBERRY PANCAKES: Wash and drain thoroughly about 1 cup fresh or frozen blueberries. (If blueberries are frozen, do not thaw before adding to pancake batter.) Stir into pancake batter gently and pour onto griddle or skillet.

BUTTERMILK PANCAKES: Substitute buttermilk instead of milk. If batter is too thick, add just a little milk. (To make buttermilk, add 1 tablespoon lemon juice or vinegar to 1 cup milk and let stand for 10 minutes.)

BANANA PANCAKES: Slice 1 or 2 ripe bananas about ¼-inch thick. When batter is poured onto griddle, place as many slices as desired on batter and lightly push bananas into batter. Cook slowly to make sure inside is firm.

TIP: Other variations include ½ cup diced apples, 1 cup cranberries, ½ cup coconut, 6 slices cooked bacon, ½ cup diced ham or 1 cup chopped pecans.

LIGHT AND CRISPY WAFFLES

2 cups biscuit mix
1 egg
½ cup oil
1⅓ cups club soda

☐ Preheat waffle iron. Combine all ingredients in mixing bowl and stir with whisk.

☐ Pour just enough batter to cover waffle iron, but not run over. Serves 4.

TIP: *To have waffles for a "company weekend", make waffles in advance. Freeze separately on baking sheet and place in large resealable plastic bags. To heat, warm in oven at 350° for about 10 minutes.*

PECAN WAFFLES

2 cups self-rising flour
½ cup oil
½ cup milk
⅔ cup finely chopped pecans

☐ Preheat waffle iron. In bowl, combine flour, oil and milk. Beat until they mix well. Stir in chopped pecans. Pour approximately ¾ cup batter into hot waffle iron and bake until brown and crispy. Serves 4.

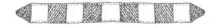

FRENCH TOAST

Olive oil
4 eggs
1 (8 ounce) carton whipping cream
2 thick slices bread, cut into 3 strips
Powdered sugar
Maple syrup

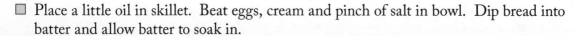

☐ Preheat oven to 325°.

☐ Place a little oil in skillet. Beat eggs, cream and pinch of salt in bowl. Dip bread into batter and allow batter to soak in.

☐ Fry bread in skillet until brown, turn and fry on other side. Transfer to baking sheet. Bake for about 4 minutes or until puffed.

☐ Sprinkle with powdered sugar and serve with maple syrup. Serves 2.

ORANGE-RAISIN FRENCH TOAST

1 egg, beaten
½ cup orange juice
5 slices raisin bread
1 cup crushed graham crackers
2 tablespoons butter

☐ Combine egg and orange juice in bowl. Dip bread in mixture and then in graham cracker crumbs.

☐ Heat skillet to medium heat and melt butter. Fry toast in butter until brown. Serves 4.

Monkey Bread

½ cup white sugar
2 tablespoons cinnamon
4 (10 biscuit) cans refrigerated biscuits
½ cup chopped pecans and/or raisins
¾ cup (1½ sticks) butter
1¼ cups packed brown sugar

☐ Preheat oven to 350°.

☐ Combine white sugar and cinnamon in plastic bag. Cut each biscuit into quarters, place 6 to 7 pieces at a time in sugar-cinnamon mixture and shake well.

☐ Layer these pieces in well-sprayed 10-inch tube pan. Sprinkle pecans and/or raisins among biscuit pieces as you are layering. Repeat steps to continue layering all biscuits in pan.

☐ In saucepan, melt butter with brown sugar over medium heat and bring to a boil. Stirring constantly, boil for 1 minute and pour over layered biscuits.

☐ Bake for 35 to 40 minutes. Let bread cool in pan for 10 to 15 minutes; turn out onto round platter. This is a "pull apart" bread. Serves 8.

Monkey bread recipes first appeared in community cookbooks in the 1950's. It has sections of soft dough placed next to each other in a cake pan, then covered in butter, cinnamon, sugar and nuts and baked. It is sometimes referred to as sticky bread.

STRAWBERRY BREAD

Wonderful toasted for breakfast!

3 cups flour
2 cups sugar
1 teaspoon baking soda
2 teaspoons ground cinnamon
3 large eggs, beaten
1 cup canola oil
1¼ cups chopped pecans
2 (10 ounce) packages frozen sweetened strawberries with juice

☐ Preheat oven to 325°.

☐ Combine flour, sugar, 1 teaspoon salt, baking soda and cinnamon in large bowl. Add eggs and oil and mix thoroughly. Fold in pecans and strawberries and mix well.

☐ Pour into 2 sprayed 9 x 5-inch loaf pans and bake for 1 hour 10 minutes.

☐ Bread is done when toothpick inserted in center comes out clean. Cool several minutes before removing from pan. Serves 10 to 16.

The U.S. is the top strawberry-producing country in the world.

BANANA-PINEAPPLE LOAF

1 cup (2 sticks) butter, softened
2 cups sugar
4 eggs
1 cup mashed ripe bananas
3¾ cups flour
2 teaspoons baking powder
2 teaspoons baking soda
1 (15 ounce) can crushed pineapple with juice
½ cup shredded coconut
1 cup chopped pecans

☐ Preheat oven to 325°.

☐ Cream butter and sugar in bowl, add eggs and beat until fluffy. Stir in bananas.

☐ In separate bowl, combine flour, baking powder, baking soda and ½ teaspoon salt and add to butter mixture (it will be stiff). Fold in pineapple, coconut and pecans.

☐ Pour into 2 sprayed, floured 9 x 5-inch loaf pans and bake for 1 hour 10 minutes.

☐ Bread is done when toothpick inserted in center comes out clean. Cool several minutes before removing from pan. Makes 2 loaves.

COCONUT BREAD

This recipe makes a pretty plate of red and white sandwiches.

1¼ cups shredded coconut
2⅔ cups flour
1¼ cups sugar
4 teaspoons baking powder
1½ cups milk
1 egg
2 tablespoons canola oil
1¼ teaspoons coconut extract

☐ Preheat oven to 300°.

☐ Place coconut on baking sheet and bake for 15 minutes. Shake pan and stir 2 times so that it will toast evenly. Remove from oven and cool.

☐ Turn oven temperature up to 350°.

☐ Sift flour, sugar, baking powder and 1 teaspoon salt in bowl and stir in coconut.

☐ In separate bowl, combine milk, egg, oil and coconut extract. Beat a little to blend egg into milk.

☐ Add liquid mixture to dry ingredients all at once and mix well, but do not over mix.

☐ Pour batter into sprayed 9 x 5-inch loaf pan and bake for 1 hour 5 minutes. Bread is done when toothpick inserted in center comes out clean. Cool. Makes 1 loaf.

TIP: This is great with flavored butters and cream cheese.

APPLESAUCE-PECAN BREAD

1 cup sugar
1 cup applesauce
⅓ cup canola oil
2 eggs
2 tablespoons milk
1 teaspoon almond extract
2 cups flour
1 teaspoon baking soda
½ teaspoon baking powder
¾ teaspoon ground cinnamon
¼ teaspoon ground nutmeg
¾ cup chopped pecans

☐ Preheat oven to 350°.

☐ Combine sugar, applesauce, oil, eggs, milk and almond extract in bowl and mix well.

☐ In separate bowl, combine flour, baking soda, baking powder, cinnamon, nutmeg and ¼ teaspoon salt and add to sugar mixture. Mix well and fold in pecans. Pour into sprayed, floured loaf pan.

TOPPING:

½ cup chopped pecans
½ teaspoon ground cinnamon
½ cup packed brown sugar

☐ Combine pecans, cinnamon and brown sugar in bowl and sprinkle over batter. Bake for 1 hour 5 minutes. Bread is done when toothpick inserted in center comes out clean. Cool on rack. Makes 1 loaf.

BANANA-APPLE BREAD

3 bananas, mashed
3 apples, peeled, grated
2 teaspoons lemon juice
½ cup (1 stick) butter, softened
2 cups sugar
2 eggs
3 cups flour
1½ teaspoons baking powder
1½ teaspoons baking soda
1 teaspoon vanilla

☐ Preheat oven to 350°.

☐ Sprinkle bananas and apples with lemon juice in bowl.

☐ In separate bowl, cream butter, sugar and eggs and beat well. Stir in fruit. Add flour, baking powder, baking soda, vanilla and ¼ teaspoon salt and stir.

☐ Pour into 2 sprayed, floured loaf pans and bake for 50 to 55 minutes or until golden brown. Bread is done when toothpick inserted in center comes out clean. Makes 2 loaves.

Family meals planned and prepared with the children's help will be more beneficial. This instills a sense of security, safety and nurturing that will be with children through their whole lives. When they help to plan and to prepare meals, they are learning to be self-sufficient and building confidence to face the world on their own.

CHERRY-APPLE LOAF

⅔ cup (1⅓ sticks) butter
2 cups sugar
4 eggs
2 cups applesauce
⅓ cup milk
1 tablespoon lemon juice
4 cups flour
1 teaspoon ground cinnamon
2 teaspoons baking powder
1 teaspoon baking soda
1½ cups chopped pecans
¾ cup chopped maraschino cherries, well drained

☐ Preheat oven to 325°.

☐ Cream butter, sugar and eggs in bowl and beat for several minutes.

☐ Stir in applesauce, milk and lemon juice.

☐ In separate bowl, sift flour, cinnamon, baking powder, baking soda and 1 teaspoon salt; add to first mixture and mix well. Fold in pecans and cherries.

☐ Pour into 3 sprayed, floured loaf pans and bake for 1 hour. Bread is done when toothpick inserted in center comes out clean.

☐ Let cool in pans for 10 to 15 minutes, remove from pans and cool on rack. Freezes well. Serve toasted for breakfast or spread with cream cheese for lunch. Makes 3 loaves.

APRICOT BREAD EXTRAORDINAIRE

This is "it" for apricot lovers!

3 cups flour
1½ teaspoons baking soda
2 cups sugar
1½ cups canola oil
4 eggs
1 teaspoon vanilla
1 (5 ounce) can evaporated milk
Apricot Butter (see below recipe)
1¼ cups chopped pecans

☐ Preheat oven to 350°.

☐ Combine flour, baking soda and ½ teaspoon salt in bowl. Add sugar, oil, eggs, vanilla and evaporated milk. Mix thoroughly. Add apricot butter and pecans and blend.

☐ Pour into 2 sprayed, floured loaf pans and bake for 1 hour 10 minutes or until toothpick inserted in center comes out clean. Makes 2 loaves.

APRICOT BUTTER:

1¼ cups finely chopped apricots
1 cup sugar

☐ Cover apricots with water in bowl and soak overnight. Combine apricots and sugar in saucepan and simmer for 10 minutes or until soft. Cool completely before adding to recipe.

PILGRIM PUMPKIN BREAD

This is fabulous served with lots of butter or for sandwiches with cream cheese filling.

1 cup canola oil
3 cups sugar
4 eggs
1 teaspoon vanilla
1 (15 ounce) can pumpkin
2 teaspoons baking soda
2 teaspoons ground cinnamon
¼ teaspoon ground allspice
3 cups flour
1 (8 ounce) box chopped dates
1½ - 2 cups chopped pecans

☐ Preheat oven to 350°. Combine oil and sugar in bowl; add eggs one at a time and beat well after each addition. Add vanilla and pumpkin and mix well.

☐ In separate bowl, sift together 1 teaspoon salt, baking soda, cinnamon, allspice and flour. Add to sugar-pumpkin mixture and beat well. Stir in dates and pecans.

☐ Pour into 2 sprayed, floured 9 x 5-inch loaf pans. Bake for 1 hour 10 minutes to 1 hour 15 minutes. Bread is done when toothpick inserted in center comes out clean. Serves 12 to 16.

Quick Pumpkin Bread

1 (16 ounce) package pound cake mix
1 cup canned pumpkin
2 eggs
⅓ cup milk
1 teaspoon allspice

☐ Preheat oven to 350°.

☐ Beat all ingredients in bowl and blend well. Pour into sprayed, floured 9 x 5-inch loaf pan.

☐ Bake for 1 hour. Bread is done when toothpick inserted in center comes out clean. Cool for 15 minutes and turn out onto cooling rack. Serves 15.

There are nine regional cuisines that are distinctively different in the United States. They are Southern, Tex-Mex, Southwest, Cajun-Creole, Pacific Rim, Midwest, New England, Pennsylvania Dutch and Floribbean.

CHRISTMAS CRANBERRY BREAD

2 cups flour
1 cup sugar
1½ teaspoons baking powder
½ teaspoon baking soda
¼ cup shortening
¾ cup orange juice
1 tablespoon grated orange peel
1 egg, well beaten
½ cup chopped nuts
1 (14 ounce) can whole cranberry sauce

☐ Preheat oven to 350°. Sift flour, sugar, baking powder, baking soda and 1 teaspoon salt in bowl. Cut in shortening until mixture resembles coarse cornmeal.

☐ In separate bowl, combine orange juice, orange peel and egg and pour into dry ingredients. Mix just enough to dampen. Fold in nuts and cranberry sauce. Spoon mixture into sprayed loaf pan and spread corners and sides slightly higher than center.

☐ Bake for 1 hour until crust is brown and center is done. Remove, cool and store overnight for easy slicing. Serves 6 to 8.

Store spices away from heat in a cool, dark place.
They lose their maximum flavor in about six months.

QUICKIE GINGER MUFFINS

1 (16 ounce) box gingerbread mix
1 egg
2 (1.5 ounce) boxes seedless raisins

☐ Preheat oven to 350°.

☐ Combine gingerbread mix, 1¼ cups lukewarm water and 1 egg in bowl and mix well. Stir in raisins. Pour into sprayed muffin cups to half full.

☐ Bake for 20 minutes or until toothpick inserted in center comes out clean. Serve warm with butter. Makes 8 to 12 muffins.

The Produce for Better Health Foundation suggests using a color guide to help with your selections.

> *Purple – helps prevent heart disease*
>
> *White – promotes good cholesterol and blood pressure levels*
>
> *Yellow/Orange – may lower risk of heart attack*
>
> *Green – helps prevent cancer and maintain eye health*

FRESH BLUEBERRY MUFFINS

1¼ cups sugar
2 cups flour
1½ teaspoons baking powder
½ cup (1 stick) butter, softened
1 egg, beaten
1 cup milk
1½ cups fresh blueberries
½ cup chopped pecans

☐ Preheat oven to 375°.

☐ Combine sugar, flour, baking powder and ½ teaspoon salt in large bowl. Cut in softened butter until mixture is coarse.

☐ Stir in egg and milk and beat well. Gently fold in blueberries and pecans, but do not beat.

☐ Spoon into sprayed, floured muffin cups (or cups with paper liners) and bake for 35 minutes or until light brown. Makes 12 muffins.

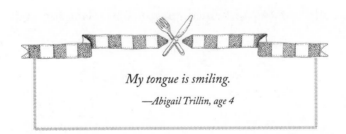

My tongue is smiling.

—Abigail Trillin, age 4

MAPLE-SPICE MUFFINS

1¼ cups flour
1½ cups whole-wheat flour
½ cup quick-cooking oats
1 teaspoon baking soda
2 teaspoons baking powder
2 teaspoons ground cinnamon
½ teaspoon ground cloves
2 eggs
1 (8 ounce) carton sour cream
1 cup maple syrup
1 cup packed brown sugar
½ cup canola oil
½ teaspoon maple flavoring
1 banana, mashed
1 cup chopped walnuts

☐ Preheat oven to 375°.

☐ Combine flours, oats, baking soda, baking powder, cinnamon and cloves in bowl. Add eggs, sour cream, maple syrup, brown sugar, oil, maple flavoring and mashed banana. Stir well with spoon.

☐ Add walnuts and pour into 24 paper-lined muffin cups. Bake for 18 to 20 minutes. Makes 24 muffins.

BLUEBERRY-ORANGE MUFFINS

1 (16 ounce) package blueberry muffin mix with blueberries
2 egg whites
½ cup orange juice
Orange marmalade

☐ Preheat oven to 375°.

☐ Wash blueberries with cold water and drain. Combine muffin mix, egg whites and orange juice in bowl and break up any lumps.

☐ Gently fold blueberries into batter. Pour into muffin cups (with paper liners) about half full.

☐ Bake for 18 to 20 minutes or until toothpick inserted in center comes out clean. Spoon orange marmalade over tops of hot muffins. Makes 6 to 10 muffins.

Family meals offer quality time for all members of the family. Meals should be interactive with each family member sharing something about their day, their friends, their job, soccer practice, etc. Family meals provide stability and a sense of community that children need. By listening to adults, they increase their vocabulary, their social skills and their confidence.

APRICOT-PINEAPPLE MUFFINS

This is a winner!

½ cup (1 stick) butter, softened
1 cup sugar
1 egg
1 (8 ounce) can crushed pineapple with juice
1¼ cups flour
½ teaspoon baking soda
½ cup quick-cooking oats
⅓ cup finely cut dried apricots

☐ Preheat oven to 350°.

☐ Cream butter and sugar in bowl until smooth. Add egg and pineapple and beat well. Add flour, baking soda, oats and ½ teaspoon salt and mix well. Fold in apricots.

☐ Spoon into sprayed muffin cups or use paper liners and bake for 20 minutes. Makes 12 muffins.

How many times during our childhoods did we hear the adage "An apple a day keeps the doctor away." As it turns out, the truth is the apple is a very nutritious food. Apples contain Vitamin C plus many other antioxidants, which are cancer fighters.

HIDDEN SECRET MUFFINS

FILLING:

1 (8 ounce) package cream cheese, softened
1 egg
⅓ cup sugar
1 tablespoon grated orange peel

MUFFINS:

1 cup (2 sticks) butter, softened
1¾ cups sugar
3 eggs
3 cups flour
2 teaspoons baking powder
1 cup milk
1 teaspoon almond extract
1 cup chopped almonds, toasted

☐ Preheat oven to 375°.

☐ To prepare filling, beat cream cheese, eggs, sugar and orange peel in bowl and set aside.

☐ To prepare batter, cream butter and sugar in bowl until light and fluffy. Add eggs one at a time and beat after each addition.

☐ In separate bowl, combine flour and baking powder and add alternately with milk to butter-sugar mixture. Begin and end with flour. Add almond extract and fold in almonds.

☐ Fill 24 lightly sprayed muffin cups half full with batter. Spoon 1 heaping tablespoon filling in each muffin cup and top with a little more muffin batter.

☐ Bake muffins for 20 to 25 minutes or until muffin bounces back when pressed or until light brown. Makes 24 muffins.

Banana-Bran Muffins

1 cup bran flakes
1 cup milk
2 medium bananas, mashed
⅓ cup canola oil
1 cup flour
4 teaspoons baking powder
¼ teaspoon baking soda
⅔ cup sugar
1 egg

☐ Preheat oven to 400°.

☐ Combine bran flakes, milk, bananas and oil in bowl and mix; let soften for 5 minutes.

☐ In separate bowl, sift flour, baking powder, baking soda and ½ teaspoon salt; add to banana mixture. Add sugar and egg and mix only until combined.

☐ Fill 12 sprayed, large-size muffin cups and bake for 16 to 20 minutes. Makes 1 dozen muffins.

When I was a boy of 14, my father was so ignorant I could hardly stand to have the old man around. But when I got to be 21, I was astonished at how much the old man had learned in seven years.

– Mark Twain

GRAHAM-STREUSEL COFFEE CAKE

2 cups graham cracker crumbs
¾ cup chopped pecans
¾ cup firmly packed brown sugar
1½ teaspoons ground cinnamon
¾ cup (1½ sticks) butter, melted
1 (18 ounce) box yellow cake mix
¼ cup canola oil
3 eggs

- Preheat oven to 350°.

- Combine cracker crumbs, pecans, brown sugar, cinnamon and butter in bowl and set aside.

- In separate bowl, combine cake mix, 1 cup water, oil and eggs and blend on medium speed for 3 minutes.

- Pour half batter into sprayed, floured 9 x 13-inch pan and sprinkle with half crumb mixture. Spread remaining batter evenly over crumb mixture and sprinkle with remaining crumb mixture. Bake for 45 to 50 minutes. Cool before glazing.

GLAZE:

1½ cups powdered sugar
2 tablespoons milk

- Mix powdered sugar and milk in bowl and drizzle glaze over cake. Serves 8 to 10.

CHERRY-NUT BREAKFAST CAKE

1 (8 ounce) package cream cheese, softened
1 cup (2 sticks) butter, softened
1½ cups sugar
1½ teaspoons vanilla
3 eggs
2¼ cups flour
1½ teaspoons baking powder
1 (10 ounce) jar maraschino cherries, drained
½ cup chopped pecans

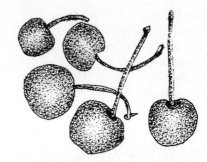

☐ Preheat oven to 350°.

☐ Combine cream cheese, butter, sugar, vanilla and eggs in bowl and beat for 3 minutes. Add flour and baking powder and beat well.

☐ Cut each cherry into 3 or 4 pieces; then fold in cherries and pecans. Pour batter into sprayed, floured 9 x 13-inch baking pan and bake for 40 minutes.

GLAZE:

1½ cups powdered sugar
2½ tablespoons milk
2 tablespoons butter, melted
½ teaspoon almond extract
½ cup chopped pecans

☐ Just before cake is done, combine powdered sugar, milk, butter and almond extract in bowl. Glaze while cake is still warm and top with pecans. Serves 8 to 10.

FRENCH APPLE COFFEE CAKE

¾ cup sugar
1 cup packed light brown sugar
⅔ cup buttermilk*
2 eggs
2½ cups flour
2 teaspoons baking soda
2 teaspoons ground cinnamon
1 (20 ounce) can apple pie filling**
¼ cup golden raisins

☐ Preheat oven to 350°.

☐ Combine sugar, brown sugar, buttermilk and eggs in bowl and mix with spoon.

☐ Add flour, baking soda, cinnamon and ½ teaspoon salt and mix well. Fold in pie filling
and raisins. Pour into sprayed, floured 9 x 13-inch baking pan.

TOPPING:

1 teaspoon ground cinnamon
¼ cup sugar
⅓ cup packed light brown sugar
⅔ cup chopped walnuts
½ cup (1 stick) butter, melted

☐ Combine cinnamon, sugar, brown sugar and walnuts in bowl and sprinkle over top of
cake. Bake for 45 minutes.

☐ When cake is done, drizzle butter over top of cake. Makes 12 big squares.

*TIP: To make buttermilk, mix 1 cup milk with 1 tablespoon lemon juice or vinegar and let milk
stand for about 10 minutes.

**TIP: If you prefer the apple slices to be in smaller pieces empty the can of pie filling on a plate and
cut each slice in half.

CRANBERRY-CROWN COFFEE CAKE

½ cup butter, softened
1 cup plus 2 tablespoons sugar
2 eggs
2 cups flour
1 teaspoon baking powder
1 teaspoon baking soda
1 (8 ounce) carton sour cream
1 teaspoon almond extract
1 (14 ounce) can whole cranberry sauce
¾ cup chopped slivered almonds

☐ Preheat oven to 350°.

☐ Combine butter and sugar and beat well. Beat in eggs one at a time.

☐ In separate bowl, combine flour, baking powder and baking soda, and add alternately with sour cream. Stir in almond extract. Spoon one-half of batter in sprayed, floured bundt or tube pan.

☐ Stir cranberry sauce in small bowl so it can be spread easily. Spread three-fourths of cranberry sauce over batter and sprinkle one-half of almonds. Pour remaining batter on top and spoon remaining cranberry sauce and almonds on top. With long knife, cut through and swirl batter and cranberries.

☐ Bake for 60 minutes. Cool for about 20 minutes before removing cake from pan.

GLAZE:

¾ cup powdered sugar
1 teaspoon almond extract

☐ When cake is cool, mix glaze ingredients plus 1 teaspoon water in bowl until smooth. Drizzle on cake. Serves 8.

PEACH COFFEE CAKE

2⅓ cups flour
1½ cups sugar
¾ cup shortening
2 teaspoons baking powder
¾ cup milk
2 eggs
1 teaspoon vanilla
1 (3 ounce) package cream cheese, softened
1 (14 ounce) can sweetened condensed milk
⅓ cup lemon juice
1 (20 ounce) can peach pie filling
2 teaspoons ground cinnamon
¾ cup chopped pecans

☐ Preheat oven to 350°.

☐ Combine flour, sugar and ¾ teaspoon salt in bowl and cut in shortening until crumbly. Set aside 1 cup crumb mixture.

☐ To remaining crumb mixture, add baking powder, milk, eggs and vanilla. Beat on medium speed for 2 minutes.

☐ Spread batter in sprayed, floured 9 x 13-inch baking dish. Bake for 25 minutes.

☐ In separate bowl, beat cream cheese and sweetened condensed milk until fluffy. Gradually fold in lemon juice, peach pie filling and cinnamon. Spoon mixture over baked cake.

☐ Add pecans to set aside crumb mixture and sprinkle on top of cake. Bake for additional 30 minutes. Serve warm. Serves 8.

APRICOT COFFEE CAKE

1 cup (2 sticks) butter, softened
1 (3 ounce) package cream cheese, softened
1½ cups sugar
2 eggs
1 teaspoon vanilla
1½ teaspoons baking powder
2¼ cups flour
1 (20 ounce) can apricot pie filling

☐ Preheat oven to 350°.

☐ Combine butter, cream cheese and sugar in bowl and beat on low speed. Add eggs and vanilla and beat on medium speed. Add baking powder and flour and beat well.

☐ Spread one-third batter in sprayed, floured 9 x 13-inch baking pan. Spread pie filling over batter. Using spoon, drop remaining batter over pie filling. Bake for 40 to 45 minutes. Cool.

ICING:

1½ cups powdered sugar
2 tablespoons milk
2 tablespoons butter, melted
½ teaspoon almond extract

☐ Mix powdered sugar, milk, butter and almond extract in bowl and beat until smooth. Drizzle icing over cake. Serves 8.

TIP: This is great with other pie fillings as well.

VEGGIE BREAKFAST TACOS

6 - 8 flour tortillas
1 cup frozen hash-brown potatoes, thawed
1 onion, chopped
1 bell pepper, seeded, chopped
1 (4 ounce) can diced green chilies, drained
4 eggs
2 - 3 tablespoons milk
Salsa

☐ Wrap flour tortillas in foil and warm in oven at 200°. Cook hash browns on griddle or
large skillet. Brown onions, bell peppers and green chilies.

☐ Beat eggs with milk in bowl. Move potato mixture to one side, pour in beaten eggs
and scramble.

☐ Mix hash-browns, onions, bell peppers, green chilies and eggs and spoon into flour
tortilla. Roll tortilla and serve hot with salsa. Serves 6 to 8.

*Egg substitutes are made mostly from egg whites,
contain less fat than whole eggs and have no
cholesterol. Use ¼ cup refrigerated egg substitute for
1 whole egg.*

Breakfast Burritos

6 large flour tortillas
½ pound bulk sausage
2 fresh green onions, chopped
5 large eggs, slightly beaten
2 tablespoons milk
⅔ cup shredded cheddar cheese
Salsa

☐ Wrap tortillas tightly in foil and heat in oven at 250° for about 15 minutes. Brown sausage and onions in skillet, drain and set aside.

☐ Combine eggs, milk, and a little salt and pepper in bowl. Pour into separate skillet and cook, stirring constantly. When eggs are still slightly moist, remove from heat. Add sausage-onion to eggs.

☐ Spoon sausage-egg mixture into middle of tortillas. Top with cheese and about 1 tablespoon salsa, roll and tuck ends inside the rolls. Serves 6.

The best way to tell if an egg is fresh is to place it in a bowl with enough water to cover it. If it stays on the bottom of the bowl on its side, the egg is fresh. If the egg stands on its end and bobs slightly, it is not as fresh. And, if the egg floats, it should be discarded.

BAGGIE OMELET FOR ONE

This is so easy, it's funny.

2 eggs
Shredded cheese
Chopped bell peppers
Chopped tomatoes
Chopped onions
Chopped mushrooms
Crumbled bacon
Chopped ham

☐ Crack eggs in 7-inch resealable plastic bag. Choose favorite ingredients, place in bag and seal. Shake to mix ingredients and "scramble" eggs.

☐ Place in boiling water for 13 minutes. Pick up bag with tongs and cool for several minutes before opening. Roll omelet out of baggie onto plate and serve. Serves 1.

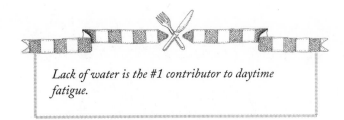

Lack of water is the #1 contributor to daytime fatigue.

BREAKFAST BAKE

1 pound hot sausage, cooked, crumbled
2 tablespoons dried onion flakes
1 (8 ounce) package shredded cheddar cheese
1 cup biscuit mix
5 eggs
2 cups milk

☐ Preheat oven to 350°.

☐ Place cooked and crumbled sausage in sprayed 9 x 13-inch glass baking dish. Sprinkle with onion flakes and cheese.

☐ Combine biscuit mix, eggs, and ¼ teaspoon each of salt and pepper in bowl and beat well. Add milk, stir until fairly smooth and pour over sausage mixture. Bake for 35 minutes.

☐ If you desire, prepare a day ahead, refrigerate and cook the following morning. Add 5 more minutes to cooking time if recipe is refrigerated. Serves 8.

Breakfast is the most important meal of the day because it sets our metabolism in motion. You need quick, high-energy foods to sustain you. Fruit and yogurt, whole grain hot cereal, eggs and high protein drinks are all great.

PINEAPPLE-CHEESE CASSEROLE

This is good served at a brunch or luncheon or as a side dish to sandwiches or ham. It's also great served at a morning bridge club along with coffee cake and a delicious strawberry spread.

1 cup sugar
5 tablespoons flour
2 (20 ounce) cans pineapple chunks, drained
1½ cups shredded cheddar cheese
1 stack round, buttery crackers, crushed
½ cup (1 stick) butter, melted

☐ Preheat oven to 350°.

☐ Mix sugar and flour together. Layer ingredients as follows: pineapple, sugar-flour mixture, cheese and cracker crumbs in sprayed 9 x 13-inch baking dish. Drizzle butter over casserole.

☐ Bake for 25 minutes or until bubbly. Serves 6 to 8.

Casseroles, as we know them today, are relatively new to American households. Cultures everywhere have cooked foods in dutch oven-type containers, but in the 1950's casseroles became well liked and widespread. As cooking containers or casserole dishes became lighter and easier to use, casseroles have found a permanent place in the American home.

QUESADILLA PIE

1 (4 ounce) can diced green chilies, drained
½ pound sausage, cooked, crumbled, drained
1 (16 ounce) package shredded cheddar cheese
3 eggs, well beaten
1½ cups milk
¾ cup biscuit mix
Hot salsa

☐ Preheat oven to 350°.

☐ Sprinkle green chilies, sausage and cheddar cheese in sprayed 9-inch pie pan.

☐ Combine eggs, milk and biscuit mix in bowl. Pour mixture over green chilies-sausage mixture and bake for 30 to 40 minutes. Serve with salsa. Serves 8.

Quesadillas originated in Mexico and have quickly permeated the American food scene. As our world becomes more global, our regional borders break down when we learn about other cultures. We "Americanize" many of the things from other countries, until one day we think we invented them.

QUICK QUICHE

½ cup (1 stick) butter, melted
1½ cups half-and-half cream
3 green onions with tops, chopped
½ cup biscuit mix
1 cup shredded Swiss cheese
¾ cup cooked, chopped ham
4 eggs, beaten

☐ Preheat oven to 350°.

☐ Combine butter, half-and-half cream, ½ teaspoon salt, ¼ teaspoon pepper, green onions and biscuit mix in bowl and blend well with mixer.

☐ Pour into sprayed 10-inch pie pan and sprinkle batter with cheese and ham. Push meat below surface with back of spoon.

☐ Beat eggs in same bowl and pour over ham and cheese. Bake for about 30 minutes or until top is golden brown. Let stand at room temperature for about 5 minutes before slicing. Serves 6 to 8.

Family meals help children learn financial responsibility. They see how a family must live within their means and provide nutritional meals to avoid health problems like diabetes and heart disease. Eating out is more expensive, the food has more calories and the family time is lost.

SAUSAGE AND CHILIES QUICHE

1 (9 inch) refrigerated piecrust
1 (7 ounce) can whole green chilies, drained
1 pound hot sausage, cooked, crumbled, drained
4 eggs, slightly beaten
2 cups half-and-half cream
½ cup grated parmesan cheese
¾ cup shredded Swiss cheese

☐ Preheat oven to 350°.

☐ Place piecrust in 9-inch pie pan. Line bottom of piecrust with green chilies. Sprinkle sausage over chilies.

☐ Combine eggs, half-and-half cream, cheeses, ½ teaspoon salt and ¼ teaspoon pepper in bowl and pour over sausage.

☐ Cover edge of pastry with foil to prevent excessive browning.

☐ Bake for 35 minutes or until top is golden brown. Let quiche stand for about 5 minutes before serving. Serves 6 to 8.

When you shop at the grocery store, you are paying the farmer, processor, packager, distributor and grocer for goods. Locate locally grown produce and visit farmers' markets. Also, check out "pick your own" farms and make an event out of buying food.

HAM AND CHEESE BARS

These are good made for a brunch or lunch, using as bread.

2 cups biscuit mix
1 heaping cup cooked, finely chopped ham
4 ounces shredded cheddar cheese
½ onion, finely chopped
½ cup grated parmesan cheese
¼ cup sour cream
1 teaspoon garlic powder
1 cup milk
1 egg

☐ Preheat oven to 350°.

☐ Combine all ingredients plus ½ teaspoon salt in bowl and mix with spoon.

☐ Spread in sprayed 9 x 13-inch baking pan and bake for 30 minutes or until light brown. Cut in rectangles, about 2 x 1-inch. Serves 8.

TIP: Cook and store in refrigerator. Reheat to serve. Heat at 325° for 20 minutes and they will be good and crispy heated a second time.

An excellent health tip:

Throw Something Away That You Haven't Used or Seen in the Past Year.

GRILLED BACON AND BANANAS

Butter, softened
4 English muffins, halved
Peanut butter
2 bananas, sliced
4 slices bacon, crispy cooked

☐ Butter outside of each English muffin. Spread peanut butter on inside of English muffin slices.

☐ Slice bananas and evenly arrange on top of peanut butter. Top with 2 bacon strip halves and the remaining muffin halves.

☐ Brown sandwiches in sprayed pan or skillet over medium heat. Turn and cook other side until golden brown. Serve hot. Serves 4.

Fruits and vegetables are packed with vitamins, minerals and phytonutrients or chemical compounds. These phytonutrients give produce their color and help them stay fresh. They also stimulate cell growth and regeneration in our bodies.

CINNAMON SOUFFLE

1 loaf cinnamon raisin bread
1 (20 ounce) can crushed pineapple with juice
1 cup (2 sticks) butter, softened
½ cup sugar
5 eggs, slightly beaten
½ cup chopped pecans

☐ Preheat oven to 350°.

☐ Slice very thin amount of crusts off. Tear bread into small pieces and place in sprayed 9 x 13-inch glass dish. Pour pineapple and juice over bread.

☐ Cream butter and sugar in bowl. Add eggs and pecans to creamed mixture and mix well. Pour creamed mixture over bread and pineapple.

☐ Bake for 40 minutes. Serve hot. Serves 10 to 12.

BREAKFAST FRUIT BOWL

1 cup flavored or plain yogurt
1 tablespoon honey
½ cup granola cereal
2 cups fresh pear, peach or apricot slices

☐ Mix yogurt and honey with granola in bowl and top with fruit slices. Make as individual servings in bowls or mix together and serve. Serves 4.

HAPPY TRAILS GRANOLA

6 cups old-fashioned oats
1½ cups unsweetened coconut
1 cup sliced almonds or pistachios
½ cup crushed wheat germ
½ cup sunflower seeds
½ cup sesame seeds
⅔ cup honey
½ cup canola oil
1 tablespoon vanilla
2 teaspoons ground cinnamon
1 teaspoon ground nutmeg

☐ Preheat oven to 350°. Mix oats, coconut, nuts, wheat germ and seeds in 9 x 13-inch baking pan.

☐ Mix honey, oil, vanilla, cinnamon and nutmeg in bowl and pour over granola mix. Stir well to coat all pieces with honey mixture. Bake for about 30 minutes. Cool mixture. Serves 8 to 10.

Sharing food and drink is one of the oldest rituals in the world. Whether a guest is offered a drink by the host or a special beverage in a special cup initiates an occasion, the moment is of significance.

– Pamela Vandyke Price

BREADS & SANDWICHES

**Use simple solutions
to make life easier.**

BREADS & SANDWICHES CONTENTS

You cannot do kindness too soon, for you never know how soon it will be too late.

– Ralph Waldo Emerson

CRAZY BEER BISCUITS

3¼ cups biscuit mix
1 teaspoon sugar
1⅔ cups beer

- ☐ Preheat oven to 400°.

- ☐ Combine all ingredients and ¼ teaspoon salt in bowl and spoon into 12 sprayed muffin cups.

- ☐ Bake for 15 to 20 minutes until golden. Makes 12 biscuits.

SAUSAGE-CHEESE BISCUITS

1 (8 ounce) package shredded cheddar cheese
1 pound hot bulk pork sausage
2 cups biscuit mix
¾ cup milk

- ☐ Preheat oven to 375°.

- ☐ Combine all ingredients and mix in bowl. Drop tablespoonfuls of dough onto baking sheet.

- ☐ Bake 20 to 25 minutes or until light brown. Serve hot. Makes 10 to 12 biscuits.

MOM'S QUICK NEVER-FAIL BREAD

This whole process takes less than 5 hours.

1½ yeast cakes
½ cup milk, room temperature
1 tablespoon sugar
2 tablespoons butter, melted
5 - 6 cups flour

☐ Dissolve yeast in 1½ cups warm water and warm milk in large bowl. After dissolved, mix in sugar, 1½ teaspoons salt and butter until it blends well.

☐ Slowly pour flour into mixture and stir after each addition. Add flour until dough is stiff enough to knead. Place on lightly floured board and knead until dough is smooth and springs back when touched.

☐ Cover and set aside in warm place until dough doubles in size. Punch down lightly and divide into 2 equal parts. Place in sprayed, floured loaf pans, cover and let stand in warm place until dough doubles in size again.

☐ When ready to bake, preheat oven to 450°. Bake for 15 minutes. Reduce heat to 350° and bake for 30 minutes or until golden brown on top. Makes 2 loaves.

You don't have to cook fancy or complicated masterpieces — just good food from fresh ingredients.

– Julia Child

EASY BRAN BREAD

1 cup bran flour
1 yeast cake
1 teaspoon sugar
6 tablespoons shortening
8 cups flour

☐ Pour 2 cups boiling water over bran. In separate bowl mix yeast and sugar in 1 cup warm water and let stand until it bubbles. Combine all ingredients plus additional 1 cup water in large bowl. If dough isn't stiff enough to knead and punch down, add a little more flour.

☐ Knead dough for about 3 or 4 minutes and let stand in warm place until it doubles in size. Divide into 2 large balls and place in sprayed, floured loaf pans. Let stand until it doubles in size again.

☐ When ready to bake, preheat oven to 350°. Bake for 45 minutes or until brown on top. Makes 2 loaves.

My mother was the making of me. She was so true, so sure of me and I felt that I had someone to live for, someone I must not disappoint.

– Thomas Edison

BEER BREAD

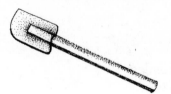

3 cups self-rising flour
¼ cup sugar
1 (12 ounce) can beer, room temperature
1 egg, beaten
2 tablespoons butter, melted

☐ Preheat oven to 350°.

☐ Combine flour, sugar and beer in bowl; mix until blended well. Spoon into 9 x 3-inch loaf pan.

☐ To give bread a nice glaze, combine egg and 1 tablespoon water in bowl; brush top of loaf with mixture. Bake for 40 to 45 minutes.

☐ Remove loaf from oven and brush top with melted butter. Serves 8.

PARMESAN BREAD DELUXE

1 loaf Italian bread
½ cup refrigerated creamy Caesar dressing
⅓ cup grated parmesan cheese
3 tablespoons finely chopped green onions

☐ Cut loaf into thick slices.

☐ Combine dressing, cheese and onion in small bowl. Spread dressing mixture on each bread slice.

☐ Place bread on baking sheet. Broil until golden brown. Serve warm. Serves 8.

SESAME TOAST

2 tablespoons sesame seeds
½ cup (1 stick) plus 2 tablespoons (¼ stick) butter, divided
¼ teaspoon basil
½ teaspoon rosemary
¼ teaspoon marjoram
½ teaspoon garlic powder
½ loaf French bread

☐ Brown sesame seeds in 2 tablespoons butter in saucepan. Add ½ cup butter, melt and add seasonings. Refrigerate overnight.

☐ When ready to bake, preheat oven to 300°.

☐ To make toast, soften and stir butter mixture. Generously spread on bread slices.

☐ Bake for 20 minutes or until slightly brown. Serves 4.

For a special treat for the kids or anyone, serve lemonade or punch with sugar on the rim. Just add a drop of food coloring to sugar in a dish. Rub the rim of a glass with an orange wedge and dip the glass into the sugar. It's easy and fun and the kids' eyes will pop out.

GREEN CHILE-CHEESE BREAD

1 loaf Italian bread
½ cup (1 stick) butter, melted
1 (4 ounce) can diced green chilies, drained
¾ cup grated Monterey Jack cheese

☐ Preheat oven to 350°.

☐ Slice bread horizontally almost all the way through. Combine melted butter, green chilies and cheese in bowl. Spread between bread slices.

☐ Cover loaf with foil. Bake for 25 minutes. Slice and serve hot. Makes 10 to 16 slices.

BUTTERY RANCH BREAD

1 loaf French bread
½ cup (1 stick) butter, softened
1 tablespoon ranch-style dressing mix
1 tablespoon mayonnaise, optional

☐ Preheat oven to 350°.

☐ Cut loaf in half horizontally. Blend butter, dressing mix and mayonnaise in bowl. Spread butter mixture on bread.

☐ Wrap bread in foil. Bake for 15 minutes. Makes 10 to 16 slices.

FANCY SAUSAGE CORNBREAD

1 (10 ounce) can cream of celery soup
2 eggs
¼ cup milk
1 (8 ounce) package corn muffin mix
⅓ pound pork sausage, crumbled, cooked, drained

☐ Preheat oven to 375°.

☐ Combine soup, eggs and milk in medium bowl. Stir in corn muffin mix just until it blends. Fold in sausage.

☐ Pour mixture into sprayed 9-inch square baking pan. Bake for 25 minutes or until golden brown. Cut into squares. Makes 6 to 8 squares.

CHEESY CORNBREAD

1 (8 ounce) box Mexican Velveeta® cheese, cubed
¾ cup milk
2 (8 ounce) packages corn muffin mix
2 eggs, beaten

☐ Preheat oven to 375°.

☐ Melt cheese with milk in saucepan over low heat and stir constantly. Combine corn muffin mix and eggs in bowl. Fold in cheese and mix just until moist.

☐ Pour into sprayed, floured 9 x 13-inch baking pan. Bake for about 25 minutes or until light brown. Makes 12 to 16 squares.

TEX-MEX CORNBREAD

2 eggs, beaten
1 cup sour cream
1 (15 ounce) can cream-style corn
½ cup canola oil
1 (8 ounce) package shredded cheddar cheese
1 (4 ounce) can diced green chilies
3 tablespoons chopped onion
3 tablespoons chopped bell pepper
1½ cups cornmeal
2½ teaspoons baking powder

☐ Preheat oven to 350°.

☐ Mix eggs, sour cream, corn, oil, cheese, green chilies, onion and bell pepper in bowl.

☐ In separate bowl, mix cornmeal, baking powder and 1 teaspoon salt and quickly add to sour cream mixture. Pour in sprayed 9 x 13-inch baking pan and bake for 45 minutes. Serves 8.

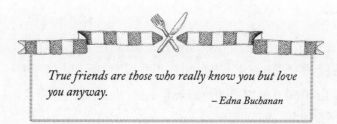

True friends are those who really know you but love you anyway.

– Edna Buchanan

EASY CHEDDAR CORNBREAD

2 (8.5 ounce) packages cornbread-muffin mix
2 eggs, beaten
1 cup plain yogurt
1 (15 ounce) can cream-style corn
½ cup shredded cheddar cheese

☐ Preheat oven to 400°.

☐ Combine cornbread mixes, eggs and yogurt in bowl and blend well. Stir in corn and cheese.

☐ Pour into sprayed 9 x 13-inch baking dish. Bake for 18 to 20 minutes or until slightly brown. Serves 8 to 10.

Cornbread dates back to as long ago as corn was first harvested. By drying the corn and grinding it down to a meal or flour, Native American Indians made bread with a course cornmeal. It was one of the simplest of breads, but provided a good source of food.

CUCUMBER SANDWICHES

1 (8 ounce) package cream cheese, softened
1 tablespoon mayonnaise
1 teaspoon lemon juice
1 (1 ounce) packet ranch dressing mix
⅛ teaspoon cayenne pepper
½ teaspoon garlic powder
1 tablespoon dry parsley flakes
2 cucumbers, peeled, seeded, grated
White sandwich bread

☐ Beat cream cheese, mayonnaise and lemon juice in bowl until creamy. Add all remaining ingredients except bread. Mix well.

☐ Cut crusts off bread and spread cucumber mixture on bread to make sandwiches. Store in refrigerator. Serves 8 to 14.

Sandwiches have been around since before Christ, but they rose to prominence with John Montagu, 4th Earl of Sandwich, First Lord of the Admiralty and patron of Captain James Cook. Montagu was an enthusiastic gambler who stayed at the tables for hours without leaving for meals. His valet brought him meat between two slices of bread and a tradition took on an official name.

GREEN CHILE GRILLED CHEESE SANDWICHES

4 slices American cheese
4 slices bread
1 (4 ounce) can diced green chilies, drained
3 tablespoons butter, softened

☐ Place 1 slice cheese on 2 slices bread. Sprinkle with green chilies. Top with 2 remaining cheese slices and second slice of bread. Butter outside of sandwiches.

☐ Brown sandwiches in large skillet over medium heat on both sides until golden brown and cheese melts. Serves 2.

SPINACH SANDWICHES

2 (10 ounce) packages frozen chopped spinach, thawed
1 (8 ounce) package cream cheese, softened
1 cup mayonnaise
2 eggs, hard-boiled, mashed
1 (1 ounce) packet vegetable soup mix
¾ cup chopped pecans
Large loaf of bread

☐ Squeeze spinach between paper towels to completely remove excess moisture.

☐ Beat cream cheese in bowl until smooth. Add spinach, mayonnaise and beat until mixture mixes well. Stir in mashed eggs, soup mix and pecans.

☐ Refrigerate for several hours before spreading sandwiches. This is enough spread for a large loaf of bread. Serves 8 to 14.

PIZZA BURGERS

1 pound lean ground beef
½ cup pizza sauce, divided
4 slices mozzarella cheese
Hamburger buns

☐ Combine beef, ½ teaspoon salt and ¼ cup pizza sauce in bowl. Mold into 4 patties and pan-fry over medium heat for 5 to 6 minutes on each side or until cooked through.

☐ Just before burgers are done, top each with 1 spoonful pizza sauce and 1 slice cheese. Cook until cheese melts. Serve on hamburger buns. Serves 4.

BRATWURST HEROES

1 (8 ounce) carton marinara sauce
1 (6 - 8 count) package bratwurst sausages
Hot dog buns
1 (8 ounce) jar roasted bell peppers
6 - 8 slices pepper-Jack cheese

☐ In saucepan, heat marinara sauce and simmer on low.

☐ Cook bratwurst on medium grill until cooked throughout, turning frequently. When brats are just about done, toast buns cut-side down on grill.

☐ Place brats on toasted buns and layer bell peppers, marinara sauce and cheese over bratwurst. Serves 6 to 8.

MEATBALL HOAGIES

1 small onion, diced
1 small green bell pepper, diced
1 (15 ounce) can sloppy Joe sauce
24 - 30 frozen cooked meatballs, thawed
6 hoagie buns

☐ Saute onion and bell pepper in 1 tablespoon oil in skillet. Add sauce and meatballs, cook for 10 minutes or until thoroughly hot; stir often.

☐ Spoon meatballs and sauce onto each hoagie bun. Serves 6.

Making sandwich spreads from leftover meats is far cheaper than buying it at the grocery store. Use a food processor, blender or food chopper to chop meats into small bits and add mayonnaise, sweet relish or chopped pickles, celery, onion, or cheese and a little salt and pepper. You'll be surprised how good it is and no one thinks of it as a "leftover".

HOT WESTERN-STYLE SANDWICHES

3 pound boneless chuck roast
¼ cup ketchup
2 teaspoons dijon-style mustard
¼ cup packed brown sugar
1 tablespoon Worcestershire sauce
½ teaspoon liquid smoke
French rolls or hamburger buns

☐ Place roast in sprayed slow cooker.

☐ Combine ketchup, mustard, brown sugar, Worcestershire, liquid smoke, ½ teaspoon salt and a little pepper in bowl and mix well. Pour mixture over roast. Cover and cook on LOW for 8 to 9 hours.

☐ Remove roast and let cool 10 to 15 minutes. Place on cutting board and shred using 2 forks. Place in warm bowl and add about 1 cup sauce from slow cooker. Spoon shredded roast-sauce mixture onto warmed (or toasted) rolls or buns. Makes 10 to 12 sandwiches.

TIP: *Pickles and onions are classic additions for this sandwich.*

CHICKEN PARTY SANDWICHES

3 pounds boneless, skinless chicken thighs
2 tablespoons Caribbean jerk seasoning
1 (10 ounce) package frozen chopped bell peppers and onions, thawed
⅔ cup chicken broth
¼ cup ketchup
⅓ cup packed brown sugar
8 hoagie buns, split

☐ Rub chicken thighs with jerk seasoning and a little pepper. Place in sprayed slow cooker and add bell peppers and onions.

☐ Combine broth, ketchup and brown sugar in bowl and pour over chicken. Cover and cook on LOW for 6 to 8 hours.

☐ Remove chicken from cooker with slotted spoon and shred chicken using 2 forks. Return chicken to slow cooker and mix well. Fill buns with chicken mixture. Makes 8 sandwiches.

Some people like to paint pictures, or do gardening, or build a boat in the basement. Other people get a tremendous pleasure out of the kitchen, because cooking is just as creative and imaginative an activity as drawing, or wood carving, or music.

— Julia Child

Hot Open-Face Turkey Sandwiches

1 (2 pound) package turkey breast tenderloins
2 (12 ounce) jars roasted turkey gravy
1 (28 ounce) package frozen home-style mashed potatoes
½ teaspoon poultry seasoning
1 teaspoon Worcestershire sauce
6 slices white or whole wheat bread, toasted
Paprika

☐ Place turkey in sprayed slow cooker and sprinkle with a little pepper. Pour gravy over top of turkey. Cover and cook on LOW for 8 to 10 hours.

☐ About 10 minutes before serving, prepare potatoes according to package directions.

☐ Remove turkey from cooker and cut into thin slices. Stir poultry seasoning and Worcestershire sauce into gravy in cooker.

☐ Place 2 slices turkey on each toasted slice of bread; top with ¼ cup mashed potatoes and spoon gravy over potatoes. Sprinkle with paprika. Makes 6 sandwiches.

TIP: You can also use instant or leftover mashed potatoes instead of frozen.

The first Thanksgiving was held at Plymouth Colony located on Cape Cod in Massachusetts in 1621. George Washington declared a one-time national holiday to give thanks in 1789, but Thanksgiving Day did not become a permanent national holiday until 1863 under Abraham Lincoln.

OPEN-FACE APPLE-HAM SANDWICHES

Mayonnaise and mustard
4 Kaiser rolls
16 slices American cheese
8 thin slices deli, boiled ham
1 red delicious apple with peel, finely chopped

☐ Spread a little mayonnaise and mustard on top and bottom halves of kaiser rolls and place on baking sheet.

☐ On top of bottom half of each roll place 1 slice cheese, 1 slice ham, about 2 tablespoons chopped apple, second slice cheese and top half of roll.

☐ Broil 4 to 5 inches from heat just until cheese melts. Serve immediately. Serves 4.

The Walleye Sandwich is a favorite in the Great Lakes area. Walleye is breaded and deep-fried, pan-fried or grilled and placed on French rolls or hamburger buns. Lettuce, tomatoes and tartar sauce make the sandwich, but the walleye is always the star.

HAM AND CHEESE CRESCENT POCKETS

1 (8 ounce) can refrigerated crescent rolls
2 tablespoons mayonnaise
2 teaspoons mustard
1 cup finely chopped ham
½ cup shredded Swiss cheese

☐ Preheat oven to 375°.

☐ Unroll dough, separate into 4 rectangles. Combine mayonnaise and mustard and spread over rectangles, leaving ½-inch border.

☐ Sprinkle ham and cheese evenly over half of each rectangle. Moisten edges of dough with water, fold over and pinch edges to seal.

☐ Bake for 10 minutes or until puffed and golden. Serves 4.

John F. Kennedy held a gathering in the White House for a group of 49 Nobel prize recipients. He made this statement: "This is perhaps the assembly of the most intelligence ever to gather at one time in the White House with the exception of when Thomas Jefferson dined alone."

FAMILY HAM AND CHEESE SANDWICHES

1 (8 ounce) loaf French bread
1 (12 ounce) jar mayonnaise
6 ounces sliced Swiss cheese
6 ounces sliced deli-sliced ham
8 sandwich-sliced dill pickles

☐ Preheat oven to 375°.

☐ Cut in bread in half horizontally and spread mayonnaise over cut sides of bread.

☐ Arrange half of cheese and half of ham on bottom slice and top with pickle slices. Arrange remaining cheese and ham on top of pickles.

☐ Cover with top of bread, press down on sandwich and cut into quarters. Place on cookie sheet and bake 5 minutes. Serve hot. Serves 4.

After its start-up in 1921, Wonder Bread brought sliced bread to the national market in 1930. It packaged the bread in a wrapper of colorful circles inspired by the "wonder" of hot air balloons. The popularity of sliced bread was the inspiration for the saying "The greatest thing since sliced bread".

HOT BUNWICHES

8 hamburger buns
8 slices Swiss cheese
8 slices ham
8 slices turkey
8 slices American cheese

☐ Preheat oven to 325°.

☐ Lay out all 8 buns. On bottom half of bun, layer a slice of Swiss cheese, ham, turkey and American cheese. Place top bun over American cheese slice. Wrap each sandwich individually in foil.

☐ Heat for 30 to 40 minutes and serve hot. Serves 8.

TIP: Instead of ham and turkey, use thin-sliced deli meats such as pastrami or corned beef. Switch cheese to slices of Mexican cheese.

TIP: These freeze great. When ready to serve, remove from freezer 2 to 3 hours before serving. Now you can have Sunday night supper ready in the freezer!

Delicatessens are small shops similar to small grocery stores with a counter and stools for patrons. First operated by Germans in the U.S., delicatessens serve cooked meats and prepared dishes. They grew to be a Jewish tradition because they were open on Sundays and served kosher. The center of delicatessens is in New York City.

CALIFORNIA CLUB SANDWICH

1 cup mayonnaise
¼ cup chili sauce
12 slices white bread, toasted
2 large tomatoes, sliced
4 thick slices cooked turkey
½ pound bacon, cooked
2 avocados, peeled, sliced

☐ Combine mayonnaise and chili sauce. Spread on all bread slices.

☐ Layer all ingredients to form double-decker sandwiches. Quarter sandwiches and secure with toothpicks. Serves 4.

TIP: Baby spinach is a great addition to this sandwich.

ALL-IN-ONE FISH SANDWICHES

1 (18 - 20 ounce) loaf Italian bread
1 (12 ounce) box frozen breaded fish fillets, thawed
1 cup prepared deli coleslaw
1 cup potato chips

☐ Slice bread in half lengthwise and broil, cut side up. Cook fish fillets according to package directions.

☐ Layer coleslaw, fish fillets and potato chips in between bread halves. To serve, cut into 4 quarters and serve immediately. Serves 4.

SWISS TUNA GRILLED SANDWICHES

1 (7 ounce) can white tuna, drained, flaked
½ cup shredded Swiss cheese
1 rib celery, finely chopped
¼ onion, finely chopped
¼ cup mayonnaise
¼ cup sour cream
Rye bread
Butter, softened

- ☐ Combine tuna, cheese, celery, onion, mayonnaise, sour cream, ½ teaspoon salt and ¼ teaspoon pepper and mix well. Spread on rye bread and top with another slice rye bread.

- ☐ Spread tops of sandwiches with butter and place top down on hot griddle. Brown over medium heat; spread butter on sandwich bottoms, flip and brown bottoms. Serve hot. Serves 2 to 4.

MARSHMALLOW SANDWICHES

White bread or whole wheat bread
Marshmallow creme
Chunky peanut butter
Butter, softened, optional

- ☐ On 1 slice bread, spread marshmallow creme. On second slice bread, spread peanut butter.

- ☐ Put marshmallow and peanut butter sides together. Eat sandwich as is or brown sandwich in skillet with a little butter.

SOUPS & STEWS

**Comforting, hearty meals
make everyone feel at home.**

SOUPS & STEWS CONTENTS

SOUPS & STEWS CONTENTS

I think age is a very high price to pay for maturity.

– Tom Stoppard

RICH CHEDDAR CHOWDER

2 (14 ounce) cans chicken broth
4 baking potatoes, peeled, diced
1 onion, chopped
1 cup shredded carrots
1 green bell pepper, seeded, chopped
1 red bell pepper, seeded, chopped
¼ cup (½ stick) butter
⅓ cup flour
1 (16 ounce) carton half-and-half cream
1½ cups milk
1 (16 ounce) package shredded sharp cheddar cheese
⅛ - ¼ teaspoon hot sauce

☐ Combine broth, potatoes, onion, carrots and bell peppers in large soup pot. Bring to a boil, reduce heat and simmer for 15 minutes or until vegetables are tender.

☐ Melt butter in large saucepan, add flour and stir until smooth. Cook for 1 minute and stir constantly. Gradually add half-and-half cream and milk; cook over medium heat and stir constantly until mixture thickens. Add to vegetable mixture along with cheese and hot sauce.

☐ Cook just until thoroughly hot; do not boil. Serves 6 to 8.

Money-Saving Tip:

Next time you're surfing the internet, go to your grocery store's website. Most have printable coupons or specials they advertise only online.

HEARTY CHEESE SOUP

5 slices bacon
1 small onion, finely chopped
2 ribs celery, finely sliced
2 (14 ounce) cans chicken broth
⅔ cup quick-cooking oats
1 cup shredded Swiss cheese
1 (8 ounce) carton whipping cream

☐ Cook bacon in large saucepan until crisp, drain and crumble. Save drippings in saucepan. Cook onion and celery in pan drippings over medium heat for 10 minutes or until tender; stir often.

☐ Add broth and oats. Bring to a boil, reduce heat and simmer for 15 minutes. Cool slightly.

☐ Place half soup in blender and process until smooth. Repeat with remaining soup.

☐ Return all soup mixture to saucepan and stir in cheese and cream; heat until cheese melts. Do not boil. Ladle soup into bowl and sprinkle with crumbled bacon. Serves 4.

Soups and stews have been around probably as long as fire. Combining ingredients in a large pot is a ritual enjoyed by all cultures and cuisines. It's as simple or as complicated as you want to make it and it's always a pleasing and comforting dish.

QUICK HOMEMADE TOMATO SOUP

4 cups canned stewed, chopped tomatoes
3 - 4 cups chicken stock
2 ribs celery, minced
1 carrot, minced
1 onion, minced
2 tablespoons basil

☐ In large soup pot, combine tomatoes, chicken stock, celery, carrot and onion on high heat.

☐ After soup begins to boil, reduce heat to low and simmer for 15 to 30 minutes. Add basil. Season with salt and pepper to taste. Serves 4.

CREAMY BROCCOLI-WILD RICE SOUP

This is a hardy, delicious soup that is full of flavor.

1 (6 ounce) package chicken-flavored wild rice mix
1 (10 ounce) package frozen chopped broccoli, thawed
2 teaspoons dried minced onion
1 (10 ounce) can cream of chicken soup
1 (8 ounce) package cream cheese, cubed

☐ Combine rice mix and 6 cups water in large saucepan. Bring to a boil, reduce heat, cover and simmer for 10 minutes, stirring once.

☐ Stir in broccoli and onion and simmer for 15 minutes, or until vegetables are tender. Stir in soup and cream cheese. Cook and stir until cheese melts. Serves 6 to 8.

INCREDIBLE BROCCOLI-CHEESE SOUP

You will have many requests for this soup!

3 tablespoons butter
½ onion, minced
¼ cup flour
1 (16 ounce) carton half-and-half cream
1 (14 ounce) can chicken broth
⅛ teaspoon cayenne pepper
1 (16 ounce) package cubed, Velveeta® Mexican Mild cheese
1½ cups chopped broccoli, cooked

☐ Melt butter in large saucepan and cook onion until it is translucent. Add flour, stir and gradually add half-and-half cream, chicken broth, ½ teaspoon salt, ¼ teaspoon pepper and cayenne pepper and stir constantly.

☐ Heat until mixture thickens. (Do not boil.) Add cheese and broccoli and stir constantly until cheese melts. Serves 4.

We may live without poetry, music and art;
We may live without conscience, and live
without heart;
We may live without friends, we may live
without books;
But civilized man cannot live without cooks.

– Owen Meredith

CREAMED BROCCOLI SOUP

4 slices bacon
1 small onion, minced
3 potatoes, shredded
1 (10 ounce) package frozen chopped broccoli, thawed
¼ cup (½ stick) butter
3 tablespoons flour
1 (16 ounce) carton half-and-half cream

☐ Fry bacon in deep skillet, drain and set aside. With bacon drippings still in skillet, add
onion, potatoes, 2 cups water and 1 teaspoon salt. Cover and cook for about 15 minutes.
Add broccoli and cook for additional 5 minutes or until vegetables are tender.

☐ In separate large saucepan, melt butter and add flour. Stir and cook until mixture bubbles.
Gradually add half-and-half cream, cook and stir constantly until it thickens.

☐ Stir in potato-broccoli mixture and heat just until thoroughly hot. Crumble bacon and
sprinkle on top of each serving. Serves 4.

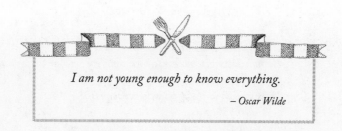

I am not young enough to know everything.

– Oscar Wilde

EASY POTATO SOUP

1 (18 ounce) package frozen hash-brown potatoes
1 cup chopped onion
1 (14 ounce) can chicken broth
1 (10 ounce) can cream of celery soup
1 (10 ounce) can cream of chicken soup
2 cups milk

☐ Combine potatoes, onion and 2 cups water in large saucepan and bring to a boil. Cover, reduce heat and simmer for 30 minutes.

☐ Stir in broth, soups and milk and heat thoroughly. Serves 6 to 8.

FARMHOUSE BACON-POTATO SOUP

2 (14 ounce) cans chicken broth with garlic
2 potatoes, peeled, cubed
1 onion, finely chopped
6 strips bacon, cooked, crumbled

☐ In large saucepan, combine broth, potatoes and onion. Bring to a boil, reduce heat to medium-high and cook about 10 minutes or until potatoes are tender.

☐ Season with a little pepper. Ladle into bowls and sprinkle with crumbled bacon. Serves about 4.

HEARTY NAVY BEAN SOUP

With cornbread on the side, this is a meal by itself.

3 (15 ounce) cans navy beans with liquid
1 (14 ounce) can chicken broth
1 cup cooked, chopped ham
1 large onion, chopped
½ teaspoon garlic powder

☐ Combine all ingredients in large saucepan, add 1 cup water and bring to a boil.

☐ Reduce heat and simmer until onion is tender-crisp. Serve hot with cornbread. Serves 6 to 8.

I cldnuot blviee that I cluod aulaclty uesdnatnrd waht I was rdanieg. The phaonmneal pweor of the hmuan mnid. Aoccdrnig to rscheearch at Cmabrigde Uinervtisy, it deosn't mttaer in waht odrer the ltteers in a wrod are, the olny iprmoatnt tnhig is taht the frist and lsat ltteer be in the rghit pclae

SOUTHWESTERN BEAN SOUP

Don't let the number of ingredients discourage you. Ask yourself this question, "Can I open cans?"

¼ cup (½ stick) butter
1 onion, chopped
1 bell pepper, seeded, chopped
2 teaspoons minced garlic
2 (15 ounce) cans Mexican stewed tomatoes
1 (15 ounce) can pinto beans, drained
1 (15 ounce) can kidney beans, rinsed, drained
1 (15 ounce) can black beans, rinsed, drained
1 tablespoon chili powder
¼ teaspoon ground coriander
1 cup shredded Mexican 4-cheese blend
1 cup shredded Monterey Jack cheese

☐ Melt butter in large saucepan on medium heat and cook onion, bell pepper and garlic for 5 minutes. Stir in tomatoes, all 3 cans beans, chili powder, coriander, and a little salt and pepper.

☐ Bring to a boil, reduce heat, cover and simmer for 25 minutes.

☐ Stir in Mexican cheese and cook over low heat, stirring occasionally just until cheese melts.

☐ Ladle into individual soup bowls and sprinkle Jack cheese over each serving. Serves 8.

AT-HOME BLACK BEAN SOUP

2 onions, finely chopped
3 teaspoons minced garlic
Olive oil
3 (15 ounce) cans black beans, rinsed, drained, divided
2 (14 ounce) cans beef broth, divided
1½ teaspoons dried cumin
2 teaspoons chili powder
Shredded sharp cheddar cheese

☐ Saute onions and garlic in soup pot with a little oil and cook on medium heat for 5 minutes. Place 1 can beans and about ½ cup broth in food processor and process until beans are smooth.

☐ Transfer to soup pot and stir in remaining beans, remaining broth, cumin, chili powder, and a little salt and pepper. Bring to a boil, reduce heat and simmer for 15 minutes. Sprinkle cheese over each serving. Serves 6 to 8.

If you season vegetables with fat, make sure it's high-quality fat that is monounsaturated and not saturated fat. High-quality fat not only helps your food taste good, it also reduces cravings for fat from junk food, improves the assimilation of fat-soluble vitamins in the veggies and satisfies more completely. (Monounsaturated fats include canola and olive oil, almond butter, cashews, peanuts, and avocado.)

GARBANZO BEAN SOUP

2 tablespoons olive oil
1 (16 ounce) package frozen chopped onions and peppers
2 teaspoons minced garlic
½ teaspoon dried sage
1 (15 ounce) can stewed tomatoes
2 (14 ounce) cans vegetable broth
1 (15 ounce) can garbanzo beans, drained
½ cup elbow macaroni
1 teaspoon Italian seasoning
1 (5 ounce) package grated parmesan cheese

☐ Combine olive oil, onions and peppers and garlic in soup pot and cook, stirring often on medium heat for 5 minutes or until onions are translucent. Stir in sage, tomatoes, broth, garbanzo beans, and a little salt and pepper. Cook for 10 minutes.

☐ Stir in macaroni and Italian seasoning and cook for about 15 minutes or until macaroni is al dente (tender, but not overdone). Place about 1 heaping tablespoon parmesan cheese over each serving. Serves 6.

When your family is hungry and the budget is tight, few dishes are so satisfying as a hearty soup or stew.

CREAMY CORN SOUP

¼ cup (½ stick) butter
1 (16 ounce) package frozen onions and bell peppers
1 (16 ounce) package frozen corn
1 (15 ounce) can cream-style corn
1 (10 ounce) can diced tomatoes and green chilies
2 (14 ounce) cans chicken broth
¼ cup flour
1 (16 ounce) carton half-and half-cream

☐ Melt butter and saute onions and bell peppers in soup pot on medium heat for 5 minutes. Stir in whole kernel corn, cream-style corn, tomatoes and green chilies, and chicken broth.

☐ Bring to a boil, reduce heat and simmer for 20 minutes. Mix ¼ cup water with flour in bowl and mix until they blend well. Stir into soup and heat, stirring constantly until soup thickens.

☐ Stir in half-and-half cream and heat soup, stirring constantly until thoroughly hot. Serves 8.

Be who you are and say what you feel because those who mind don't matter and those who matter don't mind.

— Dr. Seuss

QUICKIE CORNY SOUP

2 strips bacon
1 small bunch green onions, minced
1 (15 ounce) can cream-style corn
1 (10 ounce) can cream of celery soup
1 soup can milk

☐ Fry bacon in large saucepan or deep skillet; set bacon aside. In same skillet, add onions and saute until translucent. Crumble bacon and add back to skillet.

☐ Add cream-style corn, soup, milk, and a little salt and pepper. Heat almost to boiling, stir often and pour into soup bowls. Serves 4.

TIP: If you want to add some type of garnish on top of the soup, fry some extra bacon and crumble it over the top or chop the green onion tops and sprinkle them on top. It looks and tastes great.

By the time you learn the rules of life, you're too old to play the game.

Mexican-Style Minestrone Soup

1 (16 ounce) package frozen garlic-seasoned pasta and vegetables
1 (16 ounce) jar thick-and-chunky salsa
1 (15 ounce) can pinto beans with liquid
1 teaspoon chili powder
1 teaspoon ground cumin
1 (8 ounce) package shredded Mexican 4-cheese blend

☐ Combine pasta and vegetables, salsa, beans, chili powder, cumin, and 1 cup water in large saucepan. Bring to a boil, reduce heat, and simmer for about 10 minutes or until pasta and vegetables are heated through; stir occasionally.

☐ When ready to serve, top each serving with Mexican cheese. Serves 4 to 6.

Money-Saving Tip:

Make the most of leftover foods. One of the very best ways to use all kinds of leftovers is with delicious soups and stews. Save even small amounts of meats, vegetables, gravies and sauces together or in separate containers. Freeze containers until you have enough for a dish.

WARM YOUR SOUL SOUP

3 (14 ounce) cans chicken broth
1 (10 ounce) can Italian-stewed tomatoes with liquid
½ cup chopped onion
¾ cup chopped celery
½ (12 ounce) box fettuccini

☐ Combine chicken broth, tomatoes, onion and celery in large soup pot. Bring to a boil and simmer until onion and celery are almost tender.

☐ Add fettuccini and cook according to package directions. Season with a little salt and pepper; serve immediately. Serves 8.

SPEEDY VEGETABLE-BEEF SOUP

1 pound lean ground beef
2 (15 ounce) cans stewed tomatoes
3 (14 ounce) cans beef broth
1 (16 ounce) package frozen mixed vegetables
½ cup instant brown rice

☐ Brown ground beef in skillet, cook and stir until beef crumbles. Transfer to soup pot and add tomatoes, beef broth and vegetables.

☐ Bring to a boil, reduce heat and simmer for 20 minutes, stirring occasionally. Add brown rice and cook on medium heat for 10 minutes, or until rice is tender. Serves 4 to 6.

Italian Beefy Veggie Soup

1 pound lean ground beef
2 teaspoons minced garlic
2 (15 ounce) cans Italian stewed tomatoes
2 (14 ounce) cans beef broth
2 teaspoons Italian seasoning
1 (16 ounce) package frozen mixed vegetables
⅓ cup shell macaroni
1 (8 ounce) package shredded Italian cheese

☐ Brown beef and garlic in large soup pot for 5 minutes. Stir in tomatoes, broth, 1 cup water, seasoning, mixed vegetables, macaroni and a little salt and pepper.

☐ Bring to a boil, reduce heat and simmer for 10 to 15 minutes or until macaroni is tender.

☐ Ladle into individual serving bowls and sprinkle several tablespoons cheese over top of soup. Serves 6 to 8.

When Clarence Birdseye went on an expedition to northern Canada in 1912, he saw Eskimos storing their catch in ice. Birdseye worked to perfect the process for freezing and delivering frozen foods to stores for ten years. Once frozen foods arrived in stores, our lives and eating habits were changed forever. Today, more than half the American population eat some kind of food each week that was first frozen.

TACO SOUP

1½ pounds lean ground beef
1 large onion, chopped
2 (15 ounce) cans pinto beans with liquid
1 (15 ounce) can ranch-style beans or chili beans, drained
2 (15 ounce) cans whole kernel corn with liquid
2 (15 ounce) cans Mexican stewed tomatoes
2 (1 ounce) packets taco seasoning

☐ Brown beef and onion in large soup pot, stir until beef crumbles and drain. Add beans, corn, tomatoes and 1½ cups water.

☐ Bring to a boil, reduce heat and stir in taco seasoning. Simmer for 25 minutes. Serves 8.

QUICK ENCHILADA SOUP

1 pound lean ground beef, browned, drained
1 (15 ounce) can Mexican stewed tomatoes
2 (15 ounce) cans pinto beans with liquid
1 (15 ounce) can whole kernel corn with liquid
1 onion, chopped
2 (10 ounce) cans enchilada sauce
1 (8 ounce) package shredded 4-cheese blend

☐ Combine beef, tomatoes, beans, corn, onion, enchilada sauce and 1 cup water in soup pot.

☐ Bring to a boil, reduce heat and simmer for 35 minutes. When serving, sprinkle a little shredded cheese over each serving. Serves 6.

EASY BEEF-NOODLE SOUP

1 pound lean ground beef
1 (46 ounce) can vegetable juice
1 (1 ounce) packet onion soup mix
1 (3 ounce) package beef-flavored ramen noodles
1 (16 ounce) package frozen mixed vegetables

☐ Cook beef in large saucepan over medium heat until no longer pink and drain.

☐ Stir in vegetable juice, soup mix, noodle seasoning and mixed vegetables and bring to a boil.

☐ Reduce heat and simmer for 6 minutes or until vegetables are tender. Return to boil and stir in noodles.

☐ Cook for 5 minutes or until noodles are tender and serve hot. Serves 6 to 8.

QUICK VEGETABLE-BEEF STEW

1 pound stew meat
1 (14 ounce) can beef broth
1 (28 ounce) can stewed tomatoes
2 (15 ounce) cans mixed vegetables with liquid
½ cup barley

☐ Combine meat, broth, 2 cups water, and a little salt and pepper in large stew pot and bring to a boil. Reduce heat to low and cook for 1 hour. Stir in all remaining ingredients and cook on medium heat for 30 minutes or until barley is cooked. Serves 6.

BRONCO STEW

2 pounds ground round beef
1 (16 ounce) package frozen chopped onions and bell peppers
1 (14 ounce) can beef broth
1 (1 ounce) packet taco seasoning
2 (15 ounce) cans Mexican stewed tomatoes
2 (15 ounce) cans pinto beans with jalapenos
1 (16 ounce) package cubed Velveeta® cheese
1 (13 ounce) package tortilla chips, crushed

☐ Brown beef in stew pot and stir often. Add onion and bell peppers, and cook on high for 5 minutes. Add broth and taco seasoning, reduce heat and simmer for 35 to 45 minutes.

☐ Stir in tomatoes and beans and heat just until mixture is thoroughly hot. Add cheese and stir until cheese melts.

☐ Place about ¾ cup crushed chips in bottom of individual soup bowls, spoon stew over chips and serve immediately. Serves 8.

California is the largest producer of processed tomatoes in the world, producing almost half of the world's total production.

STROGANOFF STEW

1 (1 ounce) packet onion soup mix
2 (10 ounce) cans cream of mushroom soup
2 pounds stew meat
1 (8 ounce) carton sour cream
Egg noodles, cooked

☐ Preheat oven to 275°.

☐ Combine soup mix, soup and 2 soup cans water and pour over stew meat in roasting pan.

☐ Cover tightly and bake for 6 to 8 hours.

☐ When ready to serve, stir in sour cream, return mixture to oven until it heats thoroughly and serve over noodles. Serves 6.

BORDER-CROSSING STEW

1½ pounds round steak, cubed
2 onions, chopped
1 (14 ounce) can beef broth
1 (15 ounce) can Mexican stewed tomatoes
1 (7 ounce) can diced green chilies
3 baking potatoes, peeled, cubed
2 teaspoons minced garlic
2 teaspoons ground cumin

☐ Brown cubed steak and onion in stew pot, cook for 10 minutes; stir often.

☐ Mix in beef broth, tomatoes, green chilies, potatoes, garlic, cumin, 1 cup water, and a little salt and pepper. Cover and cook on medium-low heat for 35 minutes or until potatoes are tender. Serves 6.

OVEN-BAKED BEEF STEW

1 tablespoon flour
¾ pound beef chuck, cubed
2 potatoes, peeled, cubed
2 carrots, peeled, sliced
¾ cup chopped onion
¼ teaspoon basil
¼ cup dry red wine
1 (10 ounce) can tomato soup

☐ Preheat oven to 325°.

☐ Combine flour with a little salt and pepper and pat onto both sides of meat. Brown meat in large iron skillet. Transfer to large deep skillet; add vegetables.

☐ Combine basil, red wine and soup with 1¼ cups water. Mix well and pour over beef and vegetables. Cover and bake for about 1 hour. Serves 4.

Simplicity is the ultimate sophistication.

– Leonardo da Vinci

STEAKHOUSE STEW

1 pound boneless beef sirloin steak, cubed
Olive oil
1 (15 ounce) can stewed tomatoes
1 (10 ounce) can French onion soup
1 (10 ounce) can tomato soup
1 (16 ounce) package frozen stew vegetables, thawed

☐ Cook steak in skillet with a little oil until juices evaporate. Transfer to stew pot or roasting pan.

☐ Add 1 cup water, tomatoes, soups and vegetables and heat to boiling. Reduce heat to low and simmer for 35 minutes. Serves 6.

GREEN CHILE STEW POT (CALDILLO)

Caldillo or stew is a traditional Mexican dish served on special occasions.

2 pounds round steak, cubed
Canola oil
2 onions, chopped
2 potatoes, peeled, diced
2 cloves garlic, minced
6 - 8 fresh green chilies, roasted, peeled, seeded, diced

☐ Sprinkle round steak with 1 tablespoon salt; heat oil in large skillet and brown meat. Put onions, potatoes and garlic in same skillet and cook until onions are translucent.

☐ Pour all ingredients from skillet into large stew pot. Add chilies, 1 teaspoon salt, ½ teaspoon pepper and enough water to cover. Bring to a boil, lower heat and simmer for 1 to 2 hours or until meat and potatoes are tender. Serves 6.

BEEFY BEAN CHILI

2 pounds lean ground beef
3 ribs celery, sliced
1 onion, chopped
1 bell pepper, seeded, chopped
2 teaspoons minced garlic
1 (15 ounce) can tomato sauce
3 tablespoons chili powder
2 (15 ounce) cans pinto beans with liquid
1 - 2 cups crushed tortilla chips

☐ Brown and cook ground beef in large soup pot over medium heat until meat crumbles. Add celery, onion, bell pepper and minced garlic. Cook for 5 minutes or until vegetables are tender, but not brown.

☐ Stir in tomato sauce, chili powder, 2 cups water, and a little salt and pepper and mix well. Bring mixture to a boil, reduce heat and simmer for 20 minutes.

☐ Add beans and continue to simmer for 15 minutes. Ladle into individual serving bowls and top each serving with several tablespoons crushed tortilla chips. Serves 8.

When you are transferring a liquid from one container to another, pour liquid over the back of a spoon to minimize splashing.

EASY CHUNKY CHILI

2 pounds premium cut stew meat
1 (10 ounce) can beef broth
1 onion, chopped
2 (15 ounce) cans diced tomatoes
1 (10 ounce) can diced tomatoes and green chilies
2 (15 ounce) cans pinto beans with liquid
1½ tablespoons chili powder
2 teaspoons ground cumin
1 teaspoon oregano

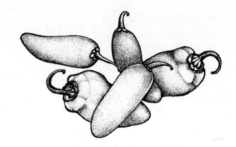

☐ If stew meat is in fairly large chunks, cut each chunk in half. Brown stew meat in large skillet and add all remaining ingredients.

☐ Bring to a boil, reduce heat and cook on low for 1 hour. Serves 8.

At one time chili was just another bowl of stew until a Dallas newspaperman, Frank X. Tolbert, challenged Wick Fowler, another newspaperman, and H. Allen Smith, a humorist, to a chili cookoff. They began the first World Championship Chili Cookoff held in the ghost town of Terlingua, Texas in the Big Bend country. Today, chili cookoffs are held all over the world, but the most famous chili cookoff was and still is what is now known as the Original Terlingua International Championship Chili Cookoff in Terlingua, Texas.

BAKED CHILI

1½ cups dried pinto beans
1½ pounds beef round steak, cubed
3 onions, finely chopped
3 teaspoons minced garlic
3 (8 ounce) cans tomato sauce
3 tablespoons chili powder
1 tablespoon ground cumin
½ teaspoon cayenne pepper
1 (8 ounce) package shredded Mexican 4-cheese blend

☐ Preheat oven to 325°.

☐ Heat beans and 6 cups water to boiling in large, heavy pot and boil for 2 minutes.

☐ Stir in all remaining ingredients except cheese, cover and bake for about 3 hours. Remove from oven and stir well. Return to oven and bake for additional 1 hour. Garnish each individual serving with cheese. Serves 6 to 8.

The first commercially packaged chili powder and canned chilies were produced by William Gebhardt of New Braunfels, Texas. In 1911 Gebhardt built a factory in San Antonio to meet the demand.

ANCHO-SPIKED CHILI

5 ancho chilies
2 tablespoons olive oil
2 onions, chopped
2 cloves garlic, minced
1 pound lean boneless beef, cubed
1 pound lean boneless pork, cubed
1 fresh or canned jalapeno pepper, seeded, minced
1 teaspoon dried, crushed oregano
1 teaspoon ground cumin
½ cup dry red wine

☐ Rinse ancho chilies, remove stems, seeds and veins and place in saucepan with 2 cups water. Bring to a boil, turn off heat and let stand covered for 30 minutes or until chilies soften. Pour chilies with liquid into blender and process until smooth.

☐ Heat oil in soup pot and saute onion, garlic and meats until meat is light brown. Add jalapeno pepper, 1 teaspoon salt, oregano, cumin, wine and ancho puree.

☐ Bring to a boil, reduce heat, cover and simmer for 2 hours. Uncover and simmer for about 30 minutes or until chili thickens slightly. Serves 8.

Gratitude is one of the sweet shortcuts to finding peace of mind and happiness inside. No matter what is going on outside of us, there's always something we could be grateful for.

— Barry Neil Kaufman

CHILE VERDE CON CARNE

"Chile con carne" means chili with meat. Verde refers to the fresh green chilies.

2 - 3 pounds sirloin or tenderloin, cubed
½ cup (1 stick) butter
2 onions, chopped
4 - 6 cloves garlic, minced
8 - 10 fresh whole green chilies, peeled, seeded, chopped
1 tablespoon ground cumin
2 teaspoons oregano

☐ Brown sirloin in butter in large skillet. Reduce heat to low and add all remaining ingredients, 1 cup water, and 1 teaspoon each of salt and pepper. Cover and simmer for about 2 to 3 hours.

☐ Stir occasionally and add ½ to 1 cup water if necessary. Remove cover, taste for flavor and adjust seasonings, if needed. Serves 6.

TIP: *To save time, chili powder may be used instead of roasting fresh green chilies, but the flavor of fresh chilies is the secret to the best chili.*

A drop in body water can trigger fuzzy short-term memory, trouble with basic math and difficulty focusing on the computer screen or the printed page.

MOM'S BEST CHICKEN SOUP

3 (14 ounce) cans chicken broth
4 boneless, skinless chicken breast halves
2 tablespoons butter
3 medium new (red) potatoes, cut into wedges
2 ribs celery, chopped
1 carrot, peeled, shredded
1 (10 ounce) package frozen green peas
1 (10 ounce) package frozen corn
1½ cups buttermilk*
½ cup flour
½ teaspoon cayenne pepper
1 teaspoon Worcestershire sauce

☐ Bring broth to a boil in large saucepan and add chicken breasts. Cover and remove from heat; let sit for 12 to 15 minutes or until chicken is no longer pink. Remove chicken with slotted spoon and let rest for 10 minutes; save broth. Cut chicken into bite-size pieces.

☐ Melt butter in soup pot, add potatoes and cook for about 10 minutes. Add reserved broth, chicken, celery, carrot, peas and corn and simmer for 30 minutes.

☐ In bowl stir buttermilk and flour until smooth, add to chicken-potato mixture and cook, stirring constantly for 5 minutes. Stir in cayenne pepper and Worcestershire sauce. Serves 8.

*TIP: *To make buttermilk, mix 1 cup milk with 1 tablespoon lemon juice or vinegar and let milk stand for about 10 minutes.*

BROCCOLI-RICE SOUP

1 (6 ounce) package chicken and wild rice mix
1 (10 ounce) package frozen chopped broccoli, thawed
2 (10 ounce) cans cream of chicken soup
1 (12 ounce) can chicken breast chunks

☐ Combine rice mix and 5 cups water in soup pot. Bring to a boil, reduce heat and simmer for 15 minutes.

☐ Stir in broccoli, soup and chicken. Cover and simmer for additional 5 minutes. Serves 6 to 8.

CHICKEN-VEGGIE SOUP

1 (32 ounce) carton chicken broth
2 small carrots, thinly sliced
1 rib celery, diced
1 baby leek, halved lengthwise, sliced
1 (8 ounce) can green peas
1 cup cooked rice
1 cup cooked, sliced chicken
2 teaspoons chopped fresh tarragon

☐ Pour broth in large saucepan and add carrots, celery and leek. Bring to a boil, reduce heat and simmer, partially covered for 10 minutes.

☐ Stir in peas, rice and chicken and continue cooking for 10 to 15 minutes or until vegetables are tender. Add tarragon and a little salt and pepper. Serves 4 to 6.

CHEESY CHICKEN SOUP

1 (10 ounce) can fiesta nacho cheese soup
1 (10 ounce) can cream of chicken soup
1 soup can milk
1 (12 ounce) can chicken breasts with liquid

☐ Mix all ingredients in saucepan on medium heat and stir until thoroughly hot. Serve hot.
Serves 4.

CHICKEN-RICE SOUP WITH GREEN CHILIES

2 boneless, skinless chicken breast halves, cooked
2 (14 ounce) cans chicken broth
1 cup chopped celery
1 cup rice
2 - 4 large fresh green chilies, seeded, chopped

☐ Cut cooked chicken into small pieces and place in large saucepan.

☐ Add chicken broth, celery, rice, green chilies, 1 teaspoon salt and ¼ teaspoon pepper and
simmer for about 35 minutes or until rice is tender. Serves 4.

An excellent health tip:
Read More Books Than You Did Last Year.

CREAMY CHICKEN-SPINACH SOUP

1 (9 ounce) package refrigerated cheese tortellini
2 (14 ounce) cans chicken broth, divided
1 (10 ounce) can cream of chicken soup
1 (12 ounce) can white chicken meat with liquid
1 (10 ounce) package frozen chopped spinach
2 cups milk
½ teaspoon dried thyme

☐ Cook tortellini in soup pot according to package directions. Drain and add tortellini back to soup pot.

☐ Stir in remaining ingredients, 1 teaspoon salt and ½ teaspoon pepper. Bring to a boil, reduce heat to low and simmer for 10 minutes. Serves 4.

Science confirms our grandmother's cure for the common cold is homemade chicken soup. Clinical studies at the University of Nebraska found that chicken soup and its ingredients had properties that fight inflammation in nasal passages offering relief for cold sufferers. But, it's not hard to figure out that just holding a bowl of hot, steaming, homemade chicken soup makes anybody feel better.

COLD NIGHT BEAN SOUP

1½ cups dried navy beans
3 (14 ounce) cans chicken broth
¼ cup (½ stick) butter
1 onion, chopped
1 clove garlic, minced
3 cups chopped, cooked chicken
1 (4 ounce) can diced green chilies
1½ teaspoons ground cumin
½ teaspoon cayenne pepper
Shredded Monterey Jack cheese

☐ Sort, wash beans and place in soup pot. Cover with water 2 inches above beans and soak overnight.

☐ Drain beans and add broth, butter, 1 cup water, onion and garlic. Bring to a boil, reduce heat and cover. Simmer for 2 hours and stir occasionally. Add more water if needed.

☐ With potato masher, mash half beans. Add chicken, green chilies, cumin and cayenne pepper. Bring to a boil, reduce heat and cover. Simmer for additional 30 minutes.

☐ When ready to serve, spoon in bowls and top with 1 to 2 tablespoons cheese. Serves 8.

QUICK CHICKEN-NOODLE SOUP

2 (14 ounce) cans chicken broth
2 boneless, skinless chicken breast halves, cooked, cubed
1 (8 ounce) can sliced carrots, drained
2 ribs celery, sliced
½ (8 ounce) package medium egg noodles

☐ Combine broth, chicken, carrots, celery and generous dash of pepper in large saucepan. Bring to a boil and cook for 3 minutes.

☐ Stir in noodles, reduce heat and cook for 10 minutes or until noodles are done; stir often. Serves 4.

FEEL-BETTER CHICKEN-NOODLE SOUP

1 (3 ounce) package chicken-flavored ramen noodles, broken
1 (10 ounce) package frozen green peas, thawed
2 teaspoons butter
1 (4 ounce) jar sliced mushrooms, drained
2 cups cooked, cubed chicken

☐ Heat 2¼ cups water in large saucepan to boiling. Add ramen noodles, contents of seasoning packet, peas and butter.

☐ Heat to boiling, reduce heat to medium and cook for about 5 minutes. Stir in mushrooms and chicken.

☐ Continue cooking over low heat until all ingredients heat through. To serve, spoon into serving bowls. Serves 4.

SPEEDY GONZALES SOUP

1 (12 ounce) can chicken with liquid
1 (14 ounce) can chicken broth
1 (16 ounce) jar mild thick-and-chunky salsa
1 (15 ounce) can ranch-style beans or chili beans

☐ Combine all ingredients in large saucepan.

☐ Bring to a boil, reduce heat and simmer for 15 minutes. Serves 4.

TIP: If you have 1 (15 ounce) can whole kernel corn, add it for a crunchy texture.

FAST FIESTA SOUP

1 (15 ounce) can Mexican stewed tomatoes
1 (15 ounce) can whole kernel corn
1 (15 ounce) can pinto beans with liquid
2 (14 ounce) cans chicken broth
1 (10 ounce) can fiesta nacho cheese soup
1 (12 ounce) can chicken breast with liquid

☐ Combine tomatoes, corn, beans, broth and soup in large soup pot, heat for 10 minutes over medium heat and mix well.

☐ Stir in chicken with liquid and heat until thoroughly hot. Serves 6.

TEMPTING TORTILLA SOUP

Don't let the number of ingredients keep you from serving this. It's really easy.

2 large boneless, skinless chicken breast halves, cooked, cubed
1 (10 ounce) package frozen corn, thawed
1 onion, chopped
3 (14 ounce) cans chicken broth
2 (10 ounce) cans diced tomatoes and green chilies
2 teaspoons ground cumin
1 teaspoon chili powder
1 clove garlic, minced
4 corn tortillas

☐ Combine all ingredients except tortillas in large soup pot. Bring to a boil, reduce heat and simmer for 35 minutes.

☐ Preheat oven to 350°.

☐ While soup simmers, cut tortillas into 1-inch strips and place on baking sheet. Broil for 3 to 5 minutes per side, or until crisp. Serve tortilla strips with each serving of soup. Serves 6.

Cut loss; don't toss. Bits of leftovers can easily go into soups, stews, stir-fry, sandwiches, etc., later in the week.

Turkey with Avocado Soup

3 large potatoes, peeled, cubed
2 (14 ounce) cans chicken broth
1 teaspoon ground thyme
½ pound smoked turkey breast, cubed
1 (10 ounce) package frozen corn
3 slices bacon, cooked crisp, drained
1 large avocado
2 plum tomatoes, coarsely chopped
1 lime

☐ Combine potatoes, broth and thyme in soup pot, cover and bring to a boil. Reduce heat and simmer until potatoes are tender, for about 15 minutes.

☐ With slotted spoon transfer half of potatoes to blender or food processor, puree and pour back into soup pot. Add turkey and corn; simmer for 5 minutes.

☐ Crumble bacon; peel and slice avocado. In separate bowl, combined bacon, avocado, tomatoes, juice of lime, and a little salt and pepper; mix.

☐ Ladle soup in individual bowls and place heaping spoonfuls of bacon-avocado mixture on top. Serves 4 to 6.

TIP: *Peel and cut avocado just before serving because they turn dark so quickly.*

LAST-MINUTE TURKEY HELP

2 (14 ounce) cans chicken broth
1 small zucchini, sliced
1 (16 ounce) package frozen vegetable and pasta mix
1½ cups cooked, cubed turkey
2 fresh green onions, sliced

☐ Combine broth, ¼ cup water, zucchini, vegetable mix and cubed turkey in large saucepan.

☐ Bring to a boil, reduce heat and simmer for 10 to 12 minutes or until vegetables and pasta are tender. Garnish each serving with sliced green onions before serving. Serves 4 to 6.

SO EASY, CREAMY TURKEY SOUP

1 (10 ounce) can cream of celery soup
1 (10 ounce) can cream of chicken soup
1 soup can milk
1 cup finely diced turkey

☐ Combine all ingredients in large saucepan and heat thoroughly. Serve hot. Serves 4.

To safely handle leftover soup, cool the hot soup quickly by placing it in a bowl set over another bowl filled with ice water. Then, refrigerate or freeze. This procedure allows less time for growth of bacteria, keeping the soup safe for eating later.

HEARTY 15-MINUTE TURKEY SOUP

This is great served with cornbread.

1 (14 ounce) can chicken broth
3 (15 ounce) cans navy beans with liquid
1 (28 ounce) can stewed tomatoes with liquid
3 cups cooked, cubed white turkey
2 teaspoons minced garlic
¼ teaspoon cayenne pepper
1 (6 ounce) package baby spinach, stems removed

☐ Combine broth, beans, stewed tomatoes, turkey, garlic, cayenne pepper, and a little salt and pepper in soup pot. Bring to a boil, reduce heat and simmer on medium heat for about 10 minutes.

☐ Stir in baby spinach, bring to a boil and cook, stirring constantly for 5 minutes. Serves 8.

FAST GOBBLER FIX

1 (16 ounce) package frozen chopped onions and bell peppers
Olive oil
2 (3 ounce) packages chicken-flavored ramen noodles
2 (10 ounce) cans cream of chicken soup
1 cup cooked, cubed turkey

☐ Cook onions and peppers in soup pot with a little oil just until tender but not brown. Add ramen noodles with seasoning packets and 4 cups water. Boil for 5 minutes or until noodles are tender.

☐ Stir in chicken soup and cubed turkey. Reduce heat to medium, stirring constantly, until thoroughly hot. Serves 4.

TURKEY AND RICE SOUP

¼ cup (½ stick) butter
1 onion, chopped
3 ribs celery, finely chopped
1 bell pepper, seeded, chopped
2 (14 ounce) cans turkey broth
1 (6 ounce) box roasted-garlic long grain-wild rice
2 (10 ounce) cans cream of chicken soup
2 cups cooked, diced white meat turkey
1 cup milk

☐ Melt butter in soup pot over medium heat. Add onion, celery and bell pepper and cook for 10 minutes. Add turkey broth, 1½ cups water and rice and bring to a boil. Reduce heat and cook on low for about 15 minutes or until rice is tender.

☐ Stir in chicken soup, turkey, milk and ¾ teaspoon pepper. Stir constantly and cook on medium heat until mixture is thoroughly hot. Serves 6.

Money-Saving Tip:
Don't buy non-grocery items at the grocery store.

CHICKEN-SAUSAGE STEW

1 (16 ounce) package frozen stew vegetables
2 (12 ounce) cans chicken breast with liquid
½ pound Italian sausage, sliced
2 (15 ounce) cans Italian stewed tomatoes
1 (14 ounce) can chicken broth
¼ teaspoon cayenne pepper
1 cup cooked instant rice

☐ Combine all ingredients except rice and add a little salt in large heavy soup pot.

☐ Bring to a boil, reduce heat and simmer for 25 minutes. Stir in cooked rice during last 5 minutes of cooking time. Serves 6 to 8.

Rice came to the South by way of a storm-ravaged merchant ship sailing from Madagascar and reaching the port of Charleston for safe haven. As a gift to the people, the ship's captain gave a local planter "Golden Seed Rice" and by 1700, rice was a major crop in the colonies. The success of the crop gave rise to the name "Carolina Gold Rice".

FAVORITE CHICKEN-TOMATO STEW

1 pound boneless, skinless chicken breast halves, cut into strips
1 onion, chopped
1 green bell pepper, seeded, chopped
2 (14 ounce) cans chicken broth
2 (15 ounce) cans Mexican stewed tomatoes
2 (15 ounce) cans navy beans with liquid
1 cup salsa
2 teaspoons ground cumin
1½ cups crushed tortilla chips

☐ Brown and cook chicken in stew pot on medium heat for 10 minutes.

☐ Add onion, bell pepper, broth, tomatoes, navy beans, salsa, cumin, and a little salt and pepper. Bring to a boil, reduce heat and simmer for 25 minutes, stirring often.

☐ Ladle into individual soup bowls and sprinkle crushed tortilla chips on top of stew. Serve immediately. Serves 8.

Use leftover meats in soups and sandwich spreads. Use a food processor or food chopper to cut the meat into small pieces and combine with chicken, beef or vegetable broth with leftover vegetables. For sandwich spreads, cut the meat into very small pieces and add mayonnaise, relish, onion, and a little salt and pepper and you're ready to make sandwiches.

TASTY TURKEY-VEGGIE STEW

2 (14 ounce) cans chicken broth
2 teaspoons minced garlic
1 (16 ounce) package frozen corn
1 (10 ounce) package frozen cut green beans
1 (10 ounce) package frozen sliced carrots
2 (15 ounce) cans stewed tomatoes
2½ cups cooked, cubed turkey
1 cup shredded mozzarella cheese

☐ Combine broth, 1 cup water, garlic, corn, green beans, carrots, tomatoes, turkey and
1 teaspoon salt in large, heavy soup pot.

☐ Bring to a boil, reduce heat and simmer for 15 minutes. To serve, top each bowl
of soup with mozzarella cheese. Serves 6 to 8.

CHICKEN AND RICE GUMBO

3 (14 ounce) cans chicken broth
1 pound boneless, skinless chicken breasts, cubed
2 (15 ounce) cans whole kernel corn, drained
2 (15 ounce) cans stewed tomatoes with liquid
¾ cup white rice
1 teaspoon Cajun seasoning
2 (10 ounce) packages frozen okra, thawed, chopped

☐ Combine chicken broth and chicken in soup pot and cook on medium-high heat for
15 minutes.

☐ Add remaining ingredients and 1 teaspoon pepper and bring to a boil. Reduce heat and
simmer for 30 minutes or until rice is done. Serves 8.

CHICKEN-BROCCOLI CHOWDER

2 (14 ounce) cans chicken broth
1 (10 ounce) package frozen chopped broccoli
1 bunch fresh green onions, finely chopped, divided
1½ cups dry mashed potato flakes
2½ cups cooked, cut-up chicken breasts
1 (8 ounce) package shredded mozzarella cheese
1 (8 ounce) carton whipping cream
1 cup milk

☐ Combine broth, broccoli and half green onions in large saucepan. Bring to a boil, reduce heat, cover and simmer for 5 minutes.

☐ Stir in dry potato flakes and mix until they blend well. Add chicken, cheese, cream, milk, 1 cup water, and a little salt and pepper. Heat over medium heat and stir occasionally until hot and cheese melts, about 5 minutes.

☐ Ladle into individual soup bowls and garnish with remaining chopped green onions. Serves 8.

MAMA MIA CHICKEN CHOWDER

2 (12 ounce) cans chicken breasts with liquid
¼ cup Italian salad dressing
1 (15 ounce) can stewed tomatoes
1 (10 ounce) can chicken broth
2 small zucchini, chopped
½ cup elbow macaroni
1 teaspoon dried basil
1 cup shredded mozzarella cheese

☐ Combine chicken, salad dressing, tomatoes, broth, zucchini, macaroni, basil, ½ cup water, and a little salt and pepper in large soup pot.

☐ Bring to a boil, reduce heat and simmer for 10 minutes or until macaroni is tender. Serve in individual soup bowls and sprinkle cheese over each serving. Serves 4 to 6.

CHEESY TOMATO CHILI

1 (28 ounce) can diced tomatoes
1 (15 ounce) can kidney beans, rinsed, drained
1 (15 ounce) can pinto beans, drained
2 (14 ounce) cans chicken broth
2 (12 ounce) cans chicken breasts with liquid
1 tablespoon chili powder
1 (8 ounce) package shredded Mexican 4-cheese blend, divided

☐ Combine tomatoes, kidney beans, pinto beans, broth, chicken, chili powder, and a little salt and pepper in soup pot. Bring to a boil, reduce heat and simmer for 25 minutes.

☐ Stir in half cheese and spoon into individual soup bowls. Sprinkle remaining cheese on top of each serving. Serves 8.

WHITE BEAN CHILI

1 pound dried great northern beans
2 onions, finely chopped
2 ribs celery, sliced
2 tablespoons olive oil
1 (7 ounce) can diced green chilies
2 tablespoons minced garlic
1 tablespoon ground cumin
2 teaspoons dried oregano
½ teaspoon cayenne pepper
3 (14 ounce) cans chicken broth
1 rotisserie chicken, boned, cubed
1 (12 ounce) package shredded Monterey Jack cheese, divided

☐ Rinse beans and place in soup pot. Cover with water 2 inches above beans and soak overnight. Drain beans and set aside.

☐ Saute onions and celery in hot oil in saucepan. Add green chilies, garlic, cumin, oregano and cayenne pepper; cook for 2 minutes and stir constantly.

☐ Transfer to soup pot and add beans, chicken broth and ½ cup water. Bring to a boil and reduce heat. Cover, simmer for about 2 hours or until beans are tender; stir occasionally.

☐ Add chicken and 1 cup cheese. Bring to a boil, reduce heat and simmer for 10 minutes, stirring often. Ladle chili into individual soup bowls and top each serving with remaining cheese. Serves 8.

HAM AND BLACK BEAN SOUP

Half of the ingredients listed for this recipe are seasonings, so don't be scared about time and effort for this soup. It doesn't take much time to measure seasonings.

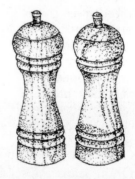

2 cups dried black beans
1 cup cooked, diced ham
1 onion, chopped
1 carrot, chopped
2 ribs celery, chopped
3 jalapeno peppers, seeded, chopped
2 (14 ounce) cans chicken broth
2 teaspoons ground cumin
2 tablespoons snipped fresh cilantro
1 teaspoon oregano
1 teaspoon chili powder
½ - 1 teaspoon cayenne pepper
1 (8 ounce) carton sour cream

☐ Wash beans, soak overnight and drain. Except for sour cream, place all ingredients, 1 teaspoon salt and 10 cups water in large, heavy soup pot. Bring to a boil, reduce heat and simmer for 3 hours or until beans are tender.

☐ Add more water as needed and stir occasionally. Make sure there is enough water in pot to make soup consistency and not too thick.

☐ Place few cups at a time in food processor (using steel blade) or blender and puree until smooth. Add sour cream and reheat soup. Serve in individual bowls. Serves 8.

WILD RICE AND HAM SOUP

1 (6 ounce) box long grain-wild rice
1 (16 ounce) package frozen onions and bell peppers
1 (10 ounce) can cream of celery soup
2 (14 ounce) cans chicken broth
2 cups cooked, diced ham
2 (15 ounce) cans black-eyed peas with jalapenos with liquid
1 (8 ounce) carton sour cream

▢ Cook rice according to package directions.

▢ Combine rice, onions and bell peppers, celery soup, broth, ham and black-eyed peas in soup pot. Bring to a bring to a boil, reduce heat and simmer for 20 minutes.

▢ When ready to serve, stir in sour cream. Serves 6.

...devote all the time and resources at your disposal to the building up of a fine kitchen. It will be, as it should be, the most comforting and comfortable room in the house.

– Elizabeth David

FRIJOLE SOUP

1½ pounds dried pinto beans
5 slices thick sliced bacon, cut in pieces
2 onions, chopped
1 teaspoon garlic powder
½ teaspoon thyme
½ teaspoon oregano
½ teaspoon cayenne pepper
Flour tortillas
Butter

☐ Wash beans, place in large soup pot and cover with water. Soak overnight and drain.

☐ Cook bacon and onions in skillet for about 5 minutes. Transfer with pan drippings to bean pot. Bring to a boil and add all seasonings.

☐ Lower heat and cook for 4 hours. Add hot water when liquid goes below original level. When beans are done, remove about half of beans.

☐ Mash beans with potato masher or process in blender. Return to pot and add 1 tablespoon salt. Serve with hot, flour tortillas and butter. Serves 4.

One of the most wonderful things about life is that we must regularly stop what we are doing and devote our attention to eating.

—Samuel Johnson

NAVY BEAN SOUP

This soup tastes great with cornbread.

3 (15 ounce) cans navy beans with liquid
1 (14 ounce) can chicken broth
1 cup cooked, chopped ham
1 large onion, chopped
½ teaspoon garlic powder

☐ Combine all ingredients with 1 cup water in large saucepan and bring to a boil.

☐ Simmer until onion is tender-crisp and serve hot. Serves 6.

GOOD OL' BEAN SOUP

3 tablespoons olive oil
1 cup shredded carrots
1 (16 ounce) package frozen chopped onions and peppers
2 (14 ounce) cans chicken broth
2 (15 ounce) cans pinto beans with jalapenos with liquid
2 cups cooked, diced ham

☐ Combine oil, carrots, and onions and peppers in soup pot and cook for 10 minutes.

☐ Add broth, pinto beans, ham and ½ cup water. Bring to a boil, reduce heat and simmer for 15 minutes. Serves 6.

TIP: *We use canned beans in many of these recipes as a time-saver. Bean soups are filling and inexpensive and are great for family meals or side dishes. You can always use dried beans after soaking in water overnight and cooking slowly for several hours.*

TOMATO AND WHITE BEAN SOUP

2 tablespoons olive oil
1 onion, chopped
1 green bell pepper, seeded, chopped
1 (15 ounce) can diced tomatoes
2 (14 ounce) cans chicken broth
2 (15 ounce) cans navy beans, rinsed, drained
1½ cups cooked, cubed ham
½ cup chopped fresh parsley

☐ Combine olive oil, onion and bell pepper in large saucepan; saute for 5 minutes and stir constantly.

☐ Stir in tomatoes, broth, navy beans and ham and bring to boil. Reduce heat and simmer for 10 minutes.

☐ Pour into individual soup bowls and sprinkle parsley on top. Serves 4.

HAM AND FRESH OKRA SOUP

1 ham hock
1 (10 ounce) package frozen butter beans or lima beans
2 - 4 cups cooked, cubed ham or chicken
1 (15 ounce) can stewed tomatoes
3 cups small, whole okra
2 large onions, diced
Rice, cooked

☐ Boil ham hock in 1½ quarts water for about 1 hour 30 minutes in soup pot.

☐ Add remaining ingredients with a little salt and pepper and simmer for additional 1 hour. Remove ham hock (pick off any remaining meat and add back to pot) and serve over rice. Serves 6.

CABBAGE-HAM SOUP

1 (16 ounce) package cabbage slaw
1 onion, chopped
1 red bell pepper, seeded, chopped
1 teaspoon minced garlic
2 (14 ounce) cans chicken broth
1 (15 ounce) can stewed tomatoes
2 cups cooked, cubed ham
¼ cup packed brown sugar
2 tablespoons lemon juice

☐ Combine slaw, onion, bell pepper, garlic, broth and 1 cup water in large, heavy soup pot. Bring to a boil, reduce heat and simmer for 20 minutes.

☐ Stir in tomatoes, ham, 1 teaspoon salt, brown sugar, lemon juice and a little pepper. Heat just until soup is thoroughly hot. Serves 6.

Children who eat at home almost every night during the week are more likely to make better grades and perform better in school than those who do not. In 1994 in a national poll of high school seniors for Reader's Digest, *Lou Harris reported higher school scores among seniors who ate with their families. He also found that high school seniors were happier with themselves and prospects for the future than seniors who did not eat at home regularly.*

SPLIT PEA SOUP

This is great for leftover ham.

1 (16 ounce) package dried green split peas
1 onion, chopped
1 large potato, peeled, diced
2 ribs celery, chopped
1 cup cooked, shredded or chopped ham
1 cup shredded carrots
1 teaspoon minced garlic
Croutons

☐ Sort and rinse peas and place in large, heavy soup pot. Cover with water 2 inches above peas and soak overnight.

☐ Drain, add 2 quarts water, onion, potato, celery, ham, carrots, garlic, and a little salt and pepper. Bring to a boil, reduce heat, cover and simmer for 2 hours 30 minutes to 3 hours and stir occasionally. (If you happen to have a meaty ham bone, you can use that instead of chopped ham.)

☐ Cool slightly and process mixture in batches in blender until smooth. Return mixture to soup pot, cover and simmer for 5 minutes or until thoroughly hot. Garnish with seasoned croutons. Serves 6.

In the childhood memories of every good cook, there's a large kitchen, a warm stove, a simmering pot and a mom.

— Barbara Costikyan

LUCKY PEA SOUP

Lucky Pea Soup is great on New Year's Day. Black-eyed peas are said to bring good luck in the New Year.

1 onion, chopped
Olive oil
1 cup cooked, cubed ham
1 (15 ounce) can black-eyed peas with jalapenos with liquid
1 (14 ounce) can chicken broth
1 teaspoon minced garlic
1 teaspoon dried sage

☐ Saute onion in a little oil in large saucepan. Add ham, black-eyed peas, broth, garlic and sage and cook on high heat.

☐ Bring to a boil, reduce heat and simmer for 20 minutes; stir occasionally. Serves 4.

You cannot help the poor by destroying the rich. You cannot strengthen the weak by weakening the strong.

You cannot bring about prosperity by discouraging thrift. You cannot lift the wage earner up by pulling the wage payer down.

You cannot further the brotherhood of man by inciting class hatred. You cannot build character and courage by taking away people's initiative and independence.

You cannot help people permanently by doing for them, what they could and should do for themselves.

– William J. H. Boetcker (Attributed to Abraham Lincoln)

CHEESY POTATO-HAM SOUP

1 (32 ounce) carton chicken broth
3 baking potatoes, peeled, grated
2 onions, finely chopped
3 ribs celery, sliced
1 (8 ounce) can peas, drained
1 (7 ounce) can diced green chilies
3 cups cooked, chopped ham
1 (16 ounce) package cubed Velveeta® Mexican Mild cheese
1 (16 ounce) carton half-and-half cream

☐ Combine broth, potatoes, onions, celery, peas, green chilies and ham in soup pot. While stirring, bring to a boil, reduce heat to medium-low and simmer for 30 minutes.

☐ Add cheese and cook on medium heat; stir constantly until cheese melts. Stir in half-and-half cream and continue cooking until soup is thoroughly hot; do not boil. Serves 8.

POTATO-SAUSAGE SOUP

1 pound pork sausage link
1 cup chopped celery
1 cup chopped onion
2 (10 ounce) cans potato soup
1 (14 ounce) can chicken broth

☐ Cut sausage into 1-inch diagonal slices. Brown sausage in large heavy soup pot, drain and place in separate bowl. Leave about 2 tablespoons sausage drippings in skillet and saute celery and onion.

☐ Add potato soup, ¾ cup water, chicken broth and sausage. Bring to a boil, reduce heat and simmer for 20 minutes. Serves 4.

SUPPER-READY HASH BROWN SOUP

1 (18 ounce) package frozen hash-brown potatoes with onions and peppers, thawed
2 (14 ounce) cans chicken broth
3 ribs celery, finely chopped
2 (10 ounce) cans cream of chicken soup
2 cups milk
2 cups cooked, chopped ham
2 teaspoons minced garlic
1 teaspoon dried parsley flakes

☐ Combine hash-brown potatoes, broth and celery in large soup pot and bring to a boil. Reduce heat and simmer for 25 minutes.

☐ Pour in soup and milk; stir until mixture is smooth. Add ham, garlic, parsley and ½ teaspoon pepper. Bring to a boil, stirring constantly, immediately reduce heat and simmer for 10 minutes. Serves 6.

When we gather at the dinner table, we form bonds that translate into who we are and where we come from. For one brief moment when we sit down to enjoy a meal, carry on conversations and listen to each other, we become a true family.

SAUSAGE-TORTELLINI SOUP

1 pound Italian sausage
1 onion, chopped
3 ribs celery, sliced
2 (14 ounce) cans beef broth
½ teaspoon dried basil
1 (15 ounce) can sliced carrots, drained
1 medium zucchini, halved, sliced
1 (15 ounce) can Italian stewed tomatoes
1 (9 ounce) package refrigerated meat-filled tortellini
Mozzarella cheese

☐ Cook and stir sausage, onion and celery in soup pot on medium heat until sausage is light brown.

☐ Drain and stir in beef broth, 1½ cups water, basil, carrots, zucchini, tomatoes, tortellini, and a little salt and pepper.

☐ Bring to a boil, reduce heat and simmer for 20 minutes or until tortellini are tender.

☐ Ladle into individual soup bowls and sprinkle each serving with cheese. Serves 4 to 6.

President James Monroe said of the most respected ethics courses taught in colleges that "The question to be asked at the end of an educational step is not 'What has the student learned?' but 'What has the student become?'"

SAUSAGE-VEGETABLE SOUP

1 pound bulk Italian sausage
2 onions, chopped
2 teaspoons minced garlic
1 (1 ounce) packet beefy soup mix
1 (15 ounce) can sliced carrots, drained
2 (15 ounce) cans Italian stewed tomatoes
2 (15 ounce) cans garbanzo beans, drained
1 cup elbow macaroni, cooked

☐ Brown sausage, onions and garlic in large soup pot. Drain and add 4 cups water, soup mix, carrots, tomatoes and garbanzo beans. Bring to a boil, reduce heat and simmer for 25 minutes.

☐ Add elbow macaroni and mix well. Serves 6.

EASY MEATY MINESTRONE

2 (26 ounce) cans minestrone soup
1 (15 ounce) can pinto beans with liquid
1 (18 ounce) package frozen Italian meatballs, thawed
1 (5 ounce) package grated parmesan cheese

☐ Combine soup, beans, meatballs and ½ cup water in large saucepan. Bring to a boil, reduce heat and simmer for about 15 minutes.

☐ To serve, sprinkle each serving with parmesan cheese. Serves 6.

MEATBALL SOUP

1 (18 ounce) package frozen cooked Italian meatballs
2 (14 ounce) cans beef broth
2 (15 ounce) cans Italian stewed tomatoes
1 (16 ounce) package frozen stew vegetables

☐ Place meatballs, beef broth and stewed tomatoes in large saucepan. Bring to a boil, reduce heat and simmer for 10 minutes or until meatballs are thoroughly hot.

☐ Add vegetables and cook on medium heat for 10 minutes. Serves 6 to 8.

TIP: If you like your soup thicker, mix 2 tablespoons cornstarch in ¼ cup water and stir into soup, bring to boiling and stir constantly until soup thickens.

NO-BRAINER HEIDELBERG SOUP

2 (10 ounce) cans potato soup
1 (10 ounce) can cream of celery soup
1 soup can milk
6 slices salami, chopped
10 green onions, chopped

☐ Heat potato soup, celery soup and milk in large saucepan on medium heat, stirring constantly, just until thoroughly hot.

☐ Saute salami and onions in sprayed skillet and add to soup.

☐ Heat thoroughly and serve hot. Serves 4.

SISTER'S BRUNSWICK STEW

This signature southern dish takes longer than most dishes, but it is so worth it. Cook meat one day and put stew together the next day. You'll have enough to freeze and serve for several meals. It makes an excellent one-dish meal.

1 (2 pound) boneless pork loin
3 pounds boneless, skinless chicken pieces
4 medium potatoes, quartered
3 (28 ounce) cans stewed, diced tomatoes
2 teaspoons sugar
1 medium onion, chopped
2 (16 ounce) packages frozen butter beans, thawed
2 (16 ounce) packages frozen corn, thawed

☐ Cut pork and chicken into bite-size pieces. Cover with water and cook in stew pot for 1 hour, very slowly or until tender. Skim off excess fat.

☐ Add potatoes and cook on medium about 30 minutes or until tender. When done, mash potatoes to thicken broth. Add tomatoes, sugar, and a little salt and pepper; mix well and cook until heated thoroughly.

☐ Add onion and butter beans. Cook for 10 minutes on low and stir frequently.

☐ Add corn and cook for 5 minutes. Keep scraping bottom of pan to prevent sticking. Serves 10.

*Some days you're the dog,
some days you're the hydrant.*

SOUTHWEST PORK STEW

2 tablespoons olive oil
2 onions, chopped
1 green bell pepper, seeded, chopped
3 teaspoons minced garlic
2 pounds pork tenderloin, cubed
2 (14 ounce) cans chicken broth
2 baking potatoes, peeled, cubed
2 (15 ounce) cans Mexican stewed tomatoes
1 (15 ounce) can yellow hominy, drained
2 teaspoons chili powder
1 teaspoon ground cumin
1 tablespoon lime juice

☐ Place oil in stew pot and saute onion, bell pepper and garlic for 5 minutes.

☐ Add cubed pork and chicken broth and bring to a boil. Reduce heat and simmer for 25 minutes.

☐ Add potatoes and cook for additional 15 minutes or until potatoes are tender. Stir in tomatoes, hominy, chili powder, cumin, lime juice and a little salt. Heat just until stew is thoroughly hot. Serves 6.

Two cannibals are eating a clown. One says to the other, "Does this taste funny to you?"

PANCHO VILLA STEW

1 pound smoked sausage
3 cups cooked, diced ham
3 (14 ounce) cans chicken broth
1 (15 ounce) can diced tomatoes with liquid
2 (7 ounce) cans diced green chilies
1 large onion, chopped
1 teaspoon garlic powder
2 teaspoons ground cumin
2 teaspoons cocoa
1 teaspoon dried oregano
2 (15 ounce) cans pinto beans with liquid
1 (15 ounce) can hominy with liquid
1 (8 ounce) can whole kernel corn, drained
Flour tortillas or cornbread

☐ Cut sausage into ½-inch slices. Combine sausage, ham, broth, tomatoes, green chilies, onion, garlic powder, cumin, cocoa, oregano and ½ teaspoon salt in stew pot. Bring to a boil, reduce heat and simmer for 45 minutes.

☐ Add pinto beans, hominy and corn and bring to a boil. Reduce heat and simmer for additional 15 minutes.

☐ Serve with buttered, flour tortillas or cornbread. Serves 8.

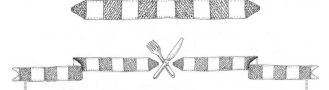

Two antennas met on a roof, fell in love and got married. The ceremony wasn't much, but the reception was excellent.

POLISH VEGETABLE STEW

Olive oil
1 onion, sliced
2 carrots, peeled, sliced
1 bell pepper, seeded, chopped
2 (15 ounce) cans stewed tomatoes
2 (15 ounce) cans new potatoes, drained, quartered
1 pound Polish sausage, sliced
1 (9 ounce) package coleslaw mix

☐ Place a little oil in large stew pot. Cook onion, carrots and bell peppers for 3 minutes or until tender-crisp. Add tomatoes and ½ cup water; stir well.

☐ Stir potatoes and sausage in soup mixture. Bring to a boil, reduce heat and simmer for 10 minutes.

☐ Stir in coleslaw mix and cook on medium heat for additional 8 minutes, stirring occasionally. Serves 6.

When leftovers are used in soups, casseroles, skillet meals, etc. there are no "leftover" flavors. The dish has a completely new taste.

BLACK BEAN STEW SUPPER

1 pound pork sausage link, thinly sliced
2 onions, chopped
3 ribs celery, sliced
Olive oil
3 (15 ounce) cans black beans, drained, rinsed
2 (10 ounce) cans diced tomatoes and green chilies
2 (14 ounce) cans chicken broth

☐ Place sausage slices, onion and celery in stew pot with a little oil, cook until sausage is light brown and onion is soft; drain. Add beans, tomatoes and green chilies, and broth.

☐ Bring to a boil, reduce heat and simmer for 30 minutes. Take out about 2 cups stew mixture, pour into food processor and pulse until almost smooth.

☐ Return mixture to pot and stir to thicken stew. Return heat to high until stew is thoroughly hot. Serves 6.

When you use leftovers in a completely different dish, no one knows they are eating leftovers. If you have leftovers from a dinner of roast, potatoes, carrots and onions, freeze all the leftovers with the gravy. Keep saving leftovers until you have enough for a great new soup or stew.

SOUTHERN GUMBO

This is great for leftover ham and no one will know it's a "leftover" meal.

2 tablespoons butter
2 tablespoons flour
1 (14 ounce) can chicken broth
1 (15 ounce) can diced tomatoes
1 cup cooked, shredded ham
2 cups fresh, sliced okra

☐ Mix butter and flour in large saucepan. Cook over medium heat and stir constantly until a paste-like roux turns light brown. Stir in broth, tomatoes, ham and okra and bring to a boil.

☐ Reduce heat to low and simmer for 25 minutes, stirring often, until gumbo thickens slightly. Serves 4.

Gumbo is part of the state cuisine of Louisiana. It originated with three different groups: the native Indians who used a filé powder from sassafras leaves as a thickener. Africans used okra and the French mixed flour and fat to make a roux.

HAM AND CORN CHOWDER

3 medium potatoes, cubed
2 (14 ounce) cans chicken broth, divided
2 ribs celery, chopped
1 onion, chopped
Olive oil
¼ cup flour
1 (16 ounce) carton half-and-half cream
½ teaspoon cayenne pepper
1 (15 ounce) can whole kernel corn
1 (15 ounce) can cream-style corn
3 cups cooked, cubed ham
1 (8 ounce) package shredded Velveeta® cheese

☐ Cook potatoes with 1 can chicken broth in saucepan.

☐ Saute celery and onion in large soup pot with a little oil. Add flour and mix well on medium heat. Add second can broth and half-and-half cream. Cook, stirring constantly, until mixture thickens.

☐ Add potatoes, cayenne pepper, corn, cream-style corn, ham, cheese, and a little salt and pepper. Heat slowly and stir several times to keep from sticking. Serves 8.

An excellent health tip:

Smile and Laugh More.

EASY VEGGIE-HAM CHOWDER

1 carrot, grated
2 ribs celery, sliced
1 onion, chopped
1 (4.5 ounce) box julienne potato mix
3 cups milk
2 cups cooked, cubed ham
Shredded sharp cheddar cheese

☐ Combine 2¾ cups water with carrot, celery, onion and potato mix in soup pot. Bring to a boil, reduce heat, cover and simmer for 20 minutes.

☐ Stir in milk and packet of sauce mix from potatoes, mix well and bring to a boil. Simmer for 2 minutes and stir in ham. When serving, garnish with sharp cheddar cheese. Serves 4 to 6.

SAUSAGE-BEAN CHOWDER

2 pounds pork sausage
1 (15 ounce) can pinto beans with liquid
1 (15 ounce) can navy beans with liquid
1 (15 ounce) can kidney beans, drained
2 (15 ounce) cans Mexican stewed tomatoes
2 (14 ounce) cans chicken broth
1 teaspoon minced garlic

☐ Brown and cook sausage in soup pot and stir until sausage crumbles. Add remaining ingredients and bring to a boil. Reduce heat to low and simmer for 20 minutes. Serves 8.

SEAFOOD BISQUE

¼ cup (½ stick) butter
1 (8 ounce) package frozen salad shrimp, thawed
1 (6 ounce) can crab, drained, flaked
1 (15 ounce) can whole new potatoes, drained, sliced
1 teaspoon minced garlic
½ cup flour
2 (14 ounce) cans chicken broth, divided
1 cup half-and-half cream

☐ Melt butter in large saucepan on medium heat. Add shrimp, crab, new potatoes and garlic and cook for 10 minutes.

☐ Stir in flour and cook, stirring constantly for 3 minutes. Gradually add chicken broth, cook and stir until mixture thickens.

☐ Stir in half-and-half cream and a little salt and pepper, stirring constantly and cook just until mixture is thoroughly hot; do not boil. Serves 6.

Use fish from only the best schools.

CREOLE SOUP

2 tablespoons butter
1 (16 ounce) package frozen chopped onions and peppers
2 ribs celery, sliced
1 teaspoon minced garlic
1 (6 ounce) package garlic butter-flavored rice
2 (15 ounce) cans stewed tomatoes
1 teaspoon Creole seasoning
1 (8 ounce) package frozen salad shrimp, thawed

☐ Melt butter and saute onions and peppers, celery, and garlic in large skillet. Stir in 1 cup water, rice, tomatoes and Creole seasoning and bring to a boil.

☐ Reduce heat to medium and cook, stirring often, for 6 minutes. Add shrimp, cover and simmer for additional 5 minutes. Serves 4 to 6.

Harry: Did you hear the joke about the broken egg?

Ralph: Yes, it cracked me up!

FROGMORE STEW

Frogmore Stew originated in South Carolina's Low Country and dates back many years. According to one story passed down through the years, an old fisherman gathered up whatever he could find to put in a stew. Other stories credit specific people on St. Helena Island with the invention, but there's no disagreement to the fact that Frogmore Stew is a combination of sausage, seafood and corn. Here's one version of the famous dish.

½ cup seafood seasoning
1 lemon, sliced, seeded
1 - 2 pounds small new potatoes
2 pounds smoked link sausage, sliced
½ cup (1 stick) butter
6 ears corn, halved
2 pounds large shrimp peeled

☐ Combine about 1½ gallons water, seasoning and lemon in very large stew pot and bring to a boil. Add potatoes and boil 15 to 20 minutes. Add sausage and boil about 5 minutes.

☐ Add butter and corn and cook for 7 minutes. Add shrimp and boil about 5 minutes or until shrimp turn pink. Immediately drain water and serve. Serves 8.

FRESH OYSTER STEW

2 (1 pint) cartons fresh oysters with liquor
3 slices bacon
1 small onion, chopped
2 ribs celery, chopped
1 (4 ounce) can sliced mushrooms
1 (10 ounce) can cream of potato soup
3 cups half-and-half cream
⅓ cup fresh chopped parsley

☐ Drain oysters and save liquor.

☐ Fry bacon in deep skillet until crisp; crumble and set aside.

☐ Cook onion and celery in bacon drippings on medium heat until tender.

☐ Add mushrooms, soup, oyster liquor, half-and-half cream, and a little salt and pepper. Heat over medium heat, stirring occasionally, until mixture is thoroughly hot.

☐ Stir in bacon and oysters and heat for additional 4 to 5 minutes or until edges of oysters begin to curl. Sprinkle with parsley. Serves 6 to 8.

While fresh herbs provide a more authentic flavor, dried herbs can be very convenient. Because dried herbs are more potent, use half the amount of fresh herbs called for in a recipe.

CLAM CHOWDER SNAP

1 (10 ounce) can New England clam chowder
1 (10 ounce) can cream of celery soup
1 (10 ounce) can cream of potato soup
1 (6.5 ounce) can chopped clams, drained
2 soup cans milk

☐ Combine all ingredients in saucepan. Heat and stir. Serves 6.

COD AND CORN CHOWDER

8 slices bacon
1 pound cod, cut into bite-size pieces
2 large baking potatoes, thinly sliced
3 ribs celery, sliced
1 onion, chopped
1 (15 ounce) can whole kernel corn
1 (8 ounce) carton whipping cream

☐ Fry bacon in large, heavy soup pot. Crumble bacon and set aside.

☐ Drain bacon grease from soup pot and stir in 2½ cups water, cod, potatoes, celery, onion, corn, and a little salt and pepper. Bring to a boil, reduce heat, cover and simmer for about 20 minutes or until fish and potatoes are done.

☐ Stir in cream and heat just until chowder is thoroughly hot. When serving, sprinkle crumbled bacon over each serving. Serves 4 to 6.

CRAB-CORN CHOWDER

1 (1.8 ounce) packet dry leek soup mix
2 cups milk
1 (8 ounce) can whole kernel corn, drained
½ (8 ounce) package cubed Velveeta® cheese
1 (7 ounce) can crabmeat, flaked

☐ Combine soup mix and milk in large saucepan, cook over medium heat and stir constantly until soup begins to thicken. While still on medium heat, stir in corn and cheese and stir until cheese melts.

☐ Just before serving, add crabmeat and stir until thoroughly hot. Serves 4.

It is generally thought that most people get plenty of protein and carbohydrates in their daily diets, but are missing some of the important nutrients. Half of a sweet red pepper provides about a day's worth of vitamin C, more than twice the amount of vitamin C in 6 ounces of orange juice. Pumpkin seeds are loaded with magnesium and are great snacks.

CAULIFLOWER-CRAB CHOWDER

1 (16 ounce) package frozen cauliflower
¼ cup (½ stick) butter
¼ cup flour
1 (14 ounce) can chicken broth
1½ cups milk
1 (3 ounce) package cream cheese, cubed
1 (2 ounce) jar chopped pimento, drained
1 teaspoon dried parsley
1 (8 ounce) package refrigerated imitation crabmeat, drained

☐ Cook cauliflower in ¾ cup water in large saucepan until tender-crisp.

☐ In separate saucepan, melt butter, stir in flour and mix well. Add broth, milk and cream cheese and cook, stirring constantly, until thick and bubbly.

☐ Add mixture to saucepan with cauliflower and stir in pimento, parsley, and a little salt and pepper.

☐ Stir in crab and heat just until thoroughly hot. Serves 4 to 6.

Money-Saving Tip:

There are all kinds of sales and promotions at grocery stores. Watch for the really big sales where you can buy items for less than half price and stock up on those. If the item is less than 50% off, but still on sale, buy for the short term.

SEAFOOD GUMBO

¼ cup olive oil
½ cup flour
1 onion, finely chopped
2 teaspoons minced garlic
2 (10 ounce) packages frozen okra
1 (15 ounce) can diced tomatoes
¾ teaspoon cayenne pepper
1 pound fresh, peeled, veined shrimp
1 pound crabmeat, flaked, drained
1 (1 pint) carton oysters, drained
3 fresh green onions, sliced
Rice, cooked

☐ Mix oil and flour in large soup pot. Cook over medium heat and stir constantly until paste-like roux turns light brown. Add onion, garlic, okra and tomatoes and cook on medium heat for about 10 minutes.

☐ Stir in 1 cup water, 2 teaspoons salt and cayenne pepper and simmer for 25 minutes.

☐ Add shrimp and crabmeat and simmer for 10 minutes. Add oysters and cook for additional 5 minutes. Stir in green onions and serve over rice. Serves 6 to 8.

Before 1911, salt clumped in damp weather and dispensing was difficult. In 1911 the Morton Salt Company added magnesium carbonate to its salt so that it would flow freely. The girl with umbrella, illustrating that the salt flows even in the rain, was introduced in 1914.

SALADS

**Put great-tasting, healthy
freshness on your table.**

SALADS CONTENTS

STAINED-GLASS FRUIT SALAD

Very good and very fast.

2 (20 ounce) cans peach pie filling
3 bananas, sliced
1 (16 ounce) package frozen strawberries, thawed, drained
1 (20 ounce) can pineapple tidbits, drained

☐ Mix fruits in bowl. Refrigerate before serving. (It's even better the day after it's made.)
Serves 8 to 10.

CRUNCHY FRUIT SALAD

2 red apples with peels, chopped
⅓ cup sunflower seeds
½ cup green grapes
⅓ cup vanilla yogurt

☐ Combine apples, sunflower seeds, grapes and yogurt in bowl. Stir to coat fruit with
yogurt. Refrigerate before serving. Serves 4.

INCREDIBLE STRAWBERRY SALAD

It really is incredible!

2 (8 ounce) packages cream cheese, softened
2 tablespoons mayonnaise
½ cup powdered sugar
1 (16 ounce) package frozen strawberries, thawed
1 (10 ounce) package miniature marshmallows
1 (8 ounce) can crushed pineapple, drained
1 (8 ounce) carton frozen whipped topping, thawed
1 cup chopped pecans

☐ Beat cream cheese, mayonnaise and powdered sugar in bowl until creamy. Fold in strawberries (if strawberries are large, cut in half), marshmallows, pineapple, whipped topping and pecans.

☐ Pour into 9 x 13-inch glass dish and freeze. Remove from freezer 15 minutes before you cut and serve. Serves 12.

I've learned that people will forget what you said, people will forget what you did, but people will never forget how you made them feel.

– Maya Angelou

PISTACHIO SALAD

Perfect to serve on St. Patrick's Day.

1 (15 ounce) can crushed pineapple, drained
1 (11 ounce) can mandarin oranges, drained
1 (6 ounce) package pistachio instant pudding mix
2 cups miniature marshmallows
1 cup chopped pecans
1 cup flaked coconut
1 (12 ounce) carton frozen whipped topping, thawed

☐ Combine pineapple, oranges, pudding mix, marshmallows, pecans and coconut in bowl and blend well.

☐ Fold in whipped topping and refrigerate. Serves 8.

BROCCOLI WALDORF SALAD

4 cups fresh broccoli florets
1 large red apple with peel, cored, chopped
½ cup golden raisins
½ cup chopped pecans
½ cup coleslaw dressing

☐ Combine broccoli, apple, raisins and pecans in large bowl. Drizzle with dressing and toss to coat. Refrigerate. Serves 8.

BROCCOLI SALAD

The grapes give the recipe a special "zip".

1 large bunch broccoli cut in bite-size pieces
1 cup chopped celery
1 bunch green onions with tops, sliced
½ red bell pepper, chopped
1 cup halved seedless green grapes
1 cup halved seedless red grapes
1 cup slivered almonds, toasted
½ pound bacon, cooked crisp, drained, crumbled

☐ Wash and drain broccoli well. It will help to drain broccoli if you place pieces on cup towel, pick it up and shake well. Combine all ingredients in bowl and toss.

DRESSING:

1 cup mayonnaise
¼ cup sugar
2 tablespoons vinegar

☐ Combine mayonnaise, sugar, vinegar, 1 teaspoon salt and ½ teaspoon pepper in bowl, add to salad and toss. Refrigerate. Serves 8 to 10.

Money-Saving Tip:

Create a list of grocery prices for the items you buy most often. You can stay on top of bargains and price cycles. This will help you recognize a good deal when you see one.

RAISIN-BROCCOLI SALAD

1 bunch fresh broccoli, cut in small bite-sized florets
½ purple onion, sliced, separated
½ cup golden raisins
1 cup slivered almonds, toasted
Imitation bacon bits

☐ Make sure broccoli is well drained. Combine broccoli, onion, raisins, almonds and celery in bowl.

DRESSING:

1 cup mayonnaise
¼ cup sugar
2 tablespoons vinegar

☐ Combine mayonnaise, sugar, vinegar, 1 teaspoon salt, and ½ teaspoon pepper in bowl, pour over vegetables and toss well. Refrigerate for several hours before serving.

☐ Sprinkle bacon bits over salad just before serving. Serves 6 to 8.

Money-Saving Tip:

If you're dashing into the store for just a few items, don't use a basket. If you're limited to what you can carry, you're more likely to avoid impulse buys.

Cauliflower and Broccoli Salad

1 (8 ounce) carton sour cream
1 cup mayonnaise
1 (1 ounce) packet ranch dressing mix
1 large head cauliflower, broken into bite-size pieces
1 large bunch fresh broccoli, broken into bite-size pieces
1 (10 ounce) package frozen green peas, thawed
3 ribs celery, sliced
1 bunch green onions with tops, chopped
1 (8 ounce) can water chestnuts, drained
8 ounces mozzarella cheese, cut in chunks
2 (2.5 ounce) packages slivered almonds, toasted

☐ Mix sour cream, mayonnaise and dressing mix in bowl and set aside. Make sure cauliflower and broccoli are well drained.

☐ In separate bowl, combine cauliflower, broccoli, peas, celery, onions, water chestnuts, cheese and almonds. Add sour cream mixture and toss. Refrigerate. Serves 12.

Try lining your refrigerator's crisper drawer with paper towels; they'll absorb excess moisture and keep your vegetables from spoiling too quickly.

MARINATED BRUSSELS SPROUTS

2 (10 ounce) packages frozen brussels sprouts
½ cup olive oil
½ cup tarragon vinegar
2 tablespoons sugar
1 clove garlic, crushed
½ teaspoon seasoned salt
2 small onions, cut in rings

☐ Cook brussels sprouts according to package directions.

☐ Combine oil, vinegar, sugar, garlic, seasoned salt, and 1 teaspoon each of salt and pepper in medium container with lid.

☐ Add brussels sprouts and onion rings to dressing. Place lid on container and shake well. Refrigerate for at least 24 hours before serving. Serves 6 to 8.

CHILLED HARVEST SALAD

2 (10 ounce) packages frozen baby lima beans
1 (15 ounce) can shoe-peg corn, drained
1 bunch fresh green onions with tops, chopped
1 cup mayonnaise
2 teaspoons ranch salad dressing seasoning

☐ Cook beans according to package directions and drain.

☐ Combine all ingredients, mix well and refrigerate. Serves 8.

SUMMER CUCUMBER CRISPS

1 pint white vinegar
1½ cups sugar
1 clove garlic, chopped
1 tablespoon whole cloves
1 tablespoon whole allspice
2 bay leaves
2 sticks cinnamon
1 tablespoon whole celery seed
1 tablespoon mustard seed
1 tablespoon peppercorns
1 teaspoon powdered ginger
5 - 6 cucumbers

☐ Combine all ingredients except cucumbers in saucepan and boil for 12 to 15 minutes. Cool mixture and strain.

☐ Thinly slice cucumbers and place in large jar or bowl with lid. Add cooled marinade and cover tightly. Keep refrigerated. Serves 10 to 12.

Often in the South, homemade pickles substitute for a salad. Bread and butter pickles, watermelon pickles, pickled okra, yellow cucumber pickles, peach pickles and green tomato pickles all grace dinner tables.

CALICO SALAD

1 (15 ounce) can peas, drained
1 (15 ounce) can whole kernel white corn, drained
1 cup finely chopped celery
1 green pepper, seeded, chopped
1 small bunch green onions, chopped
1 (2 ounce) jar diced pimentos, drained

☐ Combine and mix all vegetables in bowl with lid.

DRESSING:

½ cup sugar
½ cup wine vinegar
½ cup olive oil
½ teaspoon tarragon
½ teaspoon basil

☐ Combine sugar, vinegar, oil, tarragon, basil, 1 teaspoon salt and ½ teaspoon pepper in bowl; pour over vegetables. Cover and refrigerate overnight. Salad can be stored in refrigerator for several days. Serves 8.

Twenty years from now you will be more disappointed by the things you didn't do than by the ones you did do. So throw off the bowlines. Sail away from the safe harbor. Catch the trade winds in your sails. Explore. Dream. Discover.

– Mark Twain

CRUNCHY PEA SALAD

1 (16 ounce) package frozen English peas, thawed
½ head small cauliflower, cut into small florets
1 cup chopped celery
1 (8 ounce) can water chestnuts, drained
1 (2 ounce) jar pimentos, drained
1½ cups mayonnaise
¼ cup Italian salad dressing
½ teaspoon seasoned salt
⅛ teaspoon cayenne pepper
1 cup peanuts
½ cup bacon bits

☐ Combine peas, cauliflower, celery, water chestnuts and pimentos in large bowl with lid.

☐ In small bowl combine mayonnaise, salad dressing, seasoned salt, cayenne pepper and ½ teaspoon salt and mix well. Add to vegetable bowl, toss well, cover and refrigerate.

☐ When ready to serve, add peanuts and bacon bits and toss. Serves 8 to 10.

Salads don't have to have greens in them to qualify as a salad. Chop up vegetables, toss with a salad dressing and serve them raw. These crunchy salads are great additions to any meal.

PEA-CAULIFLOWER RANCH SALAD

1 (16 ounce) package frozen green peas, thawed
1 head cauliflower, cut into bite-size pieces
1 (8 ounce) carton sour cream
1 (1 ounce) packet ranch salad dressing mix

☐ Combine peas and cauliflower in large bowl. In separate bowl, combine sour cream and salad dressing. Toss with vegetables. Refrigerate. Serves 6 to 8.

CASHEW PEA SALAD

1 (16 ounce) package frozen green peas, thawed
¼ cup diced celery
1 small bunch fresh green onions with tops, chopped
1 cup chopped cashews
½ cup mayonnaise

☐ Combine peas, celery, onions and cashews. Toss with mayonnaise and a little salt and pepper. Serves 6 to 8.

Before squeezing lemons, limes or oranges for juice, zap them in the microwave for about 20 seconds and you will get more juice.

BLACK-EYED PEA SALAD

2 (16 ounce) cans jalapeno black-eyed peas, drained
1 ripe avocado, peeled, chopped
½ purple onion, chopped
1 bell pepper, seeded, chopped

☐ Combine all ingredients in large bowl and mix well.

DRESSING:

⅓ cup olive oil
⅓ cup white vinegar
3 tablespoons sugar
¼ teaspoon garlic powder

☐ Combine oil, vinegar, sugar, garlic powder and ½ teaspoon salt in bowl and add to vegetables. Toss and refrigerate. Serves 6 to 8.

TOMATO, MOZZARELLA & BASIL

2 - 3 tomatoes, thickly sliced
6 - 9 thick slices fresh mozzarella cheese
1 sweet onion, sliced, optional
6 - 9 leaves fresh basil
3 tablespoons extra-virgin olive oil

☐ Layer a slice of tomato, mozzarella, onion and basil. Repeat with remaining ingredients. Drizzle with olive oil and sprinkle with salt and pepper. Serves 6 to 9.

POTATO SALAD REUNION

6 medium potatoes, cubed
⅓ cup Italian salad dressing
¾ cup chopped green onions with tops
3 eggs, hard-boiled, chopped
1 cup chopped celery
1 (2 ounce) jar diced pimentos, drained
½ cup pickle relish, drained
1 cup mayonnaise
½ cup sour cream
1 tablespoon mustard
1 teaspoon seasoned salt
½ teaspoon Creole seasoning
1 teaspoon sugar
Paprika

☐ Boil potatoes in saucepan until tender, about 20 minutes; drain. While still warm, pour Italian dressing over potatoes in bowl. Cool.

☐ Add onions, eggs, celery, pimentos and pickle relish and toss.

☐ In separate bowl, combine mayonnaise, sour cream, mustard, seasoned salt, Creole seasoning, sugar, ½ teaspoon salt and 1 teaspoon pepper and fold into potato mixture. Refrigerate for several hours.

☐ When ready to serve, garnish with paprika. Serves 10 to 12.

MEDITERRANEAN POTATO SALAD

2 pounds new (red) potatoes, quartered
¾ - 1 cup Caesar dressing
½ cup grated parmesan cheese
¼ cup chopped fresh parsley
½ cup chopped roasted red peppers

☐ Cook potatoes in saucepan in boiling water until fork-tender, drain and cool. Pour dressing over potatoes in large bowl.

☐ Add cheese, parsley and peppers and toss lightly. Serve warm or chilled. Serves 6 to 8.

RED CABBAGE SLAW

1 large head red cabbage
2 onions, finely chopped
½ cup coleslaw dressing
½ cup French salad dressing

☐ Cut cabbage into thin slices and combine with onions in bowl. In separate bowl, combine dressings and toss with cabbage and onions. Refrigerate before serving. Serves 4.

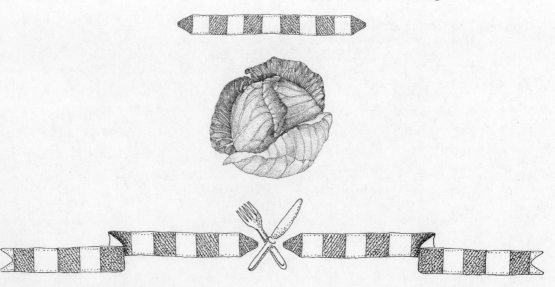

PINEAPPLE SLAW

1 (8 ounce) can pineapple tidbits with juice
3 cups finely shredded cabbage
1½ cups chopped red delicious apple with peel
½ cup chopped celery
¾ cup mayonnaise

☐ Drain pineapple and set aside 3 tablespoons juice. Combine pineapple, cabbage, apple and celery in large bowl.

☐ Combine mayonnaise and the set aside pineapple juice. Add to cabbage mixture and toss gently.

☐ Cover and refrigerate. Serves 8.

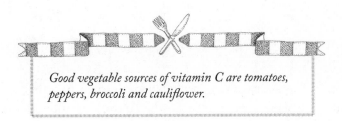

Good vegetable sources of vitamin C are tomatoes, peppers, broccoli and cauliflower.

CRUNCHY CHINESE SLAW

1 head green cabbage, grated
½ head red cabbage, grated
1 cup slivered almonds, toasted
1 bunch green onions, sliced
1 large green bell pepper, seeded, diced
1 cup sliced celery
1 (11 ounce) can mandarin oranges, drained
2 (3 ounce) packages chicken-flavored ramen noodles, crumbled (uncooked)
1 cup sunflower seeds

☐ Preheat oven to 275°.

☐ Toast almonds in oven for 15 minutes.

☐ Combine cabbage, almonds, green onions, bell pepper, celery, oranges, noodles and sunflower seeds in bowl.

DRESSING:

1 cup olive oil
¾ cup tarragon vinegar
¾ cup sugar
Seasoning packets from ramen noodles
2 dashes hot sauce

☐ Combine oil, vinegar, sugar, seasoning packets from ramen noodles, hot sauce, 2 teaspoons salt and 1 teaspoon pepper in bowl. Pour over cabbage mixture and toss well. Serves about 18.

TIP: *You can splurge on cabbage and buy 2 heads of green cabbage and use only the outer, greenest leaves to equal one head green cabbage. For the red cabbage, you can also cut only the outer red leaves.*

CORNBREAD SALAD

2 (6 ounce) packages Mexican cornbread mix
2 eggs
1⅓ cups milk
2 ribs celery, sliced
1 bunch green onions with tops, chopped
1 green bell pepper, seeded, chopped
2 firm tomatoes, chopped, drained
8 slices bacon, cooked, crumbled
1 cup shredded cheddar cheese
1 (8 ounce) can whole kernel corn, drained
½ cup ripe olives, chopped
2½ cups mayonnaise

▢ Prepare cornbread with eggs and milk according to package directions. Cook, cool and crumble cornbread in large bowl.

▢ Add remaining ingredients and mix well. Serves 16.

Money-Saving Tip:

Look at the top and bottom of grocery shelves for the best deals. Store brands are usually at the top.

Terrific Tortellini Salad

2 (14 ounce) packages refrigerated cheese tortellini
1 green bell pepper, diced
1 red bell pepper, diced
1 cucumber, peeled, chopped
1 (14 ounce) can artichoke hearts, rinsed, drained
1 (8 ounce) bottle creamy Caesar salad dressing

☐ Prepare tortellini according to package directions and drain. Rinse with cold water, drain and refrigerate.

☐ Combine tortellini, bell peppers, cucumber, artichoke hearts and dressing in large bowl. Cover and refrigerate for at least 2 hours before serving. Serves 8.

Fusilli Pasta Quick-Fix

1 (16 ounce) package fusilli or corkscrew pasta
1 (16 ounce) package frozen broccoli-cauliflower combination
1 (8 ounce) package cubed mozzarella cheese
1 (8 ounce) bottle Catalina salad dressing

☐ Cook pasta according to package directions. Drain and cool.

☐ Cook vegetables according to package directions. Drain and cool.

☐ Combine pasta, vegetables and cheese cubes in large bowl. Toss with Catalina dressing. Refrigerate for several hours before serving. Serves 6 to 8.

Bow Tie Salad

Dressing:

1¼ cups mayonnaise
⅓ cup freshly grated parmesan cheese
⅓ cup chopped fresh parsley
¼ teaspoon oregano
¼ teaspoon basil
¾ teaspoon garlic powder

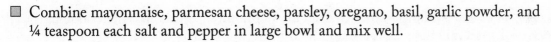

▢ Combine mayonnaise, parmesan cheese, parsley, oregano, basil, garlic powder, and ¼ teaspoon each salt and pepper in large bowl and mix well.

Salad:

4 ounces bow tie pasta, cooked, drained
4 ounces salami, cubed
1 (8 ounce) can artichoke hearts, drained, quartered
1½ cups thinly sliced zucchini
1½ cups broccoli florets
½ cup diced red pepper
½ cup pine nuts, toasted

▢ Add all salad ingredients to dressing and toss well.

▢ Cover and refrigerate for at least 2 hours before serving. Serves 8 to 10.

BROCCOLI-NOODLE CRUNCH

Who thought up the idea of grating broccoli "stems" for a salad? It was pure genius! This salad is different – and very good. It will last and still be "crispy" in the refrigerator for days!

1 cup slivered almonds
1 cup sunflower seeds
2 (3 ounce) packages chicken-flavored ramen noodles
1 (12 ounce) package broccoli slaw

☐ Preheat oven to 275°.

☐ Toast almonds and sunflower seeds in oven for 15 minutes. Break up ramen noodles (but do not cook) and mix with slaw, almonds and sunflower seeds.

DRESSING:

¾ cup olive oil
½ cup white vinegar
½ cup sugar
Ramen noodles seasoning packets

☐ Combine dressing ingredients and noodle seasoning packets in bowl. Pour over slaw mixture and mix well. Refrigerate in covered bowl for at least 1 hour; overnight is better. Serves 10 to 12

TIP: Add a handful or two of broccoli florets for extra color and texture.

HOMETOWN DEVILED EGGS

6 eggs, hard-boiled
2 tablespoons sweet pickle relish
3 tablespoons mayonnaise
½ teaspoon prepared mustard
Paprika, optional

☐ Peel eggs and cut in half lengthwise. Separate yolks and mash with fork in bowl. Add relish, mayonnaise and mustard to yolks.

☐ Place yolk mixture back into egg white halves. (Sprinkle paprika over top of devilled eggs, if you like.) Makes 12.

APPLE-WALNUT CHICKEN SALAD

3 - 4 boneless skinless chicken breast halves, cooked, cubed
2 tart green apples, peeled, chopped
½ cup chopped walnuts, toasted
⅓ cup sour cream
⅓ cup mayonnaise
1 tablespoon lemon juice

☐ Mix chicken, apples and walnuts in bowl. In separate bowl, mix sour cream, mayonnaise and lemon juice. Pour over chicken salad and toss. Refrigerate. Serves 6.

ALMOND-CHICKEN SALAD

4 cups cooked, chopped chicken breasts
1½ cups chopped celery
½ apple, peeled, diced
1 (8 ounce) can crushed pineapple, well drained
1 cup slivered almonds, toasted
1 cup halved red grapes

☐ Combine chicken, celery, apple, pineapple, almonds and grapes in bowl.

DRESSING:

1 teaspoon dry mustard
3 tablespoons lemon juice
¼ cup sour cream
1 cup mayonnaise

☐ Mix mustard, lemon juice, sour cream, mayonnaise, ½ teaspoon salt and ¼ teaspoon pepper. Add to salad, toss and refrigerate. Serves 8.

Chicken, U.S.A.

Four communities in the United States have the word "chicken" in their names: Chicken, Alaska; Chicken Bristle, Illinois; Chicken Bristle, Kentucky; and Chickentown, Pennsylvania.

CRUNCHY CHICKEN SALAD

4½ cups cooked, chopped chicken breasts
1 (8 ounce) can water chestnuts, drained
1 cup chopped celery
1 cup halved green grapes
1 (2.25 ounce) package sliced almonds, toasted

☐ Combine chicken, water chestnuts, celery, grapes and almonds in large bowl.

DRESSING:

1 (3 ounce) package cream cheese, softened
1 cup mayonnaise
1 tablespoon lemon juice
1 tablespoon dijon-style mustard

☐ Beat cream cheese and mayonnaise until smooth. Add lemon juice, mustard, ½ teaspoon black pepper and 1 teaspoon salt.

☐ Fold dressing into chicken. Refrigerate. Serves 8.

TIP: Serve over lettuce leaves or shredded cabbage.

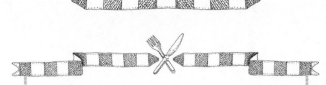

A "free-range" chicken is one that is given twice as much room as mass-produced chickens and they are free to roam indoors and outdoors. This is supposed to enhance the "chicken" flavor because they are "happy" chickens.

DERBY CHICKEN SALAD

3 - 4 boneless skinless chicken breast halves, cooked, cubed
2 avocados, peeled, diced
2 tomatoes, diced, drained
Italian salad dressing

☐ Combine chicken, avocados and tomatoes in bowl. When ready to serve, pour enough dressing over salad to coat; toss and serve immediately. Serves 6.

HAWAIIAN CHICKEN SALAD

1 cup cooked rice
3½ cups cooked, cubed chicken breasts
2 cups diced celery
1 (8 ounce) can water chestnuts, drained, chopped
1 (15 ounce) cans pineapple tidbits, well drained
1 (3 ounce) can flaked coconut
1 banana, sliced

☐ Combine all ingredients in large bowl and mix well.

DRESSING:

1¾ - 2 cups mayonnaise
2 tablespoons lemon juice
½ teaspoon white pepper
1 teaspoon curry powder

☐ Combine mayonnaise, lemon juice, white pepper, curry powder and ¼ teaspoon salt in bowl and fold into chicken salad mixture.

☐ Refrigerate for several hours before serving. Serves 10.

SOUTHWESTERN CHICKEN SALAD

4 cups cooked, cubed chicken breasts
1 (15 ounce) can black beans, drained
¾ red onion, chopped
½ red bell pepper, seeded, chopped
½ yellow bell pepper, seeded, chopped
¼ cup chopped fresh cilantro

☐ Combine chicken, beans, onion, bell peppers and cilantro in large bowl.

DRESSING:

½ cup sour cream
¼ cup mayonnaise
½ teaspoon garlic powder
1 jalapeno pepper, finely chopped
1 teaspoon lime juice
½ cup pine nuts, toasted

☐ Whisk together sour cream and mayonnaise. Stir in garlic powder, jalapeno pepper, lime juice, 1 teaspoon salt and ½ teaspoon pepper. Add to large bowl of chicken salad and toss.

☐ Refrigerate for at least 1 hour. Just before serving, toss in pine nuts. Serves 8.

QUICKIE BLACK BEAN CHICKEN SALAD

2 - 3 boneless skinless chicken breasts, cooked, cubed
1 (15 ounce) can black beans, drained
1 bunch green onions, chopped
1 cup chopped celery
Vinaigrette salad dressing

☐ Blend all ingredients in bowl and toss. Serves 6.

Tropical Chicken Salad

6 boneless, skinless chicken breast halves, cooked, cubed
2 mangoes, peeled, cubed
2 cups fresh pineapple, cubed
1 cup halved seedless green grapes
2 green onions, minced, white only
¾ cup slivered almonds, toasted
1 tablespoon fresh minced ginger (or ¼ teaspoon ground ginger)
1 tablespoon fresh minced cilantro (or ¼ teaspoon ground cilantro)
½ teaspoon white pepper
¼ teaspoon ground nutmeg
2 tablespoons lime juice
¾ cup mayonnaise
½ cup sour cream

☐ Combine chicken, mangoes, pineapple, grapes, green onions, almonds, ginger, cilantro, 1 teaspoon salt, white pepper and nutmeg in large bowl and toss lightly. Sprinkle lime juice over top and toss.

☐ In separate bowl, combine mayonnaise and sour cream. Pour dressing over salad and toss gently to coat. Serves 10 to 12.

TIP: This is great served on red cabbage leaves and garnished with peeled orange slices.

It isn't what you have, or who you are, or where you are, or what you are doing that makes you happy or unhappy. It is what you think about.

– Dale Carnegie

CRUNCHY TUNA SALAD

2 (7 ounce) cans white tuna in water, drained
¼ cup chopped onion
½ cup chopped celery
¼ cup chopped ripe olives
1 (2 ounce) jar chopped pimentos, drained
⅔ cup mayonnaise
1 tablespoon wine vinegar
1 (3 ounce) can chow mein noodles

☐ Combine all ingredients except noodles in bowl and refrigerate. Just before serving, toss
with noodles. Serves 4 to 6.

SHRIMP AND ENGLISH PEA SALAD

2 cups small frozen shrimp, cooked, cleaned
1 (10 ounce) package frozen green peas, thawed
2 ribs celery, chopped
1 cup mayonnaise
⅓ cup India relish, drained
1 tablespoon lemon juice
½ teaspoon curry powder
1 (3 ounce) can chow mein noodles
1 cup chopped cashews

☐ Using paper towels, blot shrimp well to make sure all liquid is gone.

☐ Combine peas, celery, mayonnaise, relish, lemon juice, curry powder, ¼ teaspoon salt and
½ teaspoon pepper in large bowl and mix well. Cover and refrigerate for at least 1 hour.

☐ Just before serving, add noodles and cashews and toss. Serves 4 to 6.

SIMPLY SCRUMPTIOUS SHRIMP SALAD

3 cups cooked, chopped shrimp
1 cup chopped celery
4 eggs, hard-boiled, chopped
½ cup sliced green stuffed olives, well drained
¼ cup sliced green onions
¼ cup chopped dill pickle
1 cup mayonnaise
2 tablespoons chili sauce
1 tablespoon horseradish
1 teaspoon seasoned salt
¾ teaspoon seasoned pepper

☐ Combine all ingredients in bowl, toss lightly and refrigerate. Serves 6 to 8.

SHRIMP MONTEREY SALAD

1 pound cooked tiny shrimp
2 tablespoons freshly grated parmesan cheese
¼ cup olive oil
3 tablespoons red wine vinegar
1 tablespoon lemon juice
2 teaspoons dijon-style mustard
3 medium avocados, peeled, halved
1½ cups shredded Monterey Jack cheese

☐ Combine shrimp and parmesan cheese in bowl with lid.

☐ In separate bowl, combine oil, vinegar, lemon juice, mustard, ½ teaspoon salt and
½ teaspoon pepper and mix well.

☐ Pour dressing over shrimp and marinate for 30 minutes to 1 hour. Place 1 avocado half in
each of 6 individual ramekins. Divide seafood evenly onto avocado halves. Sprinkle with
Monterey Jack cheese and serve immediately. Serves 6.

SHRIMP REMOULADE

½ cup mayonnaise
¼ cup horseradish
2 tablespoons dijon-style mustard
¼ cup olive oil
½ cup chili sauce
2 teaspoons lemon juice
¼ teaspoon cayenne pepper
1 teaspoon paprika
½ teaspoon garlic powder
1 tablespoon chopped capers
½ bunch green onions, very finely chopped
1 pound cooked, shelled, veined shrimp

☐ Combine all ingredients except shrimp in bowl and mix well.

☐ Serve sauce with shrimp. Serves 4.

A sign on the Brown Derby Restaurant states: "One night in 1937, Bob Cobb, then owner of The Brown Derby, prowled hungrily in his restaurant's kitchen for a snack. Opening the huge refrigerator, he pulled out this and that: a head of lettuce, an avocado, some romaine, watercress, tomatoes, some cold breast of chicken, a hard-boiled egg, chives, cheese and some old-fashioned French dressing. He started chopping. Added some crisp bacon swiped from a busy chef and the Cobb Salad was born. It was so good, Sid Grauman (Grauman's Chinese Theatre), who was with Cobb that midnight, asked for a 'Cobb Salad' the next day. It was so good that it was put on the menu." (See the recipe on page 232.)

CALIFORNIA COBB SALAD

1 head romaine, shredded or torn
1 boneless, skinless chicken breast half, cooked, sliced
6 strips bacon, cooked crisp, crumbled
2 eggs, hard-boiled, chopped
2 large tomatoes, chopped, drained
¾ cup plus 2 tablespoons crumbled Roquefort® cheese (or other blue cheese), divided
1 large avocado
3 green onions with tops, chopped

☐ Place romaine in large salad bowl. Arrange chicken on top of greens in one area. Repeat with separate areas of bacon, eggs, tomatoes and ¾ cup Roquefort® cheese.

☐ Peel and slice avocado and arrange slices in center. Sprinkle remaining Roquefort® and green onions over top. Serve with your favorite salad dressing. Serves 4.

EASY BACON-SESAME SALAD

1 large head romaine lettuce
2 tablespoons sesame seeds, toasted
6 strips bacon, fried, crumbled
Creamy Italian salad dressing
½ cup shredded Swiss cheese

☐ Wash and dry lettuce. Tear into bite-size pieces in bowl. When ready to serve, sprinkle sesame seeds and bacon over lettuce and toss with dressing. Top with cheese. Serves 3 to 4.

LAYERED COMPANY SALAD

1 (10 ounce) package fresh spinach, stemmed, torn into pieces, divided
1 cup sliced fresh mushrooms
1 bunch green onions with tops, chopped
1 (10 ounce) package frozen green peas
3 ribs celery, sliced
1½ cups shredded cheddar cheese, divided
1½ cups mayonnaise
1½ cups sour cream
2 teaspoons sugar, divided
4 eggs, hard-boiled, grated
1 bell pepper, seeded, chopped
1 cucumber, sliced
½ head cauliflower, chopped
1 cup shredded Monterey Jack cheese

▢ You will need a very large crystal bowl (10 inches in diameter) for this salad.

▢ Place layer half spinach. Next, layer mushrooms, green onions, frozen peas, celery and half cheddar cheese.

▢ In separate bowl, combine mayonnaise and sour cream and spread half over cheese. Sprinkle with 1 teaspoon sugar, a little salt and lots of pepper.

▢ Layer remaining spinach, eggs, bell pepper, cucumber, cauliflower and remaining cheddar cheese. Spread remaining dressing on top. Sprinkle with 1 teaspoon sugar and a little salt and pepper; top with Monterey Jack cheese.

▢ Cover with plastic wrap and refrigerate overnight. Serves 8 to 10.

ORANGE-ALMOND GREENS

⅓ cup slivered almonds
2 (11 ounce) cans mandarin oranges, drained
1 bunch green onions with tops, chopped
2 heads romaine lettuce, torn in small pieces

☐ Preheat oven to 275°.

☐ Toast almonds in oven for 15 minutes and cool. Combine almonds, oranges, green onions and lettuce in bowl and mix well.

DRESSING:

¼ cup sugar
1 teaspoon dry mustard
¼ cup cider vinegar
½ cup olive oil
2 tablespoons poppy seeds
1 cup croutons

☐ Combine sugar, mustard, vinegar, oil, poppy seeds and 1 teaspoon salt in bowl. Stir dressing well just before adding to salad. Add croutons to salad when ready to serve. Serves 4 to 6.

NUTTY GREEN SALAD

4 - 6 cups torn, mixed salad greens
1 medium zucchini, sliced
1 (8 ounce) can sliced water chestnuts, drained
½ cup peanuts
⅓ cup Italian salad dressing

☐ Toss greens, zucchini, water chestnuts and peanuts in bowl.

☐ When ready to serve, add salad dressing and toss. Serves 4 to 6.

SAVORY SPINACH SALAD

DRESSING:

½ cup olive oil
½ cup red wine vinegar
3 tablespoons ketchup
¼ cup sugar
½ teaspoon garlic powder
½ teaspoon dry mustard

☐ Combine oil, vinegar, ketchup, sugar, garlic powder, mustard, 1 teaspoon salt and a little pepper in bowl to make dressing. Refrigerate for at least 6 hours before serving.

SALAD:

1 (10 ounce) package fresh spinach, stemmed, torn
4 eggs, hard-boiled, sliced
8 slices bacon, crisply cooked, crumbled
1 cup fresh mushrooms, sliced
1 red onion, thinly sliced
1 (8 ounce) can sliced water chestnuts, optional
Croutons

☐ When ready to serve, toss spinach with eggs, bacon, mushrooms, onion and water chestnuts in bowl and add dressing. Top with croutons. Serves 6 to 8.

ORIENTAL SPINACH SALAD

1 (10 ounce) package fresh spinach
1 (15 ounce) can bean sprouts, drained
8 slices bacon, cooked crisp, drained
1 (8 ounce) can water chestnuts, chopped

☐ Combine spinach and bean sprouts in bowl. When ready to serve, add crumbled bacon and water chestnuts. Serves 4.

TIP: *Any vinaigrette or dressing mist is delicious with this salad. Mandarin oranges also give this salad a special flavor and color.*

FRESH SPINACH-APPLE SALAD

1 (10 ounce) package fresh spinach or greens
⅓ cup frozen orange juice concentrate, thawed
¾ cup mayonnaise
1 red apple with peel, diced
5 slices bacon, fried, crumbled

☐ Tear spinach into small pieces in bowl. In separate bowl, mix orange juice concentrate and mayonnaise.

☐ When ready to serve, add apple and mix with spinach. Pour orange juice-mayonnaise mixture over salad and top with bacon. Serves 4 to 6.

STRAWBERRY-ALMOND-SPINACH SALAD

10 - 14 ounces fresh baby spinach leaves, stemmed
1 quart fresh strawberries, cored, halved
½ cup slivered almonds, toasted

☐ Tear spinach leaves into smaller pieces and add strawberries and almonds on 4 to
6 individual salad plates. Refrigerate until ready to serve.

DRESSING:

⅓ cup sugar
¼ cup apple cider vinegar
½ teaspoon dried onion flakes
¼ teaspoon paprika
½ teaspoon marinade for chicken
½ cup olive oil
1 tablespoon poppy seeds

☐ Combine sugar, vinegar, onion flakes, paprika and marinade for chicken in blender.
Process for 15 to 20 seconds. Add oil and process for additional 15 seconds. Stir in
poppy seeds. Refrigerate.

☐ When ready to serve, mix well and pour over chilled salad. Serves 4 to 6.

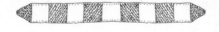

*Spread nuts, breadcrumbs and coconut out on plate
and microwave for 2 to 3 minutes on high instead
of toasting in the oven. (Stir after 1 minute if
there's no carousel.)*

RASPBERRY-TOMATO SALAD WITH BABY SPINACH

8 - 10 ounces fresh baby spinach, stemmed, torn
1 - 2 cups raspberries
1 cup grape tomatoes
½ cup sliced almonds, toasted
¼ cup red wine vinegar
½ teaspoon dry leaf tarragon, crushed
½ teaspoon dijon-style mustard
1 cup olive oil

☐ Toss spinach, raspberries, tomatoes and almonds in salad bowl and refrigerate.

☐ Mix vinegar and tarragon in small saucepan, bring to a boil and remove from heat. Pour mixture into bowl and blend in mustard and oil. Refrigerate.

☐ When ready to serve, slowly pour dressing over salad, season with a little salt and pepper and toss well. Or serve dressing on the side. Serves 3 to 4.

PEAR-WALNUT-CHEESE SALAD

Fresh lemon juice
2 medium pears, cored, peeled, sliced
¼ cup walnut pieces
4 - 6 cups butter lettuce or mixed salad greens
¼ - ½ cup goat cheese
¼ cup walnut-flavored olive oil

☐ Sprinkle lemon juice over pear slices to prevent discoloration.

☐ Toast walnut pieces on baking sheet at 225° for about 10 minutes and cool.

☐ Combine lettuce, walnuts, cheese and oil in large bowl and toss. Divide into individual servings and arrange pear slices on top. Serves 4 to 6.

SIDE DISHES

**Use delicious sides to round out
memorable table time.**

SIDE DISHES CONTENTS

SIDE DISHES CONTENTS

There is nothing more dreadful than the habit of doubt. Doubt separates people. It is a poison that disintegrates friendships and breaks up pleasant relations. It is a thorn that irritates and hurts; it is a sword that kills.

– Buddha

ALMOND ASPARAGUS

⅓ cup butter
1 - 1½ pounds fresh asparagus
⅔ cup slivered almonds
1 tablespoon lemon juice

☐ Melt butter in skillet and add asparagus and almonds. Saute for 3 to 4 minutes.

☐ Cover and steam for 3 to 5 minutes or until tender-crisp. Sprinkle lemon and a little salt and pepper over asparagus. Serve hot. Serves 5.

CREAMY ASPARAGUS BAKE

2 (15 ounce) cans cut asparagus spears with liquid
3 eggs, hard-boiled, chopped
½ cup chopped pecans
1 (10 ounce) can cream of celery soup

☐ Preheat oven to 350°.

☐ Drain liquid from asparagus and save. Arrange asparagus spears in sprayed 2-quart baking dish. Top with eggs and pecans.

☐ Heat soup and add liquid from asparagus spears. Spoon over eggs and pecans. Cover and bake for 25 minutes. Serves 8.

CHEDDAR-BROCCOLI BAKE

1 (10 ounce) can cheddar cheese soup
½ cup milk
1 (16 ounce) bag frozen broccoli florets, thawed, drained
1 (3 ounce) can french-fried onions

☐ Preheat oven to 350°.

☐ Mix soup, milk and broccoli in 2-quart baking dish. Bake for 25 minutes.

☐ Stir; sprinkle fried onions over broccoli mixture. Bake for additional 5 minutes or until fried onions are golden. Serves 4 to 6.

BROCCOLI SUPREME

2 (10 ounce) packages frozen broccoli spears, thawed
1 (6 ounce) roll garlic cheese
1 (10 ounce) can cream of mushroom soup
1 (4 ounce) can mushrooms, drained
¾ cup seasoned breadcrumbs

☐ Preheat oven to 350°.

☐ Boil broccoli in medium saucepan for 3 minutes and drain. In separate saucepan, melt cheese in mushroom soup on medium heat. Add mushrooms and combine with broccoli.

☐ Pour broccoli mixture into sprayed 2-quart baking dish and top with breadcrumbs.

☐ Bake for 30 minutes. Serves 6 to 8.

PINE NUT BROCCOLI

1 bunch fresh broccoli
¼ cup (½ stick) butter
½ cup pine nuts
⅓ cup golden raisins
2 tablespoons lemon juice

☐ Steam broccoli until tender-crisp. Combine butter, pine nuts and raisins in saucepan and saute for about 3 minutes.

☐ When ready to serve, add lemon juice to nut mixture and pour over broccoli. Serves 4.

PARMESAN BROCCOLI

1 (16 ounce) package frozen broccoli spears
½ teaspoon garlic powder
½ cup breadcrumbs
¼ cup (½ stick) butter, melted
½ cup grated parmesan cheese

☐ Cook broccoli in saucepan according to package directions.

☐ Drain and add garlic powder, breadcrumbs, butter and cheese. Add salt, if you like, and toss. Heat and serve. Serves 4.

TANGY CARROT COINS

2 (15 ounce) cans sliced carrots, drained
2 tablespoons butter
2 tablespoons brown sugar
1 tablespoon dijon-style mustard

☐ Place all ingredients in saucepan. Cook and stir over medium heat for about 2 minutes. Serve hot. Serves 4 to 6.

DILLED CARROTS

1 (12 ounce) package fresh baby carrots
3 chicken bouillon cubes or 2 teaspoons bouillon granules
¼ cup (½ stick) butter, melted
2 teaspoons dill weed

☐ Boil carrots in water with dissolved bouillon cubes until tender (about 8 minutes). Drain.

☐ Place in a skillet with butter. Cook on low heat for only a few minutes making sure the butter coats all carrots. Sprinkle dill weed over carrots and shake to cover all carrots. Serve immediately. Serves 4.

Show me another pleasure like dinner which comes every day and lasts an hour.
— *Talleyrand*

EASY CARROT CASSEROLE

So, so easy.

2 cups cooked, mashed carrots
1 cup milk
3 eggs, beaten
¼ cup (½ stick) butter, melted
1 cup chopped pecans
½ cup sugar
1 teaspoon baking powder
2 tablespoons flour
¼ teaspoon cinnamon

☐ Preheat oven to 350°.

☐ Combine carrots, milk, eggs, butter and pecans.

☐ In a separate bowl, mix sugar, 1 teaspoon salt, baking powder, flour and cinnamon;
slowly add to carrots. Mix thoroughly and pour into sprayed 2-quart casserole.

☐ Bake for 1 hour. Serves 6 to 8.

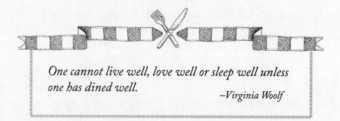

*One cannot live well, love well or sleep well unless
one has dined well.*

—Virginia Woolf

CREAMY CABBAGE

2 tablespoons (¼ stick) butter
1 tablespoon sugar
¼ teaspoon ground nutmeg
1 (4 ounce) jar diced pimentos, drained
1 medium head cabbage, sliced
1 (8 ounce) package cream cheese, softened

☐ Combine butter, sugar, nutmeg and pimentos in saucepan over medium-low heat; add cabbage. Cook until cabbage is tender-crisp, but don't overcook.

☐ Add cream cheese while on low heat and stir until it melts and cabbage is well-coated. Serves 6 to 8.

EASY STIR-FRIED CABBAGE

1 small head cabbage, finely chopped
3 tablespoons olive oil
2 tablespoons Italian salad dressing

☐ Sprinkle cabbage with ½ teaspoon salt and set aside for 30 minutes.

☐ Heat oil in skillet until very hot. Add cabbage and stir-fry for 5 to 8 minutes, stirring constantly. Remove and sprinkle with Italian dressing. Serves 6.

Keep your salads crisper longer by refrigerating the salad plates or serving bowl.

BEST CAULIFLOWER

1 (16 ounce) package frozen cauliflower
1 (8 ounce) carton sour cream, divided
1½ cups shredded American or cheddar cheese, divided
4 teaspoons sesame seeds, toasted, divided

☐ Preheat oven to 350°.

☐ Cook cauliflower in saucepan according to package directions. Drain and place half of cauliflower in sprayed 2-quart baking dish.

☐ Sprinkle a little salt and pepper on cauliflower. Spread half of sour cream and half of cheese on top.

☐ Sprinkle with 2 teaspoons sesame seeds and repeat layers. Bake for about 15 to 20 minutes. Serves 6 to 8.

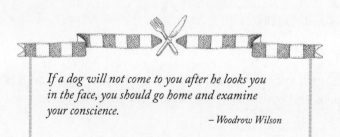

If a dog will not come to you after he looks you in the face, you should go home and examine your conscience.

– Woodrow Wilson

CAULIFLOWER MEDLEY

1 head cauliflower, cut into florets
1 (15 ounce) can Italian stewed tomatoes
1 bell pepper, seeded, chopped
1 onion, chopped
¼ cup (½ stick) butter

☐ Preheat oven to 350°.

☐ Combine all ingredients, 2 tablespoons water, and some salt and pepper in large saucepan.

☐ Cover and cook over medium-low heat for about 10 to 15 minutes or until tender. (Do not let cauliflower get mushy.) Serves 6.

CORN AND GREEN CHILE CASSEROLE

2 (10 ounce) packages frozen whole kernel corn
2 tablespoons butter
1 (8 ounce) package cream cheese
1 tablespoon sugar
1 (4 ounce) can diced green chilies

☐ Preheat oven to 350°.

☐ Cook corn according to package directions, drain and set aside. Melt butter in saucepan over low heat, add cream cheese and stir until it melts.

☐ Stir in corn, sugar and green chilies. Spoon into sprayed 2-quart baking dish. Cover and bake for 25 minutes. Serves 8.

STUFFED CORN CASSEROLE

1 (15 ounce) can cream-style corn
1 (15 ounce) can whole kernel corn, drained
½ cup (1 stick) butter, melted
1 (6 ounce) package chicken stuffing mix

☐ Preheat oven to 350°.

☐ Combine all ingredients and ½ cup water in bowl and mix well.

☐ Spoon into sprayed 9 x 13-inch baking pan. Bake for 30 minutes. Serves 6.

WILD WEST CORN

2 (15 ounce) cans whole kernel corn, drained
1 (10 ounce) can diced tomatoes and green chilies, drained
1 (8 ounce) package shredded Monterey Jack cheese
1 cup cheese cracker crumbs

☐ Preheat oven to 350°.

☐ Combine corn, tomatoes and green chilies, and cheese in large bowl and mix well.

☐ Pour into sprayed 2½-quart baking dish. Sprinkle cracker crumbs over casserole. Bake for 25 minutes. Serves 4 to 6.

SUPER CORN CASSEROLE

1 (15 ounce) can whole kernel corn, drained
1 (15 ounce) can cream-style corn
½ cup (1 stick) butter, melted
1 (8 ounce) carton sour cream
1 (6 ounce) package jalapeno cornbread mix

☐ Preheat oven to 350°.

☐ Mix all ingredients and pour into sprayed 9 x 13-inch baking dish. Bake uncovered for 35 minutes. Serves 6 to 8.

CORN AND OKRA JAMBALAYA

¼ pound bacon
1 pound fresh okra, sliced
2 onions, chopped
1 (15 ounce) can stewed tomatoes
1 (15 ounce) can whole kernel corn, drained
Rice, cooked

☐ Fry bacon in large skillet until crisp and drain bacon. In same skillet with bacon drippings, saute okra and onions, but do not brown.

☐ Add tomatoes and corn and bring to a boil. Reduce heat and simmer for about 5 to 10 minutes.

☐ Serve over hot rice. Sprinkle crumbled bacon over top of each serving. Serves 6 to 8.

FANTASTIC SKILLET CORN

This is so good, you'll ignore the calories.

2 (16 ounce) packages frozen whole kernel corn
½ cup (1 stick) butter
1 cup whipping cream
1 tablespoon sugar

☐ Place corn in large skillet and turn on medium heat. Add butter, whipping cream, sugar and 1 teaspoon salt.

☐ Stirring constantly, heat until most of whipping cream and butter absorbs into corn. Serves 10.

CHEESY BAKED EGGPLANT

1 eggplant
½ cup mayonnaise
⅔ cup seasoned breadcrumbs
¼ cup grated parmesan cheese

☐ Preheat oven to 400°.

☐ Peel eggplant and slice ½-inch thick. Spread both sides of slices with mayonnaise and dip in mixture of crumbs and parmesan. Coat both sides well.

☐ Place in single layer in shallow baking dish. Bake for 20 minutes. Serves 4.

EGGPLANT CASSEROLE

1 large eggplant
1 cup cracker crumbs
1 cup shredded cheddar cheese, divided
1 (10 ounce) can diced tomatoes and green chilies

☐ Preheat oven to 350°.

☐ Peel and slice eggplant. Place eggplant in saucepan and cover with water. Cook for 10 minutes or until tender. Drain well on paper towels.

☐ Mash eggplant. Stir in cracker crumbs, ¾ cup cheese, and tomatoes and green chilies and mix well.

☐ Spoon eggplant mixture in sprayed 1-quart baking dish. Sprinkle with remaining cheese. Bake for 30 minutes. Serves 8.

TASTY BLACK-EYED PEAS

2 (10 ounce) packages frozen black-eyed peas
1¼ cups chopped green pepper
¾ cup chopped onion
3 tablespoons butter
1 (15 ounce) can stewed tomatoes with liquid

☐ Cook black-eyed peas in saucepan according to package directions and drain. Saute green pepper and onion in butter in skillet.

☐ Add peas, tomatoes, and a little salt and pepper. Cook over low heat until thoroughly hot and stir often. Serves 8.

QUICK BAKED BEAN STANDBY

3 (15 ounce) cans baked beans
½ cup chili sauce
⅓ cup packed brown sugar
4 slices bacon, cooked, crumbled

☐ Preheat oven to 325°.

☐ Combine baked beans, chili sauce and brown sugar in sprayed 3-quart baking dish. Bake for 40 minutes.

☐ When ready to serve, sprinkle bacon on top. Serves 6.

BETTER BUTTER BEANS

1 cup sliced celery
1 onion, chopped
¼ cup (½ stick) butter
1 (10 ounce) can diced tomatoes and green chilies
½ teaspoon sugar
2 (15 ounce) cans butter beans

☐ Saute celery and onion in butter in skillet over medium-high heat for about 3 minutes or until translucent.

☐ Add tomatoes and green chilies, several sprinkles of salt, and sugar. Add butter beans, cover and simmer for about 20 minutes. Serve hot. Serves 8.

BUTTER BEANS AND GREEN ONIONS

1 (10 ounce) packages frozen butter beans
6 bacon slices
1 bunch fresh green onions, chopped
½ teaspoon garlic powder
½ cup chopped fresh parsley

☐ Cook butter beans according to package directions and set aside.

☐ Cook bacon slices in skillet until crispy; crumble and set bacon aside.

☐ Saute green onions in bacon drippings. Stir in butter beans, garlic powder, parsley, and a little salt and pepper. Cook just until thoroughly hot.

☐ Pour into serving bowl and sprinkle with bacon. Serves 4.

CREAMED PEAS

1 (16 ounce) package frozen English peas
2 tablespoons butter
1 (10 ounce) can cream of celery soup
1 (3 ounce) package cream cheese
1 (8 ounce) can water chestnuts, drained

☐ Cook peas according to package directions.

☐ Combine butter, soup and cream cheese in large saucepan. Cook on medium heat and stir until butter and cream cheese melt.

☐ Add peas and water chestnuts and mix. Serve hot. Serves 6.

PINE NUT GREEN BEANS

1 (16 ounce) package frozen green beans
¼ cup (½ stick) butter
¾ cup pine nuts
¼ teaspoon garlic powder

☐ Cook beans in water in covered 3-quart saucepan for 10 to 15 minutes or until tender-crisp and drain.

☐ Melt butter in skillet over medium heat and add pine nuts. Cook, stirring frequently, until golden.

☐ Add pine nuts and garlic powder to green beans. Serve hot. Serves 6 to 8.

QUICK SEASONED GREEN BEANS

4 slices bacon, chopped
1 medium onion, chopped
2 (15 ounce) cans green beans, drained
1 teaspoon sugar

☐ Saute bacon and onion in skillet and drain. Add green beans and sugar and heat thoroughly. Serves 8.

ITALIAN GREEN BEANS

This is so simple you would think there had to be more to it to be this good.

1 (16 ounce) package frozen Italian green beans
3 green onions with tops, chopped
2 tablespoons butter
1 teaspoon Italian seasoning

☐ Mix all ingredients plus ¼ cup water in 2-quart saucepan. Cook on medium-high heat for about 10 minutes or until beans are tender. Serves 6.

ALMOND GREEN BEANS

⅓ cup slivered almonds
¼ cup (½ stick) butter
¾ teaspoon garlic salt
3 tablespoons lemon juice
2 (15 ounce) cans French-style green beans, drained

☐ Cook almonds in butter, garlic salt and lemon juice in saucepan until slightly golden brown.

☐ Add green beans to almonds and heat. Serves 6 to 8.

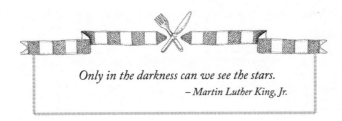

Only in the darkness can we see the stars.
– Martin Luther King, Jr.

FRESH SESAME GREEN BEANS

1 pound fresh green beans
¼ cup soy sauce
½ cup (1 stick) butter
½ cup sesame seeds, toasted

☐ Cook green beans in medium saucepan about half covered in water over medium-high heat until tender-crisp, about 10 minutes; drain.

☐ Combine soy sauce and butter in saucepan. Cook over medium heat for a few minutes.

☐ Add to green beans and toss lightly. Add sesame seeds and toss again. Serves 4 to 6.

CRUNCHY GREEN BEAN CASSEROLE

3 (15 ounce) cans whole green beans, drained
2 (10 ounce) cans cream of mushroom soup
2 (8 ounce) cans sliced water chestnuts, drained, chopped
2 (3 ounce) cans french-fried onions

☐ Preheat oven to 350°.

☐ Combine green beans, mushroom soup and water chestnuts in bowl. Pour mixture into sprayed 2-quart baking dish. Cover and bake for 30 minutes.

☐ Remove casserole from oven, sprinkle fried onions over top and bake for additional 10 minutes. Serves 8.

FRIED OKRA

Small, fresh garden okra
Milk
Cornmeal
2 - 3 tablespoons oil

☐ Thoroughly wash and drain okra. Cut off tops and ends and slice.

☐ Toss okra with a little milk (just enough to make cornmeal stick) and salt and pepper. Sprinkle cornmeal over okra and toss.

☐ Heat oil in skillet. When oil is boiling, fry okra and turn several times until okra is golden brown and crisp. Serves 4 ounces per person.

TIP: *Season to taste with salt and pepper.*

OKRA GUMBO

1 large onion, chopped
1 pound fresh okra, sliced
¼ cup (½ stick) butter
2 (15 ounce) cans tomatoes
1 potato, chopped
Cooked rice

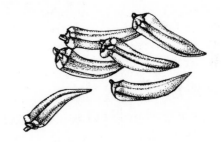

☐ Brown onion and okra in butter in skillet over medium-high heat. Add tomatoes and potato and bring to a boil.

☐ Simmer until potatoes are done, about 30 minutes. Serve over rice. Serves 6.

CHEESY ONION CASSEROLE

5 sweet onions, sliced
½ cup (1 stick) butter
1 cup shredded cheddar cheese
22 saltine crackers, crushed

☐ Preheat oven to 325°.

☐ Saute onion in butter in skillet until translucent. Layer half onions, half cheese, half crackers in sprayed 2-quart baking dish and repeat layers.

☐ Bake for 35 minutes. Serves 6.

POTATO-CHIVE SOUFFLE

3 eggs, separated
2 cups mashed potatoes*
½ cup sour cream
2 heaping tablespoons chopped chives

☐ Preheat oven to 350°.

☐ Beat egg whites in bowl until stiff and set aside. In separate bowl, beat yolks until smooth and add to potatoes.

☐ Fold beaten egg whites, sour cream, chives and 1 teaspoon salt into potato-egg yolk mixture and pour into sprayed 2-quart baking dish.

☐ Bake for 45 minutes. Serves 6.

TIP: Use leftover mashed potatoes or prepare instant mashed potatoes. Be sure potatoes have cooled before mixing in egg yolks.

BROCCOLI-CHEESE POTATOES

1 (10 ounce) can fiesta nacho cheese soup
2 tablespoons sour cream
½ teaspoon dijon-style mustard
1 (10 ounce) box frozen broccoli florets, cooked
4 medium potatoes, baked, fluffed

☐ Whisk soup, sour cream, mustard and broccoli in 1-quart microwave-safe baking dish.

☐ Heat in microwave for 2 to 2½ minutes and stir well. Spoon over baked potatoes. Serves 4.

CREAMY MASHED POTATOES

6 large potatoes
1 (8 ounce) carton sour cream
1 (8 ounce) package cream cheese, softened
½ teaspoon white pepper

☐ Preheat oven to 325°.

☐ Peel, cut up and boil potatoes in large saucepan until tender, about 20 minutes. Drain.

☐ Add sour cream, cream cheese, 1 teaspoon salt and white pepper. Whip until cream cheese melts and potatoes are mashed.

☐ Pour into sprayed 3-quart baking dish. Cover with foil and bake for about 20 minutes (about 10 minutes longer if reheating). Serves 8.

EASY POTATOES AU GRATIN

1 (8 ounce) package cubed Velveeta® cheese
1 (16 ounce) carton half-and-half cream
1 cup shredded cheddar cheese
½ cup (1 stick) butter
1 (2 pound) package frozen hash-brown potatoes, thawed

☐ Preheat oven to 350°.

☐ Melt Velveeta® cheese, half-and-half cream, cheddar cheese and butter in double boiler. (Do not burn or scorch.)

☐ Place hash browns in sprayed 9 x 13-inch baking dish and pour cheese mixture over potatoes.

☐ Bake for l hour. Serves 8 to 10.

LOADED BAKED POTATOES

6 medium potatoes
1 pound hot sausage
1 (16 ounce) package cubed Velveeta® cheese
1 (10 ounce) can diced tomatoes and green chilies

☐ Preheat oven to 375°.

☐ Wrap potatoes in foil and bake for 1 hour or until done.

☐ Brown sausage in skillet and drain. Add cheese to sausage. Heat until cheese melts and add tomatoes and green chilies.

☐ Serve sausage-cheese mixture over baked potatoes. Serves 6.

TWICE-BAKED POTATOES

8 medium baking potatoes
2 tablespoons butter
1 (10 ounce) can cheddar cheese soup
1 tablespoon chopped dried chives
Paprika

- [ ] Preheat oven to 425°.

- [ ] Bake potatoes until done, about 45 minutes. Cut potatoes in half lengthwise and scoop out flesh leaving thin shell. Whip potatoes with butter and ½ teaspoon salt in bowl.

- [ ] Gradually add soup and chives and beat until light and fluffy. (If you want a little "zip" to potatoes, add 1 (10 ounce) can fiesta nacho cheese soup instead of cheddar cheese soup.)

- [ ] Spoon into shells and sprinkle with paprika. Bake for 15 minutes. Serves 8.

HERBED NEW POTATOES

1½ pounds new (red) potatoes
6 tablespoons (¾ stick) butter, sliced
¼ teaspoon thyme
½ cup chopped fresh parsley
½ teaspoon rosemary

- [ ] Scrub potatoes and cut in halves, but do not peel.

- [ ] Boil potatoes in enough lightly salted water to cover potatoes in medium saucepan for about 20 minutes or until tender and drain well.

- [ ] Add butter, thyme, parsley and rosemary and toss gently until butter melts. Serve hot. Serves 6.

MASHED POTATOES SUPREME

1 (8 ounce) package cream cheese, softened
½ cup sour cream
2 tablespoons butter, softened
1 (.4 ounce) packet ranch salad dressing mix
6 - 8 cups prepared warm instant mashed potatoes

☐ Preheat oven to 350°.

☐ Beat cream cheese, sour cream, butter and dressing mix in bowl. Add potatoes and stir well.

☐ Transfer to 2-quart baking dish and bake for 25 minutes or until thoroughly hot. Serves 6.

NO-FRY BAKED FRIES

5 medium baking potatoes
⅓ cup olive oil
Seasoned salt

☐ Preheat oven to 375°.

☐ Scrub potatoes, cut each in 6 lengthwise wedges and place in shallow baking dish.

☐ Brush potatoes with oil and sprinkle with seasoned salt.

☐ Bake for about 50 minutes or until potatoes are tender and light brown. Baste twice with remaining oil while baking. Serves 6 to 8.

TIP: *For more of a crunch, broil the potatoes the last 3 to 5 minutes.*

SPEEDY SWEET POTATOES

2 (15 ounce) cans sweet potatoes, drained
1 (8 ounce) can crushed pineapple with juice
½ cup chopped pecans
⅓ cup packed brown sugar
1 cup miniature marshmallows, divided

☐ Layer sweet potatoes, a little salt, pineapple, pecans, brown sugar and ½ cup marshmallows in 2-quart microwave-safe dish.

☐ Cover and microwave on HIGH for 6 minutes or until bubbly around edges.

☐ Top with remaining marshmallows and heat uncovered on HIGH for 30 seconds or until marshmallows puff. If you like, sprinkle sweet potatoes with a little nutmeg. Serves 8 to 10.

MAPLE-PECAN SWEET POTATOES

½ cup chopped pecans
1 (29 ounce) can sweet potatoes, drained
½ cup pure maple syrup

☐ Preheat oven to 250°.

☐ Toast pecans in oven for about 10 minutes.

☐ In bowl, mash sweet potatoes with fork (leave some small chunks). Add maple syrup and mix well.

☐ Transfer to sprayed 7 x 11-inch baking dish. Turn oven to 350°. Sprinkle pecans over sweet potato mixture and bake uncovered for 25 minutes. Serves 4 to 6.

BAKED SWEET POTATO SPECIAL

4 sweet potatoes
6 tablespoons (¾ stick) butter, melted
½ cup sugar
½ cup packed brown sugar
1 teaspoon ground cinnamon
½ cup flaked coconut

☐ Preheat oven to 375°.

☐ Prick sweet potatoes several times with fork. Wrap each sweet potato in foil and bake for about 1 hour, or until tender.

☐ Unwrap sweet potatoes and make slit down center of each sweet potato. Use fork to fluff up potato.

☐ Combine melted butter, sugar, brown sugar, cinnamon and coconut in small bowl and mix well. Spoon one-fourth mixture over each potato and fluff with fork again to make sure sugar mixture goes into each potato. Serves 4.

SWEET POTATO WEDGES

3 pounds sweet potatoes, peeled, quartered lengthwise
6 tablespoons (¾ stick) butter, melted
6 tablespoons orange juice
¾ teaspoon ground cinnamon

☐ Preheat oven to 350°.

☐ Arrange sweet potatoes in sprayed 9 x 13-inch baking pan. Combine butter, orange juice, ½ teaspoon salt and cinnamon and drizzle over sweet potatoes.

☐ Cover and bake for 60 minutes or until tender. Serves 8.

WHIPPED SWEET POTATOES

1 (28 ounce) can sweet potatoes
1 cup (2 sticks) butter, melted, divided
1 cup packed light brown sugar
1½ cups crushed corn flakes

☐ Preheat oven to 350°.

☐ Drain most of liquid from sweet potatoes. Place sweet potatoes in bowl and cut large pieces of potatoes into small pieces.

☐ Beat sweet potatoes until creamy and fold in ¾ cup melted butter and brown sugar.

☐ Beat until butter and brown sugar thoroughly combine with sweet potatoes and pour into sprayed 2-quart baking dish.

☐ Combine crushed corn flakes and remaining ¼ cup melted butter and sprinkle over sweet potato casserole. Bake for 40 minutes. Serves 10 to 12.

TIP: *If you like, add ⅓ cup chopped pecans to corn flakes.*

The world is a dangerous place to live; not because of the people who are evil, but because of the people who don't do anything about it.
– *Albert Einstein*

HERBED SPINACH

2 (16 ounce) packages frozen chopped spinach
1 (8 ounce) package cream cheese, softened
¼ cup (½ stick) butter, melted, divided
1 (6 ounce) package herb-seasoned stuffing

☐ Preheat oven to 350°.

☐ Cook spinach according to package directions. Squeeze spinach between paper towels to completely remove excess moisture.

☐ Add cream cheese and half of butter. Stir well while spinach is still hot. Pour into sprayed baking dish.

☐ Spread herb stuffing on top and drizzle with remaining butter. Bake for 25 minutes. Serves 8.

I predict future happiness for Americans if they can prevent the government from wasting the labors of the people under the pretense of taking care of them.

– Thomas Jefferson

FAVORITE SPINACH CASSEROLE

1 (1 ounce) packet onion soup mix
1 (8 ounce) carton sour cream
2 (10 ounce) packages frozen chopped spinach, thawed, well drained*
⅔ cup shredded Monterey Jack cheese

☐ Preheat oven to 350°.

☐ Combine onion soup mix and sour cream; add spinach and mix well. Pour into sprayed 2-quart baking dish. Bake for 20 minutes.

☐ Sprinkle cheese over top and bake for additional 5 minutes. Serves 8.

*TIP: Squeeze spinach between paper towels to completely remove excess moisture.

Iceberg lettuce has very little nutritional value. Choose romaine, butter lettuce, Boston bibb, spinach, kale, chard or any the leafy greens you see in the produce section.

CREAMED SPINACH

1 (16 ounce) package frozen chopped spinach
3 eggs
½ cup flour
1 (16 ounce) carton small curd cottage cheese, drained
1 (8 ounce) package shredded cheddar cheese

☐ Preheat oven to 350°.

☐ Cook spinach in saucepan, drain very well and set aside.

☐ Beat eggs in bowl and add flour, cottage cheese, and a little salt and pepper.

☐ Stir in spinach and cheddar cheese. Pour into 1½-quart baking dish and bake
for 35 minutes. Serves 8.

SNAPPY CHEESE SQUASH

4 - 6 medium yellow squash, sliced
½ green bell pepper, seeded, chopped
1 small onion, chopped
1 (8 ounce) package shredded Mexican Velveeta® cheese

☐ Preheat oven to 350°.

☐ Combine squash, bell pepper and onion in large saucepan and just barely cover with water.
Cook over medium heat just until tender, about 10 to 15 minutes.

☐ Drain and add cheese. Stir until cheese melts and pour into sprayed 2-quart baking dish.

☐ Bake for 15 minutes. Serves 6 to 8.

DYNAMITE SQUASH BAKE

5 medium yellow squash, sliced
2 potatoes, thinly sliced
1 onion, chopped
2 (10 ounce) cans cream of chicken soup

☐ Preheat oven to 350°.

☐ Layer squash, potatoes and onion in sprayed 2-quart baking dish.

☐ Combine soup and ¾ can water in saucepan and heat just enough to mix well. Pour over vegetables.

☐ Cover and bake for 45 minutes. Serves 8.

WALNUT ZUCCHINI

3 - 4 zucchini, julienned
½ red bell pepper, seeded, julienned
¼ cup (½ stick) butter
1 cup chopped walnuts

☐ Saute zucchini and bell pepper in butter in skillet until tender. Shake pan and toss zucchini to cook evenly. Pour off any excess butter.

☐ Add chopped walnuts. When walnuts blend and heat, serve immediately. Serves 6.

Zucchini Patties

1½ cups grated zucchini
1 egg, beaten
2 tablespoons flour
⅓ cup finely minced onion
½ teaspoon seasoned salt
3 tablespoons oil

☐ Mix all ingredients except oil in bowl. Heat oil in skillet.

☐ Drop large spoonfuls of zucchini mixture into skillet and mash down a little. Cook on medium heat until heated through and both sides are golden brown.

☐ Drain on paper towels. Serves 4.

Baked Tomatoes with Basil

3 large tomatoes, cored
1½ cups seasoned breadcrumbs
¼ cup (½ stick) butter, melted
Dried basil

☐ Preheat oven to 350°.

☐ Slice tomatoes in ½ to 1-inch thick slices and place on baking sheet. Mix breadcrumbs, butter and basil.

☐ Sprinkle slices generously with breadcrumbs. Bake for 10 to 15 minutes or until light brown on top. Serves 6.

TOMATO BAKE

2 (15 ounce) cans diced tomatoes, drained
1½ cups toasted breadcrumbs, divided
A scant ¼ cup sugar
½ onion, chopped
¼ cup (½ stick) butter, melted

☐ Preheat oven to 325°.

☐ Combine tomatoes, 1 cup breadcrumbs, sugar, onion and butter in bowl.

☐ Pour into sprayed baking dish and cover with remaining breadcrumbs. Bake for 25 to 30 minutes or until crumbs are light brown. Serves 6 to 8.

BROCCOLI-STUFFED TOMATOES

4 medium tomatoes
1 (10 ounce) package frozen chopped broccoli
1 (6 ounce) roll garlic cheese, softened
½ teaspoon garlic salt

☐ Preheat oven to 375°.

☐ Cut tops off tomatoes and scoop out flesh. Cook broccoli in saucepan according to package directions and drain well.

☐ Combine broccoli, cheese and garlic salt and heat just until cheese melts. Stuff broccoli mixture into tomatoes and place on baking sheet.

☐ Bake for about 10 minutes. Serves 4.

CREAMY VEGETABLE CASSEROLE

1 (16 ounce) package frozen broccoli, carrots and cauliflower
1 (10 ounce) can cream of mushroom soup
1 (8 ounce) carton garden-vegetable cream cheese
1 cup seasoned croutons

☐ Preheat oven to 350°.

☐ Cook vegetables according to package directions, drain and place in large bowl.

☐ Combine soup and cream cheese in saucepan and heat just enough to mix easily. Pour into vegetable mixture and mix well.

☐ Pour into 2-quart baking dish. Sprinkle with croutons. Bake for 25 minutes or until bubbly. Serves 6 to 8.

VEGETABLE-CORN MEDLEY

1 (11 ounce) can cream-style corn
½ cup milk
2 cups broccoli florets
2 cups cauliflower florets
1 cup shredded cheddar cheese

☐ Heat corn and milk in large saucepan over medium heat to boiling and stir often.

☐ Stir in broccoli and cauliflower florets and return to boiling. Reduce heat to low and cover.

☐ Cook for 20 minutes or until vegetables are tender; stir occasionally. Stir in cheese and heat until cheese melts. Serves 8.

CHEESY VEGETABLE SAUCE

Use this sauce to dress up just about any vegetable dish.

½ cup shredded cheddar cheese
½ cup sour cream
¼ cup (½ stick) butter
2 tablespoons chopped fresh parsley
½ teaspoon garlic powder

☐ Combine all ingredients in 3-quart glass bowl. Microwave on MEDIUM-HIGH for 2 minutes or until cheese melts, stirring with wire whisk at 1-minute intervals.

☐ Serve over cooked broccoli, cauliflower or even potatoes. Serves 6.

NO-BRAINER BAKED MACARONI AND CHEESE

1 (8 ounce) package macaroni
2⅓ cups milk
1 (8 ounce) package cubed Velveeta® cheese

☐ Preheat oven to 350°.

☐ Cook macaroni according to package directions until tender. Drain. Stir in milk and cheese and mix well.

☐ Pour into sprayed baking dish and bake covered for 45 minutes or until set. Serves 6.

MACARONI, TOMATOES AND CHEESE

2 cups elbow macaroni
1 (14 ounce) can stewed tomatoes with liquid
1 (8 ounce) package shredded cheddar cheese
2 tablespoons sugar
1 (6 ounce) package cheese slices

☐ Preheat oven to 350°.

☐ Cook macaroni in saucepan according to package directions and drain. Combine macaroni, tomatoes, shredded cheese, sugar, ¼ cup water and a little salt in large bowl and mix well.

☐ Pour into sprayed 9 x 13-inch baking dish and place cheese slices on top. Bake for 30 minutes or until bubbly. Serves 8 to 10.

SPICED-UP MACARONI

1 (8 ounce) package spiral pasta
⅓ cup (5⅓ tablespoons) butter
1 (8 ounce) package Mexican Velveeta® cheese
1 (10 ounce) can diced tomatoes and green chilies with liquid
½ yellow onion, very finely diced
1 (8 ounce) carton sour cream

☐ Cook pasta according to package directions and drain. Add butter and stir continuously until butter melts. Cover and keep warm.

☐ Preheat oven to 325°.

☐ In large saucepan, combine Velveeta® cheese, tomatoes and green chilies, and diced onion. Stir in pasta and heat on low for 5 minutes, stir occasionally.

☐ Fold in sour cream and pour into 2-quart baking dish. Cover and bake for 20 minutes. Serves 6.

There is no dispute about the origin of macaroni and cheese in America. Thomas Jefferson served it in the White House at a State Dinner in 1802.

CREAMY SPINACH LINGUINE

4 ounces spinach linguine
1 cup whipping cream
1 cup chicken broth
½ cup freshly grated parmesan cheese
½ cup frozen English peas

☐ Cook linguine in medium saucepan according to package directions, drain and keep warm.

☐ In separate saucepan, combine whipping cream and chicken broth and bring to a low boil.

☐ Reduce heat and simmer for 25 minutes or until it thickens and reduces to 1 cup. Remove from heat, add cheese and peas and stir until cheese melts.

☐ Toss with linguine and serve immediately. Serves 6.

Two ounces dry pasta will make about 1 cup cooked pasta. Spaghetti and macaroni products usually double in volume when cooked. Egg noodles don't expand quite as much.

BASIL PASTA WITH ONION

2½ cups small tube pasta
1 small onion, chopped
2 tablespoons olive oil
2½ tablespoons dried basil
1 cup shredded mozzarella cheese

☐ Cook pasta in saucepan according to package directions.

☐ Meanwhile, saute onion until translucent in oil in skillet over medium-high heat. Stir in basil, 1 teaspoon salt and ¼ teaspoon pepper. Cook and stir for 1 minute.

☐ Drain pasta, but leave about ½ cup liquid so pasta won't dry out. Stir basil mixture into pasta.

☐ Remove from heat and stir in cheese just until it begins to melt. Serve immediately. Serves 4 to 6.

CREAMY SEASONED NOODLES

1 (8 ounce) package wide egg noodles
¼ cup (½ stick) butter
1 (.4 ounce) packet Italian salad dressing mix
½ cup whipping cream
¼ cup grated parmesan cheese

☐ Cook noodles in saucepan according to package directions and drain.

☐ In small saucepan, melt butter with remaining ingredients. Add to pasta and toss lightly to blend thoroughly. Serve hot. Serves 6.

CARNIVAL COUSCOUS

1 (6 ounce) box herbed chicken couscous
¼ cup (½ stick) butter
1 red bell pepper, seeded, finely chopped
1 yellow squash, seeded, finely chopped
¾ cup fresh broccoli florets, finely chopped

☐ Preheat oven to 325°.

☐ Cook couscous in saucepan according to package directions, but do not use butter.

☐ With butter in saucepan, saute bell pepper, squash and broccoli and cook over medium heat for about 10 minutes or until vegetables are tender.

☐ Combine couscous and vegetables in sprayed 2-quart baking dish and bake for about 20 minutes. Serves 8.

Food… can look beautiful, taste exquisite, smell wonderful, make people feel good, bring them together, inspire romantic feelings… At its most basic, it is fuel for a hungry machine…

– Rosamond Richardson

GREEN RICE AND SPINACH

1 cup instant rice
1 (10 ounce) package frozen chopped spinach
1 onion, finely chopped
3 tablespoons butter
¾ cup shredded cheddar cheese

☐ Preheat oven to 350°.

☐ Cook rice in large saucepan according to package directions.

☐ Punch holes in box of spinach and cook in microwave for about 3 minutes.

☐ Mix spinach, onion, butter, cheese, rice and ¼ teaspoon salt. If it seems a little dry, add several tablespoons water.

☐ Pour into sprayed 2-quart baking dish. Bake for 25 minutes. Serves 6.

COLORFUL BACON-RICE DISH

¾ pound bacon
2½ cups cooked rice
1 (15 ounce) can sliced carrots, drained
1 (10 ounce) package frozen green peas, thawed

☐ In large skillet, fry bacon until crisp and remove. Drain skillet partially, leaving about ½ cup bacon drippings in skillet. Crumble bacon and set aside.

☐ Add rice, carrots and peas to skillet and cook, stirring occasionally, until mixture heats thoroughly. Stir in bacon and serve hot. Serves 4 to 6.

RED RICE

1 (16 ounce) package smoked sausage, sliced
2 (10 ounce) cans diced tomatoes and green chilies
3 cups chicken broth
2 teaspoons Creole seasoning
1½ cups long grain rice

Brown sausage in large, heavy pan until brown. Stir in tomatoes and green chilies, broth, and seasoning and bring to a boil.,Stir in rice, cover and reduce heat. Simmer for 25 minutes, uncover and cook until liquid absorbs. Serves 8.

You know you're in love when you can't fall asleep because reality is finally better than your dreams.

BEEF DISHES

**The best of beef dishes will
have encore presentations.**

BEEF DISHES CONTENTS

BEEF DISHES CONTENTS

One measure of friendship consists not in the number of things friends can discuss, but in the number of things they need no longer mention.

– Clifton Fadiman

HOMER'S BEEF KEBABS

KEBABS:

2 - 2½ pounds sirloin steak
Bell peppers
Fresh mushrooms
Tiny onions
Cherry tomatoes

MARINADE:

1 cup red wine
2 teaspoons Worcestershire sauce
2 teaspoons garlic powder
1 cup canola oil
¼ cup ketchup

☐ Cut meat into 1½ to 2-inch chunks and cut bell peppers into bite-size pieces. Combine 1 teaspoon salt and marinade ingredients in bowl.

☐ Pour over steak pieces and marinate in refrigerator for 3 to 4 hours.

☐ Alternate meat, peppers, mushrooms, onions and cherry tomatoes on skewers.

☐ Preheat grill to medium heat. Grill about 10 to 15 minutes, turning to cook evenly. Serves 8.

SOUTHWESTERN ROUND STEAK

1 pound round steak, tenderized
Flour
Olive oil
1 (15 ounce) can Mexican stewed tomatoes
2 teaspoons beef bouillon granules

☐ Preheat oven to 325°.

☐ Cut beef into serving-size pieces and dredge in flour. Put a little olive oil in skillet with ovenproof handle to brown steak over medium-high heat.

☐ Mix tomatoes and beef bouillon granules in bowl and pour over steak. Cover and bake for 1 hour. Serves 6.

STEAK ITALIENNE WITH STEWED TOMATOES

2 pounds lean round steak
2 teaspoons Italian seasoning
1 teaspoon garlic salt
2 (15 ounce) cans stewed tomatoes

☐ Preheat oven to 325°.

☐ Cut steak into serving-size pieces and brown in skillet. Place in sprayed 9 x 13-inch baking dish.

☐ Combine Italian seasoning, garlic salt and stewed tomatoes. Pour over steak pieces.

☐ Cover and bake for 1 hour. Serves 4 to 6.

ON-THE-BORDER STEAKS

½ teaspoon dry mustard
2 tablespoons fajita seasoning
1 teaspoon minced garlic
1½ pounds flank steak
Oil
Hot salsa
Rice, cooked

☐ Combine ½ teaspoon pepper, dry mustard, fajita seasoning and garlic. Rub flank steak with a little oil, sprinkle seasonings over steak and refrigerate 4 to 6 hours.

☐ Grill steak on each side on covered grill 6 to 8 minutes over medium heat. Remove from heat and let rest 10 minutes.

☐ Cut steak diagonally across grain into thin strips. Serve with hot salsa over hot, cooked rice. Serves 4.

Flat-iron steak, flank steak, skirt steak and tri-tip roasts are great cooked on the grill, but they must be seared on the outside and grilled slowly over low to medium heat. In addition, these cuts should be cut in thin slices across the grain.

OREGANO LONDON BROIL

2 pounds (1-inch thick) London broil steak
½ cup bottled Greek vinaigrette dressing
1 tablespoon dried oregano
1 teaspoon lemon juice

☐ Dry steak with paper towels. Combine vinaigrette, oregano, lemon juice and ½ teaspoon pepper in large resealable bag.

☐ Add steak and press air out of bag. Seal and turn several times to distribute marinade well. Refrigerate 1 hour.

☐ Remove steak from marinade, discard marinade and grill about 5 inches from heat over medium-low heat for about 15 minutes for rare to medium steak. Remove from heat and let rest 10 minutes.

☐ Slice steak across grain. Serves 4 to 6.

The longer you cook meat, the firmer it becomes. Learn how to identify rare, medium and well done steaks by pressing your finger against the meat. A very firm steak is well done. A very soft steak is rare. With a little trial and error, you will be able to grill to perfection.

MARINATED BEEF STRIPS

2 teaspoons oil
2 teaspoons minced garlic
½ teaspoon cayenne pepper
2 tablespoons soy sauce
2 tablespoons honey
1 pound beef sirloin, thinly sliced

☐ Combine oil, garlic, cayenne pepper, soy sauce and honey and place in resealable plastic bag. Add sliced beef, seal and shake. Refrigerate for 1 hour.

☐ Place beef slices in large sprayed skillet over medium-high heat and cook 5 to 6 minutes or until done. Serves 4.

SIRLOIN WITH ITALIAN VEGETABLES

1 pound boneless sirloin steak, cut in strips
Oil
2 (15 ounce) cans Italian stewed tomatoes with liquid
1 (16 ounce) package frozen Italian green beans, thawed
1 (8 ounce) carton sour cream
Egg noodles, cooked

☐ Place sirloin strips in large skillet with a little oil. Sprinkle with salt and pepper. Cook on medium-high heat about 3 minutes, until browned on both sides.

☐ Add stewed tomatoes and green beans. Bring to boil, lower heat and simmer 5 minutes. Just before serving, fold in sour cream. Mix well and serve when heated through.

☐ Serve over hot egg noodles. Serves 4.

SEARED STEAK IN WINE SAUCE

2 pounds (¾ inch thick) round steak
Oil
1 (1 ounce) packet onion soup mix
1 cup dry red wine
1 (4 ounce) can sliced mushrooms

☐ Preheat oven to 325°.

☐ Remove all fat from steak and cut in serving-size pieces. Brown meat on both sides in a little oil in skillet over medium-high heat.

☐ Place in sprayed 9 x 13-inch baking dish.

☐ Combine onion soup mix, wine, 1 cup hot water and mushrooms in skillet. Heat for several minutes. Pour over browned steak.

☐ Cover and bake for 1 hour 20 minutes or until steak is tender. Serves 6 to 8.

Flat-iron steak, boneless blade, petite steak, top blade and round steaks are all less expensive cuts that work on the grill. They should be cooked medium rare and never well done. Less tender cuts of beef should be cut in thin slices across the grain and at a 45° angle for the best results.

EASY STEAK OUT

2 pounds (½ inch thick) round steak
Olive oil
1 onion, thinly sliced
2 (10 ounce) cans tomato bisque soup

☐ Cut steak into serving-size pieces. Brown meat in a little oil in skillet.

☐ Combine onion and soup in bowl and add to steak.

☐ Bring to a boil. Turn heat down, cover and simmer for 1 hour 20 minutes. (Add a little water if needed.) Serves 6 to 8.

TIP: *If you want a little breading on the meat, dust meat with flour and a little salt and pepper before browning in skillet. Serve over rice, noodles or toast.*

Thousand Island and Italian dressings are great, inexpensive marinades for chicken or pork.

TENDER STEAK STRIPS OVER RICE

1 pound round steak, cut in strips
1 (14 ounce) can beef broth
3 tablespoons cornstarch
1 tablespoon soy sauce
1 red bell pepper, seeded, julienned
1 green bell pepper, seeded, julienned
1 (4.6 ounce) broccoli and cheese boil-in-bag rice mix

☐ Brown steak strips in large skillet and reduce heat. Add ⅓ cup water, cover and simmer until liquid evaporates.

☐ Combine beef broth, cornstarch and soy sauce (and a little garlic powder if you like) in bowl and pour over steak strips.

☐ Add bell peppers and stir until mixture boils and thickens.

☐ Cook rice according to package directions and serve steak over rice. Serves 4.

Live life fully while you're here. Experience everything. Take care of yourself and your friends. Have fun, be crazy, be weird. Go out and screw up! You're going to anyway, so you might as well enjoy the process. Take the opportunity to learn from your mistakes: find the cause of your problem and eliminate it. Don't try to be perfect; just be an excellent example of being human.

— Anthony Robbins

SIMPLE BEEF STROGANOFF

1 pound round steak, cut into thin strips
½ cup sliced onion
2 tablespoons butter
1 (10 ounce) can cream of mushroom soup
½ cup sour cream
Cooked noodles

☐ Brown meat in skillet over medium-high heat and drain; set beef aside.

☐ Cook onion in butter in skillet until tender.

☐ Add beef, soup and sour cream to skillet. Bring to boil; reduce heat and simmer for 45 minutes or until tender. (Add a little water if needed.)

☐ Serve over noodles. Serves 4.

ROASTED GARLIC STEAK

2 (15 ounce) cans tomatoes with roasted garlic and herbs
½ cup Italian salad dressing
1½ pounds (¾ inch thick) boneless beef sirloin steak

☐ Combine tomatoes, dressing and ⅓ cup water in saucepan. Cook on medium heat and stir occasionally.

☐ Broil steaks to desired doneness. Allow about 7 minutes per side for medium. Serve heated sauce with steak. Serves 4 to 6.

SO-CAL MARINATED TRI-TIP ROAST

2 cloves garlic, minced
⅔ cup soy sauce
¼ cup canola or virgin olive oil
¼ cup packed light brown sugar
2 tablespoons red wine vinegar
1 (2 - 3 pound) tri-tip roast

☐ Mix garlic, soy sauce, oil, brown sugar and vinegar in bowl. Pour into resealable plastic bag with tri-tip.

☐ Marinate in refrigerator overnight. Turn plastic bag several times to rotate meat.

☐ Drain meat and cook slowly over charcoal fire until meat is tender.

☐ Remove from heat and rest 10 minutes. Cut thin slices across grain. Serves 6.

SMOTHERED STEAK BREAK

1 large round steak
1 (10 ounce) can mushroom soup
1 (1 ounce) packet onion soup mix
⅔ cup milk

☐ Preheat oven to 325°.

☐ Cut steak into serving-size pieces and place in sprayed 9 x 13-inch baking pan.

☐ Combine soup, soup mix and milk in saucepan. Heat just enough to mix well. Pour over steak. Seal with foil. Bake for 1 hour. Serves 4.

PEPPERED CHEESE STEAK

1 (1¼ pound) sirloin steak, cut into strips
1 (16 ounce) package frozen bell pepper and onion strips, thawed
1 (16 ounce) package cubed Mexican Velveeta® cheese
Rice, cooked

☐ Cook steak strips in sprayed, large skillet over medium heat for about 10 minutes or until no longer pink. Remove steak from skillet and set aside.

☐ Stir in vegetables and ½ cup water. Simmer vegetables for about 5 minutes until all liquid cooks out.

☐ Add cheese. Turn heat to medium-low until cheese melts. Stir in steak and serve over rice. Serves 4.

Money-Saving Tip:

Remember, the biggest package isn't always the cheapest. The only way you can be sure is to take a calculator and figure out the cost per unit. Don't be embarrassed to bring a calculator to the store. However, many stores do show price per ounce in their displays.

SMOTHERED BROCCOLI-BEEF

Try this over noodles. It's great. The flavors mix really well and the noodles soak up the creamy broccoli-flavored gravy.

1 pound beef sirloin steak
1 onion, chopped
Oil or butter
1 (10 ounce) can cream of broccoli soup
1 (10 ounce) package frozen chopped broccoli, thawed

☐ Slice beef across grain into very thin strips. Brown steak strips and onion in a little oil or butter in large sprayed skillet over medium heat and stir several times.

☐ Add a little water, reduce heat and simmer for 10 minutes. Mix in soup and broccoli and heat. Serves 4.

BEEF-BELL PEPPER SKILLET

2 pounds lean round steak
Oil
1 cup rice
1 (14 ounce) can beef broth
1 green bell pepper, seeded, chopped

☐ Cut steak into serving-size pieces and brown in very large skillet with a little oil over medium-hot heat.

☐ Add rice, beef broth, bell peppers and 1 cup water to skillet. Bring to a boil. Reduce heat, cover and simmer for 1 hour. Serves 6 to 8.

CHICKEN-FRIED STEAK AND CREAM GRAVY

2 pounds round steak, tenderized
1¼ cups flour
2 eggs, slightly beaten
½ cup milk
Canola oil

☐ Trim tenderized steak and cut into 6 to 8 pieces. Combine flour, 1 teaspoon salt and a little pepper in bowl. Dredge all steak pieces in flour mixture until lightly coated.

☐ In separate bowl, combine eggs and milk. Dip steak into egg mixture, dredge again in flour and get plenty of flour pressed into steak. Heat about ½ inch oil in heavy skillet and fry steak pieces until golden brown.

CREAM GRAVY:

6 tablespoons flour
6 - 8 tablespoons pan drippings
3 cups milk

☐ Move steaks to warm oven. Add flour to drippings in skillet, stir constantly and cook until flour begins to brown. Add milk slowly and stir until gravy thickens.

☐ Season with ½ teaspoon salt and ¼ teaspoon pepper. Serve in bowl or over steaks and mashed potatoes. Serves 4 to 6.

SEASONED BEEF TENDERLOIN

3 tablespoons dijon-style mustard
2 tablespoons prepared horseradish
1 (3 pound) center-cut beef tenderloin
½ cup seasoned breadcrumbs

☐ Combine mustard and horseradish in bowl and spread over beef tenderloin. Press breadcrumbs into horseradish-mustard mixture and wrap in foil. Refrigerate for at least 12 hours.

☐ When ready to bake, preheat oven to 375°. Remove wrap and place in sprayed pan. Bake for 30 minutes or to 145° for medium rare.

☐ Let tenderloin stand for 15 minutes before slicing. Serves 6.

Money-Saving Tip:

Look for Manager's Specials, especially in the meat department. Items that have "sell by" dates that are nearing expiration can usually be purchased at deep discounts. This is perfect for meals you plan to cook right away or you can freeze the meat for later use.

GREEN CHILE STUFFED TENDERLOIN

2 cloves garlic, minced
1 medium onion, chopped
1 tablespoon virgin olive oil
1 (4 ounce) can diced green chilies
½ cup shredded Mexican 4-cheese blend
½ cup seasoned breadcrumbs
4 (2-inch thick) beef tenderloin fillets

☐ Cook garlic and onion in oil in large skillet until they are translucent. Add green chilies, cheese and breadcrumbs. Stir several times and remove from heat.

☐ Make horizontal slice three-quarters through fillets. Place green chilies mixture in middle of fillets, fold and seal with toothpicks to hold mixture in place.

☐ Grill on oiled grate over medium-hot fire for about 5 to 10 minutes per side or until internal temperature is at least 145°. Serves 4.

Money-Saving Tip:
Search the end-caps at the end of the rows of shelves. The best deals are usually there because the store is trying to entice you to go down the aisles.

SAVORY SEASONED ROAST BEEF

1 tablespoon dried thyme
1 tablespoon dried, crushed rosemary
1 teaspoon rubbed sage
1 (4 - 5 pound) boneless beef roast

☐ Preheat oven to 325°.

☐ Combine thyme, rosemary and sage in small bowl and rub over roast. Place roast, fat-side up, in roasting pan.

☐ Bake for 2 hours to 2 hours 30 minutes or until meat reaches desired doneness.

☐ Remove roast to warm serving platter and let stand for 10 minutes before slicing. Serves 8 to 10.

EASY ROAST BEEF DINNER

1 (10 ounce) can cream of mushroom soup
1 (1 ounce) packet onion soup mix
½ cup white wine
1 (4 pound) rump roast

☐ Preheat oven to 325°.

☐ Combine mushroom soup, onion soup mix, white wine and ⅓ cup water in saucepan and heat over medium just enough to blend.

☐ Place roast in sprayed roasting pan. Pour soup mixture over roast. Cover and bake for 3 hours 30 minutes to 4 hours. Serves 8.

SIMPLE CHUCK ROAST MEAL

1 (3 - 4 pound) boneless rump roast or chuck roast
4 medium potatoes, peeled, cut into pieces
2 onions, quartered
1 (10 ounce) can cream of mushroom soup

☐ Preheat oven to 350°.

☐ Place seasoned* meat in roasting pan with 1 cup water. Cover and bake for about 1 hour.

☐ Add potatoes and onions, cover and continue cooking for additional 1 hour.

☐ Combine soup and ½ cup water in saucepan. Heat just enough to pour over roast and vegetables.

☐ Bake uncovered for additional 10 to 15 minutes. Serves 8.

*TIP: *Everyone seasons food according to their tastes. Salt and pepper work great for this roast. Lemon pepper, garlic salt or seasoned salt are excellent too. Season with your personal favorites.*

No matter how old a mother is, she watches her middle-aged children for signs of improvement.

– Florida Scott-Maxwell

LEMON-HERB POT ROAST

1 teaspoon garlic powder
2 teaspoons lemon-pepper seasoning
1 teaspoon dried basil
1 (3 - 3½ pound) boneless beef chuck roast
1 tablespoon canola oil

☐ Combine garlic powder, lemon pepper and basil in bowl and press evenly into surface of beef.

☐ Heat oil in large, heavy pan over medium-high heat and brown roast.

☐ Add 1 cup water, bring to a boil and reduce heat to low. Cover tightly and simmer for 3 hours. (Add water if necessary.) Vegetables may be added to roast the last hour of cooking. Serves 4.

Pot roast is a simple one-pot dish symbolizing the frugal nature, sensibility and love of simplicity inherent in early settlers of America. New Englanders epitomized these qualities and one such example is their use of boiling and steaming less tender cuts of meat, then adding vegetables half-way through the cooking process.

TOMORROW BEEF BRISKET

1 (5 - 6 pound) trimmed beef brisket
1 (1 ounce) packet onion soup mix
1 (10 ounce) bottle steak sauce
1 (12 ounce) bottle barbecue sauce

☐ Preheat oven to 325°.

☐ Place brisket cut-side up in sprayed roasting pan. Combine onion soup mix, steak sauce and barbecue sauce in bowl and mix. Pour over brisket.

☐ Cover and cook for 4 to 5 hours or until tender. Remove brisket from pan and pour off drippings. Refrigerate both, separately, overnight.

☐ The next day, trim all fat from meat, slice and reheat. Skim fat off drippings and reheat. Serve sauce over brisket. Serves 10.

At one time pigs roamed wild on Manhattan Island and residents built a long wall on the northern edge of what is now lower Manhattan. The wall turned into a street named Wall Street. Today it represents one of the greatest financial markets in the world.

SLOW COOKIN' BRISKET

½ cup hickory-flavored liquid smoke
1 (4 - 5 pound) beef brisket
1 (5 ounce) bottle Worcestershire sauce
¾ cup barbecue sauce

☐ Pour liquid smoke over brisket. Cover and refrigerate overnight.

☐ When ready to bake, preheat oven to 275°.

☐ Drain and pour Worcestershire sauce over brisket. Cover and bake for 6 to 7 hours.

☐ Uncover and pour barbecue sauce over brisket and bake for additional 30 minutes. Remove from heat and let rest 15 minutes.

☐ Slice very thin across grain. Serves 8.

In Texas beef brisket is synonymous with the word barbecue. In other words, when one says barbecue it means brisket. Texans don't barbecue on weekends or use the barbecue to cook on. In Texas barbecue is not a verb or an adjective. It is a noun with only one meaning and that meaning is brisket.

BEEF FLAUTAS

This is great for leftover brisket.

2 - 3 cups shredded cooked beef brisket
1 tablespoon chili powder
1 tablespoon snipped cilantro
2 teaspoons ground cumin
1 onion, chopped
2 cloves garlic, minced
Corn tortillas
Canola oil

☐ Season shredded brisket with chili powder, cilantro, cumin and a little salt and stir. Add onion and garlic and mix well.

☐ Place corn tortillas in oven under broiler or in a hot dry skillet for 2 to 3 minutes. (This will help the tortillas to be more pliable.)

☐ Place several tablespoons shredded brisket in each corn tortilla and fold up like envelope and secure with toothpick.

☐ Heat oil in deep saucepan and carefully drop flauta into oil. Fry until crispy, remove from oil and drain. Serve hot. Serves 4 to 5.

We all have hometown appetites. Every other person is a bundle of longing, for the simplicities of good taste once enjoyed on the farm or in the hometown he or she left behind.

– Clementine Paddleford.

BEEF RIBS AND GRAVY

4 pounds beef short ribs
1 onion, sliced
1 (12 ounce) jar beef gravy
1 (1 ounce) packet beef gravy mix
Mashed potatoes

☐ Place beef ribs in sprayed 6-quart slow cooker. Cover with onion and sprinkle with
   1 teaspoon pepper.

☐ Combine beef gravy and dry gravy mix in small bowl and pour over ribs and onion.

☐ Cover and cook on LOW for 9 to 11 hours. (The ribs must cook this long on LOW to
   tenderize.) Serves 4 to 6.

TIP: Serve with hot mashed potatoes and gravy.

IRISH CORNED BEEF WITH VEGETABLES

1 (4 - 5) pound corned beef brisket
4 large potatoes, peeled, quartered
6 carrots, peeled, quartered
1 head cabbage

☐ Place corned beef in roasting pan, cover with water and bring to a boil. Turn heat down
   and simmer for 3 hours. Add water if necessary.

☐ Add potatoes and carrots. Cut cabbage into eighths and lay over top of other vegetables
   and corned beef.

☐ Bring to a boil, turn heat down and cook for additional 30 to 40 minutes or until
   vegetables are tender. When slightly cool, slice corned beef across grain. Serves 8.

EASY CORNED BEEF

1 (5 pound) corned beef brisket
Whole cloves
½ cup maple syrup

☐ Preheat oven to 375°.

☐ Place corned beef in baking dish with water to almost cover beef. Bring to a boil. Lower heat and simmer until done. (Allow about 30 minutes per pound.)

☐ When corned beef is done, place on rack in shallow pan. Stick whole cloves in crosswise design. Pour syrup over meat and sprinkle with a little pepper.

☐ Place in oven to brown and glaze for about 15 minutes. When ready to serve, slice beef across grain. Serve hot or at room temperature. Serves 10.

EASY ONION-BEEF CASSEROLE

1 pound lean ground beef
¼ cup rice
1 (10 ounce) can French onion soup
1 (3 ounce) can french-fried onions

☐ Preheat oven to 325°.

☐ Brown ground beef in sprayed skillet, drain and place in sprayed 7 x 11-inch baking dish.

☐ Combine rice, soup and ½ cup water and pour over beef. Cover and bake for 40 minutes.

☐ Sprinkle fried onions over top and bake uncovered for additional 10 minutes. Serves 4.

SEASONED ONION-BEEF PATTIES

1 (1 ounce) packet onion soup mix
2 pounds ground beef
Canola oil
2 (10 ounce) cans French onion soup

☐ Preheat oven to 350°.

☐ Combine soup mix and ½ cup water in bowl; add beef. Stir well and shape into patties about ½-inch thick.

☐ Cook in large skillet with a little canola oil and brown on both sides.

☐ Move patties to sprayed 9 x 13-inch baking dish. Pour soup over patties. Cover and bake for about 35 minutes. Serves 8.

QUICK AND EASY MUSHROOM MEATLOAF

1 pound ground round beef, browned
2 (10 ounce) cans cream of mushroom
1 (1 ounce) packet dry onion soup mix
1 cup cooked rice

☐ Preheat oven to 350°.

☐ Mix all ingredients in bowl. Place into sprayed 9 x 5-inch loaf pan. Bake for 50 minutes. Serves 8.

FAMILY FAVORITE MEATLOAF

2 pounds lean ground beef
¾ cup Italian-seasoned dry breadcrumbs
2 large eggs, beaten
2 (10 ounce) cans cream of mushroom soup, divided
¼ cup (½ stick) butter
1¼ cups milk

☐ Preheat oven to 350°.

☐ Mix beef, breadcrumbs, eggs and ½ can soup. In sprayed baking pan, shape firmly into 9 x 4-inch loaf and bake 45 minutes. Let stand about 10 minutes before slicing.

☐ In saucepan, combine remaining soup, butter and milk, mix well and heat, stirring often, until sauce is thoroughly hot. Serve over slices of meatloaf. Serves 8.

A great sauce for meatloaf is a can of Sloppy Joe sauce. Just pour it over the top and everyone will ask you for the recipe.

POTATO-BEEF BAKE

1 pound ground beef
1 (10 ounce) can sloppy Joe sauce
1 (10 ounce) can fiesta nacho cheese soup
1 (32 ounce) package frozen hash-brown potatoes, thawed

☐ Preheat oven to 400°.

☐ Cook beef in skillet over medium heat until no longer pink and drain. Add sloppy Joe sauce and fiesta nacho cheese soup.

☐ Place hash browns in sprayed 9 x 13-inch baking dish. Top with beef mixture.

☐ Cover and bake for 25 minutes. Uncover and bake for additional 10 minutes. Serves 6.

TIP: If you really like a cheesy dish, sprinkle shredded cheddar cheese on top just before serving.

SMOTHERED BEEF PATTIES

1½ pounds ground beef
½ cup chili sauce
½ cup buttery cracker crumbs
1 (14 ounce) can beef broth

☐ Combine beef, chili sauce and cracker crumbs in bowl and form into 6 patties.

☐ Brown patties in sprayed skillet and pour beef broth over patties. Bring to a boil. Reduce heat, cover and simmer for about 40 minutes. Serves 6.

BEEF MEDLEY CASSEROLE

1 pound lean ground beef
1 onion, chopped
¼ cup steak sauce
1 tablespoon flour
1 (15 ounce) can baked beans with liquid
1 (8 ounce) can whole kernel corn, drained
1½ cups crushed garlic-flavored croutons

☐ Preheat oven to 325°.

☐ Brown beef and onion in large skillet and drain. Stir in all remaining ingredients except croutons.

☐ Pour into sprayed 9 x 13-inch baking dish and sprinkle crouton crumbs on top.

☐ Bake uncovered for 45 minutes or until bubbly around edges. Serves 6 to 8.

Baking, roasting, outdoor grilling and broiling in the oven are some of the best methods for low-fat cooking of meats, poultry and fish.

PINTO BEEF PIE

1 pound lean ground beef
1 onion, chopped
2 (15 ounce) cans pinto beans with liquid
1 (10 ounce) can diced tomatoes and green chilies with liquid
1 (2.8 ounce) can french-fried onions

☐ Preheat oven to 350°.

☐ In skillet, brown beef and onion and drain.

☐ In 2-quart baking dish, layer 1 can beans, beef-onion mixture, and ½ can tomatoes and green chilies. Repeat layers.

☐ Top with fried onions and bake uncovered for 30 minutes. Serves 4.

POTATO-BEEF CASSEROLE

4 medium potatoes, peeled, sliced
1¼ pounds lean ground beef, browned, drained
1 (10 ounce) can cream of mushroom soup
1 (10 ounce) can vegetable beef soup

☐ Preheat oven to 350°.

☐ In large bowl, combine all ingredients. Add a little salt and pepper. Transfer to sprayed 3-quart baking dish.

☐ Bake covered for 1 hour 30 minutes or until potatoes are tender. Serves 4.

COLD NIGHT CHILI SUPPER

1 (40 ounce) can chili with beans
1 (7 ounce) can diced green chilies
1 bunch fresh green onions, sliced
1 (8 ounce) package shredded Mexican 4-cheese blend
2½ cups crushed ranch-flavored tortilla chips, divided

☐ Preheat oven to 350°.

☐ Combine chili, green chilies, green onions, cheese and 2 cups crushed chips.
   Transfer to sprayed 3-quart baking dish and bake 25 minutes.

☐ Sprinkle remaining chips over top of casserole and bake additional 10 minutes.
   Serves 4 to 6.

*Here are some good nutritious foods to include
in your diet to supplement the protein and
carbohydrates in your daily diets.*

*½ red bell pepper = 1 day's worth of vitamin C;
   about 6 times as much as 6 ounces of orange juice*

*1 sweet potato = more than 1 day's supply of
   vitamin A; 100 calories*

Pumpkin seeds are loaded with magnesium.

*Carrots, spinach, winter squash are loaded with
   vitamin A.*

HASH BROWN DINNER

1½ pounds lean ground chuck, browned
1 (1 ounce) packet brown gravy mix
1 (15 ounce) can cream-style corn
1 (15 ounce) can whole kernel corn
1 (8 ounce) package shredded cheddar cheese, divided
1 (18 ounce) package frozen hash browns, partially thawed
1 (10 ounce) can cream of mushroom soup
1 (5 ounce) can evaporated milk

☐ Place browned beef in sprayed slow cooker and toss with dry brown gravy mix.

☐ Add cream-style corn and whole kernel corn and cover with half cheddar cheese.

☐ Top with hash browns and remaining cheese.

☐ Combine mushroom soup and evaporated milk in bowl. Mix well and pour over hash browns and cheese.

☐ Cover and cook on LOW for 6 to 8 hours. Serves 4 to 6.

Stretch meatloaf by adding cooked rice, grains,
quick-cooking grains or oatmeal, and/or vegetables.

OLD-FASHIONED BASIC BURGER

1¼ pounds ground chuck
1 egg
2 teaspoons Worcestershire sauce

☐ Mix ground chuck with egg, worcestershire, ½ teaspoon salt and ¼ teaspoon pepper. Form into 4 or 5 patties

☐ Cook on medium grill for 5 to 6 minutes per side or in skillet for 4 to 5 minutes per side. (Cook until at least 160°.) Toast hamburger buns and serve with your favorite fixings. Serves 4 to 5.

Seymour, Wisconsin claims that Charlie Nagreen made the first hamburger at the Outagamie County Fair in 1885.

Later in 1885 Frank and Charles Menches from Akron, Ohio sold pork sausages to county fairs. When the pork ran out at a fair in Hamburg, New York, the brothers substituted beef patties and put them between two pieces of bread and called them "hamburgers" after that city.

In 1891 Oscar Weber Bilby made the first hamburger on a bun on July 4, 1891 in Tulsa, Oklahoma. He cooked ground beef patties on a homemade grill. His family still uses the original grill in their restaurant to make hamburgers today.

In 1904 the St. Louis World's Fair introduced and sold hamburgers and claimed they were the first burgers.

Additional claims for the birthplace of the hamburger come from Athens, Texas and New Haven, Connecticut.

All in all, we can certainly agree that the hamburger is an American original.

TANGY SURPRISE BURGERS

1¼ pound lean ground beef
4 pineapple rings
½ cup hot and spicy ketchup
⅔ cup packed brown sugar
1 tablespoon dijon mustard
4 kaiser rolls
Deli coleslaw

☐ Prepare outdoor grill on medium-high heat. Divide beef into four portions and form patties around pineapple rings so that none of pineapple is showing.

☐ In saucepan, combine ketchup, brown sugar and mustard and heat until sugar dissolves.

☐ Grill burgers about 5 minutes on each side or at least 160°. Spoon some of brown sugar sauce over burgers several times before serving.

☐ Place patties on rolls and top with 1 heaping tablespoon of coleslaw. Cover with top bun and serve immediately. Serves 4.

The secret of good cooking is first, having a love of it… If you're convinced cooking is drudgery, you're never going to be good at it, and you might as well warm up something frozen.

— James Beard

SOUR CREAM HAMBURGERS

2 pounds ground beef
1 (8 ounce) carton sour cream
1 (1 ounce) packet dry onion soup mix
¾ cup dry breadcrumbs
1 egg, beaten
6 - 8 hamburger buns

☐ Preheat grill to medium-high heat.

☐ In bowl, combine beef, sour cream, dry onion soup mix, breadcrumbs, egg and ½ teaspoon black pepper. Form beef mixture into patties.

☐ Grill patties about 7 minutes per side, or until at least 160°.

☐ Place patties on buns and top with your favorite toppings. Serves 6 to 8.

If a man be sensible and one fine morning while he is lying in bed, count at the tips of his fingers how many things in this life truly will give him enjoyment, invariably he will find food is the first one.

– Lin Yutang

BURGERS SUPREME

1¼ pounds lean ground beef
1 egg, beaten
1 tablespoon dried parsley
2 tablespoons quick-cooking oats
½ cup mayonnaise
2 tablespoons chili sauce
¼ teaspoon cayenne pepper
4 large hamburger buns
2 avocados, peeled, sliced
4 slices from center of large onion

☐ In bowl combine beef, egg, parsley, oats and salt to taste. Form into 4 patties and cook in skillet 5 minutes on each side, or until at least 160°.

☐ In small bowl, combine mayonnaise, chili sauce and cayenne pepper. Spread on tops and bottoms of buns. Place patties on 4 bottom halves of buns and top with avocado slices and onion slices. Add shredded lettuce, if you like. Serves 4.

*No matter where I take my guests,
it seems they like my kitchen best.*

– *Pennsylvania Dutch Saying*

FIRECRACKER BURGERS

1 pound ground beef
1 cup finely chopped onion
1 (4 ounce) can diced green chilies, drained
2 teaspoons seasoned breadcrumbs
1 egg, beaten
1 teaspoon beef bouillon granules
¼ teaspoon cayenne pepper, optional
4 slices pepper Jack cheese
4 hamburger buns

☐ Preheat grill for medium-high heat.

☐ In bowl, combine beef, onion, green chilies, breadcrumbs, egg, beef bouillon granules and cayenne pepper. Mix well and shape into 4 patties.

☐ Grill patties 5 minutes on each side, or until at least 160°. Top each patty with cheese slice about 2 minutes before removing from grill.

☐ Serve on hamburger buns with your favorite toppings. Serves 4.

...even those for whom cooking is an oppressive chore or a source of self-doubting anxiety, acknowledge that a meal shared by friends and family is one of the bonding rituals without which the family, society even, can fall apart.

– Antonia Till

BIG JUICY STUFFED BURGERS

1½ pounds ground beef
1 (10 ounce) bottle steak sauce, divided
2 tablespoons fajita seasoning
2 tablespoons dried minced onion
¼ teaspoon cayenne pepper
8 slices American cheese, divided
1 (4 ounce) can diced green chilies, drained
1 (4 ounce) can sliced ripe olives

☐ In bowl, combine beef, ¼ cup steak sauce, fajita seasoning, onion and cayenne pepper. Mix well and form into 8 thin patties. On 4 patties, place one slice of cheese, a little of the green chilies and ripe olives. Top with remaining 4 patties, press down and seal edges so filling does not escape.

☐ Preheat grill to medium heat. Place patties on grill and brown on both sides. Once they begin to brown, brush tops with remaining steak sauce. Continue grilling for about 15 minutes, basting frequently with steak sauce.

☐ When meat is ready to come off the grill, place remaining 4 slices of cheese on tops of patties. Serve on buns or on their own. Serves 4.

True friends are those who really know you but love you anyway.

– Edna Buchanan

JALAPENO-BLUE CHEESE BURGERS

2 pounds ground beef
6 jalapeno peppers, seeded, chopped
1 cup crumbled blue cheese
2 tablespoons finely minced onion
2 teaspoons minced garlic
2 tablespoons soy sauce
6 slices provolone cheese
6 hamburger buns, split
½ cup mayonnaise
¼ cup ketchup
Shredded lettuce

☐ In bowl, combine beef, jalapeno peppers, blue cheese, onion, garlic, soy sauce and salt to taste. Mix well and form into 6 patties.

☐ Preheat grill to medium-high. Grill patties about 7 minutes on each side or until at least 160°. Just before removing patties, place slice of cheese on top of each and cover grill until cheese melts.

☐ Combine mayonnaise and ketchup and spread on bottom of each bun. Top with patty and shredded lettuce. Serves 6.

A smile is an inexpensive way to improve your looks.

— Anonymous

CHEESY HIDDEN BURGERS

1¼ pounds ground beef
½ finely chopped onion
1 egg, beaten
1 teaspoon hot pepper sauce
1 tablespoon dry breadcrumbs
1 teaspoon dried parsley
⅓ cup shredded pepper Jack cheese
½ teaspoon cayenne pepper
1 (2 ounce) jar chopped pimentos, drained
4 slices pickled jalapeno pepper, finely chopped

☐ Preheat oven to 350°.

☐ In bowl, combine beef, onion, egg, hot pepper sauce, breadcrumbs, parsley, and salt and pepper to taste.

☐ In a separate bowl, combine cheese, cayenne pepper, pimentos and pickled jalapeno peppers.

☐ Form beef mixture into 4 balls and press a well in center of each. Stuff each with one-fourth cheese mixture and press meat around filling to seal. Place on baking sheet and press gently into thick patties.

☐ Bake 20 minutes or until well done, turning once. Place patties on buns and add your favorite toppings. Serves 4.

Southwest Burgers

2 pounds lean ground beef
1 packet taco seasoning mix
1 cup salsa, divided
1 (8 count) package kaiser buns
8 slices hot pepper Jack cheese

☐ Combine beef, taco seasoning and ¼ cup salsa in large mixing bowl. Shape mixture into 8 patties.

☐ Preheat grill to medium-high heat. Cook patties about 7 minutes per side or until at least 160°.

☐ When patties are almost done, place buns cut side down on grill and heat 1 or 2 minutes. Place patties on bottom half of buns, top with cheese and cook an additional minute or until cheese melts.

☐ Top with heaping tablespoon salsa and top half of bun. Serves 8.

Family meals are great for finding out about your children's lives. When children talk about their day and their activities, you learn what they are learning. You can explain important points and use these times as teaching moments. It is not a time for conflict or strong discipline, but a time for love and nurturing.

SPICY CAJUN BURGERS

1 pound round beef
3 tablespoons seasoned dry breadcrumbs
1 egg
3 green onions, finely chopped
1 tablespoon plus 1 teaspoon Cajun seasoning, divided
1 tablespoon prepared mustard
¼ cup chili sauce
½ teaspoon hot sauce
4 slices pepper Jack cheese
4 hamburger buns
Shredded lettuce
4 thin slices red onion

☐ Preheat grill to high heat.

☐ In bowl, combine beef, breadcrumbs, egg, green onions, 1 tablespoon Cajun seasoning and mustard. Mix well and form into 4 patties.

☐ In small bowl, blend chili sauce, remaining 1 teaspoon Cajun seasoning and hot sauce.

☐ Cook patties about 5 minutes on each side or until at least 160°. Place slice of cheese on each burger; remove from heat when cheese starts to melt and place on bun.

☐ Serve with chili sauce mixture, plus shredded lettuce and a thin slice of red onion. Serves 4.

BURGERS ITALIAN STYLE

1½ pounds ground round beef
½ cup spaghetti sauce
¼ cup Italian seasoned breadcrumbs
1 egg
10 slices Italian bread
10 slices provolone cheese

☐ In bowl, combine ground beef, spaghetti sauce, breadcrumbs and egg; mix well. Shape into 5 patties and place in oven-safe dish. Broil patties in oven about 4 inches from heat. Broil about 6 minutes on each side, or until at least 160°.

☐ On a baking sheet, lightly toast each bread slice. Turn oven off.

☐ Place 1 slice cheese on 5 slices, top with patty and a second slice of cheese. Place another slice of bread on top and place baking sheet back in oven (oven will still be hot from broiling the patties and toast). Leave in warm oven about 5 minutes or until cheese melts slightly.

☐ Serve with additional spaghetti sauce if you like. Serves 5.

Family meals teach basic manners and social skills that children should learn to be successful in life. What they learn will help them in new situations and give them more confidence because they will know how to act and what to say and do.

FAMILY CABBAGE ROLLS

This is a wonderful way to get the kids to eat cabbage.

1 large head cabbage, cored
1½ pounds lean ground beef
1 egg, beaten
3 tablespoons ketchup
⅓ cup seasoned breadcrumbs
2 tablespoons dried minced onion flakes
2 (15 ounce) cans Italian stewed tomatoes
¼ cup cornstarch
3 tablespoons brown sugar
2 tablespoons Worcestershire sauce

☐ Preheat oven to 325°.

☐ Place head of cabbage in large soup pot of boiling water for 10 minutes or until outer leaves are tender. Drain well. Rinse in cold water and remove 10 large outer leaves*. Set aside.

☐ Slice or shred remaining cabbage. Place into sprayed 9 x 13-inch baking dish.

☐ Combine ground beef, egg, ketchup, breadcrumbs, onion flakes and 1 teaspoon salt in large bowl and mix well.

☐ Pack together about ½ cup meat mixture and put on each cabbage leaf. Fold in sides and roll leaf to completely enclose filling. (You may have to remove thick vein from cabbage leaves for easier rolling.) Place each rolled leaf over shredded cabbage.

☐ Place stewed tomatoes in large saucepan. Combine cornstarch, brown sugar and Worcestershire sauce in bowl and add to tomatoes. Cook on high heat, stirring constantly until stewed tomatoes and juices thicken. Pour over cabbage rolls. Cover and bake for 1 hour. Serves 10.

TIP: To get that many large leaves, you may have to put 2 smaller leaves together to make one roll.

CHEESEBURGER PIE

1 cup plus 2 tablespoons biscuit mix, divided
1 pound ground beef
½ cup chopped onion
1 tablespoon Worcestershire sauce
2 eggs
1 cup small curd creamed cottage cheese
2 tomatoes, sliced
1 cup shredded cheddar cheese

☐ Preheat oven to 375°.

☐ Mix 1 cup biscuit mix with ¼ cup cold water until soft dough forms; beat 20 strokes vigorously. Smooth dough into ball on floured wax paper and knead 5 times.

☐ Roll dough 2 inches larger than inverted pie pan. Ease dough into pan; flute edge if desired.

☐ Cook and stir ground beef and onion until browned; drain. Stir in ½ teaspoon salt, ¼ teaspoon pepper, 2 tablespoons biscuit mix and Worcestershire sauce. Spoon into piecrust.

☐ Mix eggs and cottage cheese and pour over beef mixture. Arrange tomato slices in circle on top; sprinkle with cheddar cheese. Bake about 30 minutes or until set. Serves 6 to 8.

TRADITIONAL SHEPHERD'S PIE

Traditionally an Irish dish and found in many Irish pubs.

1½ pounds ground beef
1 large onion, chopped
1 cup chopped carrots
1 cup sliced mushrooms or 1 (6 ounce) can sliced mushrooms
2 tablespoons butter
½ cup frozen green peas
2 teaspoons Worcestershire sauce
½ cup beef broth
2 tablespoons flour
4 cups mashed potatoes

☐ Preheat oven to 400°.

☐ Brown beef in skillet; drain fat and set aside beef.

☐ In same skillet, saute onion, carrots and mushrooms in butter until onions are translucent. Add peas, beef, Worcestershire sauce, broth, and salt and pepper. Mix well and simmer for 10 minutes.

☐ Mix flour with ¼ cup water and add to mixture; cook and stir until thickened. Place in 9 x 13-inch baking dish. Spread mashed potatoes on top and swirl into peaks.

☐ Bake for 25 to 30 minutes or until potatoes are golden. Serves 6.

Shepherd's pie is a great way to combine leftovers with mashed potatoes for a flavorful new dish.

MAC CHEESE SUPPER

1½ pounds lean ground beef
2 (7 ounce) packages macaroni and cheese dinner
1 (15 ounce) can whole kernel corn, drained
1½ cups shredded Monterey Jack cheese

☐ Preheat oven to 350°.

☐ Sprinkle ground beef with 1 teaspoon salt, brown in skillet until no longer pink and drain.

☐ Prepare macaroni and cheese according to package directions.

☐ Spoon beef and corn into macaroni. Pour into sprayed 9 x 13 baking dish and bake for 20 minutes. With 5 minutes remaining, sprinkle Jack cheese over top and leave in oven until cheese melts. Serves 4 to 6.

Thomas Jefferson's first recipe for Macaroni and Cheese is much like our recipes today. Pasta, butter, milk, seasonings, and yellow or white cheese mixed together and baked. Ronald Reagan was another American president who listed Macaroni and Cheese as his favorite food and served it in the White House.

STUFFED GREEN PEPPERS

4½ large bell peppers
¼ cup (½ stick) butter, divided
1 large onion, diced
1 rib celery, diced
½ bunch green onions, diced
2 cloves garlic, minced
½ - 1 pound ground beef
2 - 3 slices white bread, torn in small pieces
1 - 2 eggs, beaten, divided
1 carrot, grated
½ teaspoon sugar
1 cup seasoned breadcrumbs

☐ Preheat oven to 350°.

☐ Parboil 4 whole bell peppers for 3 minutes. Cut in half horizontally and set aside to cool.

☐ Finely chop remaining ½ pepper and place in saucepan with 2 tablespoons butter, onion, celery, green onions and garlic; saute vegetables.

☐ Add ground beef to mixture and brown. Remove from heat and set aside.

☐ Soak bread in ¼ cup water and 1 egg in bowl. Add bread mixture, carrot, sugar, and a little salt and pepper to meat mixture and mix well.

☐ If mixture is too stiff, add remaining egg. Fill bell pepper shells with meat mixture, cover with seasoned breadcrumbs and dot with remaining butter. Bake for 30 to 40 minutes. Serves 6 to 8.

SWISS STEAK

1 - 1½ pounds boneless, round steak
½ teaspoon seasoned salt
½ teaspoon seasoned pepper
8 - 10 medium new (red) potatoes with peel, halved
1 cup baby carrots
1 onion, sliced
1 (15 ounce) can stewed tomatoes
1 (12 ounce) jar beef gravy

☐ Cut steak in 6 to 8 serving-size pieces and sprinkle with seasoned salt and seasoned pepper. Brown in non-stick skillet.

☐ Layer steak pieces, potatoes, carrots and onion in sprayed slow cooker.

☐ Combine tomatoes and beef gravy in saucepan over heat to mix. Spoon over vegetables. Cover and cook on LOW for 7 to 8 hours. Serves 4 to 6.

TEXAS CHILI PIE

2 (20 ounce) cans chili without beans
1 (16 ounce) package corn chips
1 onion, chopped
1 (12 ounce) package shredded cheddar cheese

☐ Preheat oven to 325°.

☐ Heat chili in saucepan.

☐ Layer corn chips, chili, onion and cheese, one-third at a time, in sprayed 9 x 13-inch baking dish. Repeat layers with cheese on top.

☐ Bake for 20 minutes or until cheese bubbles. Serves 6.

BUENO TACO CASSEROLE

2 pounds lean ground beef
1½ cups taco sauce
2 (8.8 ounce) packages microwave Spanish rice, prepared
1 (8 ounce) package shredded Mexican 4-cheese blend, divided

☐ Preheat oven to 350°.

☐ Brown ground beef in skillet and drain. Add taco sauce, Spanish rice and half cheese and stir. Spoon into sprayed 3-quart baking dish.

☐ Cover and bake for 35 minutes. Sprinkle remaining cheese on top and bake uncovered for 5 minutes. Serves 8.

EASY SALSA MEATLOAF

1 (6 ounce) package stuffing mix
1 egg
½ cup salsa
1½ pounds lean ground beef

☐ Preheat oven to 350°.

☐ Combine stuffing mix, egg, salsa and ⅓ cup water in bowl and mix well. Add ground beef to stuffing mixture.

☐ Spoon into sprayed 9 x 5-inch loaf pan, shape into loaf and bake for 1 hour. Serves 4 to 6.

ROSA'S MEXICAN BEEF BASH

1 (13 ounce) bag tortilla chips, divided
2 pounds lean ground beef
1 (15 ounce) can Mexican stewed tomatoes
1 (8 ounce) package shredded Mexican 4-cheese blend

☐ Preheat oven to 350°.

☐ Partially crush half bag of chips and place in sprayed 9 x 13-inch baking dish.

☐ Brown ground beef in sprayed skillet and drain. Add stewed tomatoes and cheese and mix well. Pour over chips.

☐ Sprinkle remaining crushed chips over casserole. Bake for 40 minutes. Serves 8.

BEEF SKILLET SUPPER

1 pound lean ground beef
1 (10 ounce) can tomato soup
1 cup hot chunky salsa
6 (6 inch) flour tortillas, cut into 1-inch pieces
1½ cups shredded cheddar cheese

☐ Brown and cook ground beef on medium-high heat in large, heavy skillet; drain. Add soup, salsa, ¾ cup water, tortillas, salt to taste and half cheese; mix well.

☐ Cover and cook over low heat for 15 minutes. Top with remaining cheese and serve right from skillet. Serves 4.

BORDER TACO PIE

1 pound lean ground beef
½ bell pepper, seeded, chopped
1 (15 ounce) can Mexican stewed tomatoes
1 tablespoon chili powder
8 ounces shredded sharp cheddar cheese
1 (8 ounce) package corn muffin mix
1 egg
⅓ cup milk

☐ Preheat oven to 375°.

☐ Brown ground beef and bell pepper in a little oil in large skillet and drain well. Add a little salt, tomatoes, 1 cup water and chili powder.

☐ Cook on medium heat for about 10 minutes or until most liquid cooks out. Pour into sprayed 9 x 13-inch glass-baking dish. Sprinkle cheese on top.

☐ Combine muffin mix, egg and milk; beat well. Pour over top of cheese. Bake for 25 minutes or until muffin mix is light brown.

☐ Let cool for about 10 minutes before serving. Serves 8 to 10.

TIP: Add some jalapeno slices to give it some heat.

Nine out of every ten tomatoes grown in the U.S. are grown in California. In addition over 85% of all home gardeners in the U.S. grow tomatoes.

Black Bean Chili Casserole

1 pound lean ground beef
1 onion, finely chopped
2 (15 ounce) cans black beans, drained
1 teaspoon cumin
1 teaspoon chili powder
1½ cups thick-and-chunky salsa
1 (8 ounce) package corn muffin mix
1 egg
⅓ cup milk

☐ Preheat oven to 375°.

☐ In sprayed large skillet, cook beef and onion on medium-high heat for 8 to 10 minutes.

☐ Stir in black beans (or pinto beans if you prefer), cumin, chili powder, salsa and a little salt. Bring to a boil and reduce heat to medium. Cook 5 minutes and stir occasionally. Spoon into sprayed 3-quart round baking dish.

☐ In small bowl, prepare muffin mix according to package directions with egg and milk. Drop 8 spoonfuls batter around edge of baking dish, onto bean-beef mixture.

☐ Bake uncovered for 20 to 25 minutes or until topping is golden brown. Serves 6.

A great way to thicken soups or beans is instant mashed potato flakes. Just add a little a first and let it cook a little. If you need more, you can always add more. You can thicken a pot of beans with a can of refried beans. Just stir it in a little at a time until you get the consistency you want.

BEEF-ENCHILADA CASSEROLE

1½ pounds ground beef
1 (1 ounce) packet taco seasoning mix
Canola oil
8 corn tortillas
1 (8 ounce) package shredded cheddar cheese, divided
1 (10 ounce) can enchilada sauce
1 (4 ounce) can diced green chilies
1 cup sour cream
1 (12 ounce) package shredded Monterey Jack cheese

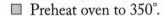

☐ Preheat oven to 350°.

☐ Sprinkle a little salt and pepper over beef, brown in large skillet and drain well.

☐ Add taco seasoning mix and 1¼ cups water to beef and simmer for 5 minutes.

☐ In separate skillet, heat a small amount of oil until hot. Cook tortillas, one at a time, until soft and limp, about 5 to 10 seconds on each side. Drain on paper towels.

☐ Spoon ⅓ cup meat mixture into center of each tortilla.

☐ Sprinkle with a little cheddar cheese, roll and place seam-side down into sprayed 9 x 13-inch baking dish.

☐ After filling all tortillas, add enchilada sauce and green chilies to remaining meat mixture. Spoon over tortillas.

☐ Cover and bake about 30 minutes.

☐ Spread sour cream over tortillas and sprinkle Monterey Jack cheese over top. Bake uncovered about 5 to 10 minutes or until cheese melts. Serves 6 to 8.

GREEN ENCHILADAS

1½ pounds lean ground beef
1 onion, chopped
1 teaspoon ground cumin
1 teaspoon minced garlic
3 cups shredded longhorn cheese
1 (10 ounce) can cream of chicken soup
¾ cup evaporated milk
1 (7 ounce) can diced green chilies, drained
1 (2 ounce) jar diced pimentos
1 (8 ounce) package shredded cheddar cheese
Canola oil
10 - 12 (8 ounce) corn tortillas

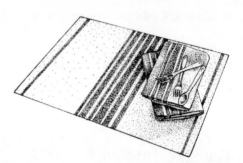

☐ Preheat oven to 350°.

☐ Brown beef and onion in skillet. Add 1 teaspoon salt, cumin and garlic; then add longhorn cheese. Stir until cheese melts and turn off heat.

☐ Combine soup, evaporated milk, green chilies, pimentos and cheddar cheese in saucepan and heat until cheese melts.

☐ In separate skillet, heat a little oil and fry tortillas only enough to soften.

☐ Roll equal amount of meat mixture into each softened tortilla until all meat is used.

☐ Place seam-side down in sprayed 9 x 13-inch baking dish. Pour cheese-milk sauce over tortillas.

☐ Bake for 30 to 35 minutes or until hot and bubbly. Serves 6 to 8.

TEXAS TAMALE PIE

1¼ pounds lean ground beef
1 onion, finely chopped
Canola oil
1 (15 ounce) can diced tomatoes
1 (10 ounce) can diced tomatoes and green chilies
1 (15 ounce) can pinto beans
1 (8 ounce) can whole kernel corn
1 teaspoon chili powder
1 (6 ounce) package cornbread mix

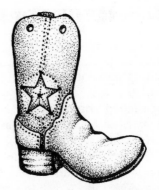

☐ Preheat oven to 375°.

☐ Brown beef and onion in skillet with a little oil. Add tomatoes and tomatoes and green chilies; simmer for about 15 minutes.

☐ Place 3 to 4 tablespoons beans on small plate and mash with fork. Add to beef-tomato mixture to thicken slightly. Add remaining beans, corn and chili powder.

☐ Spoon into sprayed 9 x 13-inch glass baking dish.

☐ Mix cornbread mix according to package directions; add extra 2 tablespoons milk for thinner batter. Spread on top of beef-bean mixture.

☐ Bake for 30 minutes. Serves 6 to 8.

My favorite animal is steak.

– *Fran Lebowitz*

MEXICAN-BEEF CASSEROLE

Tortilla chips
Canola oil
1½ pounds lean ground beef
1 onion, chopped
1 bell pepper, seeded, chopped
1 (15 ounce) can Mexican stewed tomatoes
1 (15 ounce) can ranch-style pinto beans with liquid
¼ cup salsa
1 (1 ounce) packet onion soup mix
1 teaspoon seasoned salt
1 teaspoon chili powder
¼ teaspoon garlic powder
½ teaspoon ground coriander
1 (12 ounce) package shredded cheddar cheese

☐ Preheat oven to 350°.

☐ Place about 40 chips in sprayed 9 x 13-inch baking dish. Crush slightly with your hands.

☐ Place oil in skillet and brown meat, onion and bell pepper.

☐ Add tomatoes, beans, salsa, onion soup mix, seasoned salt, chili powder, ¼ teaspoon pepper, garlic powder and coriander and mix well.

☐ Heat and simmer for 3 to 4 minutes.

☐ Spoon over chips in baking dish and cover with cheese.

☐ Cover and bake for 35 minutes. Serves 8.

NOTHING FANCY BEEF BURRITOS

1 pound ground beef
1 tablespoon chili powder
2 onions, chopped
1 (15 ounce) can refried beans
4 - 6 flour tortillas, warmed
1 (8 ounce) package shredded Mexican 4-cheese blend
1 tomato, chopped
Salsa

☐ Brown ground beef with 1 teaspoon salt and chili powder in heavy skillet. Drain grease, add onions and cook until onions are translucent.

☐ Heat refried beans in saucepan.

☐ Spread several tablespoons refried beans on warmed flour tortilla. Top with ground beef, cheese and tomato. Fold up ends of tortilla and roll to secure. Serve with salsa. Serves 4 to 6.

Mexican food is a favorite across America, but Texas has put its stamp on Tex-Mex, which is now considered one of America's nine regional food cuisines. Tex-Mex is not authentic Mexican food from the interior of Mexico, but rather an adaptation of Mexican food standardized to some extent by Texans.

CREAMY PASTA SHELLS

1¼ pounds lean ground beef
1 onion, chopped
1 (10 ounce) can cream of celery soup
1 (10 ounce) box shells and cheese sauce

☐ Brown beef and onion in skillet and stir until beef crumbles and is no longer pink. Drain grease. Add soup and mix.

☐ Prepare shells and cheese according to package directions. Stir into beef mixture. Simmer for 20 minutes. Serve hot. Serves 4.

CHEESY BEEFY GNOCCHI

2 cups gnocchi or shell pasta
1 pound lean ground beef
1 (10 ounce) can cheddar cheese soup
1 (10 ounce) can tomato bisque soup

☐ Cook pasta according to package directions and drain.

☐ Brown beef in skillet and drain. Return beef to skillet and add pasta, soups and 1½ cups water.

☐ Bring mixture to a boil and mix well. Cover, reduce heat to medium and cook for about 10 minutes; stir often. Serves 4.

SPAGHETTI AND MEATBALLS

MEATBALLS:

2 pounds lean ground round
½ pound ground pork
4 eggs
2 cups grated parmesan cheese
1½ cups dry breadcrumbs
1 onion, chopped
2 cloves garlic, pressed
½ bunch fresh parsley, minced
½ cup milk
1½ tablespoons ketchup
Olive oil

☐ Toss all ingredients except olive oil lightly and shape into balls.

☐ Place meatballs in hot skillet with olive oil and brown; drain and set aside.

SAUCE:

1 onion, minced
1 clove garlic, pressed
1 tablespoon olive oil
2 (6 ounce) cans tomato paste
1 tablespoon minced sweet basil
1 tablespoon ground oregano
Spaghetti, cooked

☐ In heavy saucepan saute onion and garlic in olive oil until soft and clear. Add tomato paste, 1½ to 2 quarts water, a little salt and pepper, basil, and oregano; mix well.

☐ Add browned meatballs and simmer for 1 hour or until sauce thickens. Serve over cooked spaghetti. Serves 6 to 8.

SIMPLE SPAGHETTI BAKE

8 ounces spaghetti
1 pound lean ground beef
1 green bell pepper, seeded, finely chopped
1 onion, chopped
1 (10 ounce) can tomato bisque soup
1 (15 ounce) can tomato sauce
2 teaspoons Italian seasoning
1 (4 ounce) can black sliced olives, drained
1 (12 ounce) package shredded cheddar cheese

☐ Cook spaghetti according to package directions and drain.

☐ Cook beef, bell pepper and onion in skillet and drain.

☐ Add remaining ingredients, ⅓ cup water, ½ teaspoon salt and spaghetti and stir well. Pour into sprayed 9 x 13-inch baking dish. Cover and refrigerate 2 to 3 hours.

☐ When ready to bake, preheat oven to 350°. Bake covered for 45 minutes. Serves 6 to 8.

The expiration dates on dairy products usually refer to freshness more than spoilage. The dairy sets the expiration date based on when the freshness begins to decline. The milk may not reach the spoilage stage for several days after the expiration date.

SPAGHETTI PIE SPECIAL

6 ounces spaghetti, cooked, drained
⅓ cup grated parmesan cheese
1 egg, beaten
1 cup small curd cottage cheese, drained
1 pound lean ground beef
½ cup chopped onion
1 (15 ounce) can tomato sauce
1 teaspoon minced garlic
1 teaspoon dried oregano
1 tablespoon sugar
½ cup mozzarella cheese

☐ Preheat oven to 350°.

☐ Mix spaghetti while still warm with parmesan and egg in large bowl.

☐ Spoon into sprayed 10-inch pie pan (or pizza pan) and pat mixture up and around sides with spoon to form crust. Spoon cottage cheese over spaghetti layer.

☐ In skillet, brown beef and onion. Drain and add tomato sauce, garlic, oregano, sugar, and salt and pepper to taste. Simmer for 15 minutes.

☐ Spoon meat mixture over cottage cheese and bake 30 minutes. Sprinkle mozzarella n top and bake for 5 minutes or just until cheese melts. To serve, cut into wedges. Serves 4 to 6.

RAVIOLI AND MORE

1 pound lean ground beef
1 teaspoon garlic powder
1 large onion, chopped
2 zucchini, grated
¼ cup (½ stick) butter
1 (28 ounce) jar spaghetti sauce
1 (25 ounce) package ravioli with portobello mushrooms, cooked
1 (12 ounce) package shredded mozzarella cheese

☐ Preheat oven to 350°.

☐ Brown ground beef in large skillet until no longer pink and drain. Add garlic powder and
½ teaspoon each of salt and pepper.

☐ Cook onion and zucchini with butter in saucepan just until tender-crisp and stir in
spaghetti sauce. Spread ½ cup sauce mixture in sprayed 9 x 13-inch baking dish.

☐ Layer half ravioli, half remaining spaghetti sauce mixture, half beef and half cheese.
Repeat layers except cheese.

☐ Cover and bake for 35 minutes. Sprinkle remaining cheese on top. Let stand 10 minutes
before serving. Serves 6.

*There has always been a food processor in the
kitchen. But once upon a time she was usually called
the missus, or Mom.*

– Sue Berkman

SLOW COOKER LASAGNA

1 pound lean ground beef
1 onion, chopped
½ teaspoon garlic powder
1 (18 ounce) can spaghetti sauce
½ teaspoon ground oregano
6 - 8 lasagna noodles, divided
1 (12 ounce) carton cottage cheese, divided
½ cup grated parmesan cheese, divided
1 (12 ounce) package shredded mozzarella cheese, divided

☐ Brown ground beef and onion in large skillet. Add garlic powder, spaghetti sauce and oregano. Cook just until thoroughly warm.

☐ Spoon layer of meat sauce in sprayed oval slow cooker. Add layer lasagna noodles (break to fit slow cooker).

☐ Top with layer of half remaining meat sauce, half cottage cheese, half parmesan cheese and half mozzarella cheese. Repeat layers starting with remaining lasagna noodles.

☐ Cover and cook on LOW for 4 to 6 hours. Serves 4 to 6.

I never did give them hell. I just told the truth and they thought it was hell.
— *Harry S. Truman*

Abundant Stuffed Shells

20 - 22 jumbo pasta shells
1 pound lean ground beef, browned, drained
½ cup finely chopped onion
1 cup shredded cheddar cheese
½ cup seasoned breadcrumbs
1 teaspoon minced garlic
1 teaspoon Italian seasoning
2 eggs, beaten
2 (26 ounce) jar spaghetti sauce
½ cup shredded mozzarella cheese

☐ Cook pasta shells for 7 minutes in boiling water (they need only be partially cooked), drain and place on sheet of wax paper.

☐ Combine beef, onion, cheddar cheese, breadcrumbs, garlic, seasoning and eggs in bowl. Carefully stuff each pasta shell with spoonful of meat mixture.

☐ Pour 1 jar spaghetti sauce in sprayed slow cooker. Place stuffed shells on top of sauce. Pour remaining sauce evenly over shells. Sprinkle with mozzarella cheese.

☐ Cover and cook on LOW heat for 4 hours. Do not overcook. Serves 4 to 6.

The press must grow day in and day out – it is our Party's sharpest and most powerful weapon.

– Joseph Stalin

EASY WINTER WARMER

This is such a good spaghetti sauce on noodles and is a great substitute for cream sauce.

1 (12 ounce) package medium egg noodles
Canola oil
3 tablespoons butter
1½ pounds lean ground round beef
1 (10 ounce) package frozen seasoning blend (chopped onions and peppers), thawed
1 (28 ounce) jar spaghetti sauce, divided
1 (12 ounce) package shredded mozzarella cheese

☐ Preheat oven to 350°.

☐ Cook noodles according to package directions in pot of boiling water with a dab of oil and salt. Drain thoroughly, add butter and stir until butter melts.

☐ Brown beef and onions and peppers in skillet and drain thoroughly.

☐ In sprayed 9 x 13-inch baking dish layer half spaghetti sauce, half noodles, half beef mixture and half cheese. Repeat for second layer.

☐ Cover and bake for about 30 minutes or until dish is hot. Serves 6 to 8.

There can be no liberty for a community that lacks the means by which to detect lies.

—Walter Lippmann

SOUTHWEST SPAGHETTI

1½ pounds lean ground beef
2½ teaspoons chili powder
1 (15 ounce) can tomato sauce
1 (7 ounce) package spaghetti
1 heaping tablespoon beef seasoning
Shredded cheddar-Monterey Jack cheese

☐ Brown ground beef in skillet until no longer pink. Place in sprayed 4 to 5-quart slow cooker.

☐ Add chili powder, tomato sauce, spaghetti, 2⅓ cups water and beef seasoning and mix well.

☐ Cover and cook on LOW for 6 to 7 hours.

☐ When ready to serve, cover with lots of shredded cheese. Serves 4 to 6.

If we did all the things we are capable of, we would literally be astounded.

— *Thomas A. Edison*

CHICKEN DINNERS

**The whole neighborhood
will love these recipes.**

CHICKEN DINNERS CONTENTS

ADOBE CHICKEN

2 cups cooked brown rice
1 (10 ounce) can diced tomatoes and green chilies
3 cups cooked, chopped chicken
2 (8 ounce) packages shredded Monterey Jack cheese, divided

☐ Preheat oven to 325°.

☐ Combine rice, tomatoes and green chilies, chicken, and half cheese.

☐ Spoon into sprayed 7 x 11-inch baking dish. Cover and bake for 30 minutes.

☐ Sprinkle remaining cheese over casserole and bake uncovered for additional 5 minutes.
Serves 4 to 6.

*A boneless chicken breast will cook in less than
10 minutes in a steamer. After you remove the
chicken, let it sit uncut for 2 to 3 minutes, and any
slight pinkness in the interior will gently finish
cooking in the chicken's own steam.*

CHICKEN CASSEROLE PEPE

1 (10 ounce) bag Doritos® chips, divided
1 onion, chopped
1 (10 ounce) can cream of chicken soup
2 (10 ounce) cans diced tomatoes and green chilies
1 (1 pound) package Velveeta® cheese, cubed
3 cups chopped chicken

☐ Preheat oven to 350°.

☐ Place half chips in sprayed 9 x 13-inch baking dish. Crush some with palm of hand.

☐ Combine onion, soup, tomatoes and green chilies, and cheese in large saucepan. Heat on medium and stir until cheese melts. Add chicken and pour over chips.

☐ Crush remaining chips in resealable plastic bag with rolling pin. Sprinkle over chicken-cheese mixture. Bake uncovered for 40 minutes or until bubbly around edges. Serves 4.

Never partially cook chicken and store to finish later. The heat may simply start cultivating bacteria that will be thriving too strongly to be fully destroyed by the briefer cooking time when you finish the chicken.

EASY CHICKEN AND DUMPLINGS

3 cups cooked, chopped chicken
2 (10 ounce) cans cream of chicken soup
3 teaspoons chicken bouillon granules
1 (8 ounce) can refrigerated buttermilk biscuits

☐ Combine chopped chicken, both cans of soup, chicken bouillon granules and 4½ cups water in large, heavy pot. Boil mixture and stir to mix well.

☐ Separate biscuits and cut into quarters.

☐ Drop biscuit pieces 1 at a time into boiling chicken mixture and stir gently.

☐ When all biscuits are dropped, reduce heat to low and simmer, stirring occasionally, for about 15 minutes. Serves 4.

TIP: *Deli turkey will work just fine in this recipe. It's a great time-saver!*

CHICKEN-BROCCOLI SKILLET

3 cups cooked, cubed chicken
1 (16 ounce) package frozen broccoli florets
1 (8 ounce) package cubed Velveeta® cheese
⅔ cup mayonnaise

☐ Combine chicken, broccoli, cheese and ¼ cup water in skillet.

☐ Cover and cook over medium heat until broccoli is tender-crisp and cheese melts. Stir in mayonnaise and heat through, but do not boil. Serves 4.

TIP: *This is great served over hot, cooked rice.*

CREAMY CHICKEN PASTA

1 (10 ounce) package penne pasta
1 tablespoon olive oil
2 (12 ounce) cans white chicken meat, drained
2 tablespoons prepared pesto
¾ cup whipping cream

☐ In large saucepan, cook penne pasta according to package directions. Drain and place back in saucepan.

☐ Gently stir in oil, chicken, pesto and whipping cream.

☐ Place saucepan over low heat, simmer just until cream is absorbed. Spoon into serving bowl and serve immediately. Serves 4.

When choosing a package of fresh chicken breasts, look for one that isn't too "juicy". Water is a sure sign of thawing. Look for medium-size, uniform breasts that will cook in the same amount of time.

CHICKEN SQUARES

2 (12 ounce) cans chicken breast chunks with liquid
1 (8 ounce) carton cream cheese, softened
¼ cup finely chopped onion
2 tablespoons sesame seeds
1 (8 count) package refrigerated crescent rolls

☐ Preheat oven to 350°.

☐ Drain chicken and pour liquid in mixing bowl. Combine chicken liquid with cream cheese and beat until creamy. Add chicken, onion and sesame seeds.

☐ Open package of crescent rolls and keep 2 triangles together to form 4 squares. Pinch seam together in middle of each square.

☐ Spoon about ½ cup chicken mixture into center of each square. Fold corners up into center and seal edges.

☐ Repeat for all squares. Place rolls on sprayed baking sheet and bake about 15 minutes. Serves 4.

Salt or sodium chloride is about 40% sodium. One teaspoon salt yields 2000 milligrams of sodium. That's only 400 milligrams less than an adult's maximum recommended daily intake of 2400 milligrams.

HURRY-UP CHICKEN ENCHILADAS

2½ - 3 cups cooked, cubed chicken breasts
1 (10 ounce) can cream of chicken soup
1½ cups chunky salsa, divided
8 (6-inch) flour tortillas
1 (10 ounce) can fiesta nacho cheese soup

☐ In saucepan, combine chicken, cream of chicken soup and ½ cup salsa and heat.

☐ Spoon about ⅓ cup chicken mixture down center of each tortilla and roll tortilla around filling. Place seam-side down in sprayed 9 x 13-inch baking dish.

☐ Mix nacho cheese soup, remaining 1 cup salsa and ¼ cup water and pour over enchiladas.

☐ Cover with wax paper and microwave on HIGH, turning several times, for 5 minutes or until bubbly. Serves 4.

Never explain – your friends do not need it and your enemies will not believe you anyway.

– Elbert Hubbard

FAMILY CHICKEN SPAGHETTI

6 frozen breaded cooked chicken breast halves
1 (8 ounce) package spaghetti, cooked
1 (18 ounce) jar spaghetti sauce
1 (12 ounce) package shredded mozzarella cheese, divided

☐ Bake chicken breasts according to package directions and keep warm. Cook spaghetti according to package directions, drain and arrange on platter.

☐ Place spaghetti sauce in saucepan with 1 cup mozzarella cheese and heat slightly, but do not boil.

☐ Spoon about half sauce over spaghetti and arrange chicken breasts on top.

☐ Spoon remaining spaghetti sauce on chicken and sprinkle remaining cheese over top. Serves 4 to 6.

CHICKEN CURRY

2 (10 ounce) cans cream of mushroom soup
2 teaspoons curry powder
⅓ cup chopped slivered almonds, toasted
4 boneless, skinless chicken breast halves, cooked, cubed

☐ Combine soup, 1 soup can water, curry powder, almonds and cubed chicken in large saucepan.

☐ Heat and cook for 5 minutes and stir frequently. Serves 4.

TIP: This is great served over white rice.

TORTELLINI-CHICKEN SUPPER

1 (9 ounce) package frozen cooked chicken breasts
1 (9 ounce) package refrigerated cheese tortellini
1 (10 ounce) package frozen green peas, thawed
1 (8 ounce) carton cream cheese with chives and onion
½ cup sour cream

☐ Prepare chicken according to package directions; set aside and keep warm.

☐ Cook tortellini in saucepan according to package directions. Place peas in colander and pour hot pasta water over peas. Return tortellini and peas to saucepan.

☐ Combine cream cheese and sour cream in smaller saucepan, heat on low and stir well until cream cheese melts. Spoon mixture over tortellini and peas, toss and keep heat on low.

☐ Spoon tortellini and peas in serving bowl and place chicken on top. Serve hot. Serves 4.

SKILLET CHICKEN AND STUFFING

1 (6 ounce) box stuffing mix for chicken
1 (16 ounce) package frozen whole kernel corn
¼ cup (½ stick) butter
4 boneless, skinless chicken breast halves, cooked

☐ Combine contents of seasoning packet from stuffing mix, corn, 1⅔ cups water and butter in large skillet.

☐ Bring to a boil. Reduce heat, cover and simmer for 5 minutes.

☐ Stir in stuffing mix just until moist. Cut chicken into thin slices. Mix with stuffing-corn mixture.

☐ Cook on low heat until thoroughly hot. Serves 4.

QUICK CHICKEN POT PIE

1 (15 ounce) package refrigerated piecrust
1 (19 ounce) can cream of chicken soup
2 cups diced cooked chicken breast
1 (10 ounce) package frozen mixed vegetables, thawed

☐ Preheat oven to 325°.

☐ Place one piecrust in 9-inch pie pan.

☐ Combine chicken soup, chicken and mixed vegetables; mix well and pour into piecrust.

☐ Cover with second layer of piecrust; fold edges under and crimp. With knife, cut 4 slits in center of piecrust. Bake uncovered for 1 hour 15 minutes or until crust is golden. Serves 4 to 6.

TIP: When you're too busy to cook a chicken, try a rotisserie chicken from the grocery store.

Pot pies have been written about since the Roman Empire and continue today as a top 100 favorite food. Pot pies usually have a meat (beef, chicken, turkey) surrounded by gravy with mixed vegetables all inside a fluffy pastry.

APRICOT-GINGER CHICKEN

2 teaspoons ground ginger
¾ cup Italian dressing
4 boneless, skinless chicken breast halves
⅔ cup apricot preserves

☐ Combine ginger and Italian dressing; set aside ¼ cup. Place remaining dressing in large resealable plastic bag.

☐ Add chicken to bag and marinate in refrigerator overnight; turn occasionally.

☐ When ready to bake, preheat oven to 350°.

☐ Remove chicken and place in sprayed 9 x 13-inch baking dish. Discard used marinade.

☐ Pour the set aside ¼ cup marinade in saucepan, bring to a boil and cook for 1 minute. Remove from heat and stir in preserves.

☐ Bake chicken for 45 minutes and baste with cooked marinade mixture last 10 minutes of cooking. Serves 4.

Chicken breast halves today are almost twice as large as they were several years ago. Breeders are growing bigger chickens with bigger chicken breasts. During processing, they inject breasts with a saline solution or broth to "plump up" the chickens. This is supposed to make the meat easier to cook and keep it from drying out. If you don't like the idea, buy organic or less-processed chicken. They tend to be smaller and may not go through the "plumping" process.

CHICKEN DELIGHT

6 boneless, skinless chicken breast halves
1 (8 ounce) carton whipped cream cheese with onion and chives
Butter, softened
6 bacon strips

- ☐ Preheat oven to 375°.

- ☐ Flatten chicken breasts to ½-inch thickness. Spread 3 tablespoons cream cheese over each. Dot with butter and a little salt and roll. Wrap each with bacon strip.

- ☐ Place seam-side down in sprayed 9 x 13-inch baking dish. Bake for 40 to 45 minutes or until at least 165°.

- ☐ To brown, broil 6 inches from heat for about 3 minutes or until bacon is crisp. Serves 6.

EASY SLOW-COOKED CHICKEN

5 boneless, skinless chicken breast halves
2 (10 ounce) cans cream of chicken soup
1 (6 ounce) box chicken stuffing mix
1 (16 ounce) package frozen green peas, thawed

- ☐ Place chicken breasts in 6-quart slow cooker and spoon soup over chicken.

- ☐ Combine stuffing mix with ingredients according to package directions. Spoon over chicken and soup.

- ☐ Cover and cook on LOW for 5 to 6 hours.

- ☐ Sprinkle drained green peas over top of stuffing. Cover and cook for additional 45 to 50 minutes. Serves 5.

SWISS CHICKEN

4 boneless, skinless chicken breast halves
4 slices Swiss cheese
1 (10 ounce) can cream of chicken soup
¼ cup chicken broth
½ cup herb-seasoned stuffing
¼ cup (½ stick) butter, melted

☐ Preheat oven to 350°.

☐ Arrange chicken in sprayed 9 x 13-inch pan. Top with cheese slices. Combine soup and broth in saucepan and heat just enough to mix well.

☐ Spoon evenly over chicken and sprinkle with stuffing mix. Drizzle butter over stuffing. Bake uncovered for 45 to 55 minutes. Serves 4.

In everyone's life, at some time, our inner fire goes out. It is then burst into flame by an encounter with another human being. We should all be thankful for those people who rekindle the inner spirit.

– Albert Schweitzer

CHICKEN DIPSTICKS

1½ cups cornbread stuffing mix plus half seasoning packet
¼ cup olive oil
4 boneless, skinless chicken breast halves
Chicken Dipsticks Sauce (recipe follows)

☐ Preheat oven to 350°.

☐ Place stuffing mix in resealable plastic bag and crush with rolling pin.

☐ Add oil to center of 9 x 13-inch baking pan and spread around entire pan.

☐ Cut chicken breasts into 3 or 4 pieces each, dip in stuffing mix and place in baking pan. Arrange chicken making sure pieces are not touching.

☐ Bake for 25 minutes. Remove from oven, turn pieces over and bake for additional 15 minutes or until brown. Serve with Chicken Dipsticks Sauce. Serves 4.

CHICKEN DIPSTICKS SAUCE

¼ cup honey
3 tablespoons spicy brown mustard

☐ Combine honey and brown mustard in bowl. Makes ⅓ cup.

Dieting is wishful shrinking.

— Author Unknown

CRISPY NUTTY CHICKEN

⅓ cup minced dry roasted peanuts
1 cup corn flake crumbs
½ cup buttermilk ranch salad dressing
4 chicken breast halves

☐ Preheat oven to 350°.

☐ Combine peanuts and corn flake crumbs on wax paper. Pour salad dressing onto plate or pie pan.

☐ Dip each piece chicken in salad dressing and roll in crumb mixture to coat. Arrange chicken in sprayed 9 x 13-inch shallow baking dish.

☐ Bake for 50 minutes until light brown. Serves 4.

FLAKED CHICKEN

4 boneless, skinless chicken breast halves
½ cup Italian salad dressing
½ cup sour cream
2½ cups crushed cornflakes

☐ Preheat oven to 375°.

☐ Place chicken in resealable plastic bag; add salad dressing and sour cream. Seal and refrigerate 1 hour.

☐ Remove chicken from marinade and discard marinade.

☐ Dredge chicken in cornflakes; place in sprayed 9 x 13-inch baking dish.

☐ Bake for 45 minutes. Serves 4.

EL PRONTO CHICKEN

4 boneless, skinless chicken breast halves
½ cup (1 stick) butter, melted
⅔ cup seasoned breadcrumbs
½ cup grated parmesan cheese

☐ Preheat oven to 350°.

☐ Dip chicken in butter. Mix breadcrumbs and parmesan cheese in bowl.

☐ Roll chicken in crumb-cheese mixture. Place in sprayed 9 x 13-inch baking dish.

☐ Cover and bake for 55 minutes. Serves 4.

TIP: Cooked rice is always a complementary addition to chicken. Try serving this dish over cooked rice.

Tomatoes that are loaded onto tomato trucks in bulk have been specially bred to have a thicker skin and to be able to withstand the weight without much damage. Tomatoes for processing are picked ripe and red. Fresh market tomatoes are picked green.

CREAM CHEESE CHICKEN

2 tablespoons butter, melted
4 boneless, skinless chicken breast halves
1 (10 ounce) can cream of mushroom soup
1 (.4 ounce) packet Italian salad dressing mix
½ cup sherry
1 (8 ounce) package cream cheese, cubed
Noodles, cooked

☐ Brush melted butter over chicken and place in sprayed slow cooker.

☐ Add remaining ingredients except noodles to saucepan, heat just enough to mix well and add to slow cooker.

☐ Cover and cook on LOW for 6 to 7 hours. Serve over noodles. Serves 4.

CREAMY CHICKEN AND POTATOES

4 boneless, skinless chicken breast halves
2 teaspoons chicken seasoning
8 - 10 small new (red) potatoes with peels
1 (10 ounce) can cream of chicken soup
1 (8 ounce) carton sour cream

☐ Place chicken breast halves, sprinkled with chicken seasoning, in sprayed slow cooker. Arrange new potatoes around chicken.

☐ Combine soup, sour cream and lots of pepper in saucepan and heat just enough to mix well. Spoon over chicken breasts.

☐ Cover and cook on LOW for 4 to 6 hours. Serves 4.

GLAZED CHICKEN OVER RICE

4 boneless, skinless chicken breast halves, cubed
Oil
1 (20 ounce) can pineapple chunks with juice
½ cup honey-mustard grill-and-glaze sauce
1 red bell pepper, seeded, chopped
2 cups instant white rice, cooked

☐ Brown chicken in a little oil in skillet. Reduce heat and cook 15 minutes. Add pineapple, honey mustard sauce and bell pepper and bring to a boil.

☐ Reduce heat and simmer for 15 minutes or until sauce thickens slightly. Serve over hot cooked rice. Serves 4.

HONEY-ROASTED CHICKEN

3 tablespoons soy sauce
3 tablespoons honey
2½ cups crushed Wheat Chex® cereal
½ cup very finely minced walnuts
5 - 6 boneless, skinless chicken breast halves

☐ Preheat oven to 400°.

☐ In shallow bowl, combine soy sauce and honey. In another shallow bowl, combine crushed cereal and walnuts.

☐ Dip both sides of each chicken breast in soy sauce-honey mixture and dredge in cereal-walnut mixture.

☐ Place each piece on sprayed foil-lined baking sheet. Bake for 25 minutes (about 35 minutes if breasts are very large). Serves 5 to 6.

SUMMERTIME LIMEADE CHICKEN

6 large boneless, skinless chicken breast halves
1 (6 ounce) can frozen limeade concentrate, thawed
3 tablespoons brown sugar
½ cup chili sauce
2 (6 ounce) packages garlic and butter-flavored rice

☐ Sprinkle chicken breasts with a little salt and pepper and place in sprayed skillet over high heat. Cook and brown on both sides for about 10 minutes. Remove from skillet and set aside, but keep warm.

☐ Add limeade concentrate, brown sugar and chili sauce to skillet and bring to a boil.

☐ Cook, stirring constantly, for 4 minutes. Return chicken to skillet and spoon sauce over chicken. Reduce heat, cover and simmer for 15 minutes or until chicken is at least 165°.

☐ Cook rice according to package directions and serve chicken over cooked rice. Serves 6.

ALMOND-MUSHROOM CHICKEN

6 boneless, skinless chicken breast halves
¼ cup (½ stick) butter
1 (10 ounce) can cream of mushroom soup
½ cup sliced almonds

☐ Preheat oven to 350°.

☐ Place chicken breasts in sprayed 9 x 13-inch baking pan.

☐ Combine butter, soup, almonds and ¼ cup water in saucepan. Heat and mix just until butter melts.

☐ Pour mixture over chicken. Cover and bake for 1 hour. Serves 6.

LEMONADE CHICKEN

6 boneless, skinless chicken breast halves
1 (6 ounce) can frozen lemonade, thawed
⅓ cup soy sauce
1 teaspoon garlic powder

☐ Preheat oven to 350°.

☐ Place chicken in sprayed 9 x 13-inch baking dish.

☐ Combine lemonade, soy sauce and garlic powder in bowl and pour over chicken.

☐ Cover and bake for 45 minutes. Uncover, baste chicken with juices and cook for additional 10 minutes. Serves 6.

MARINATED GARLIC CHICKEN

4 - 5 boneless, skinless chicken breast halves
1 tablespoon oregano
¾ teaspoon garlic powder
½ cup (1 stick) butter, melted

☐ Place chicken breasts in resealable plastic bag and add oregano, garlic powder and butter. Marinate in refrigerator for 3 or 4 hours.

☐ When ready to bake, preheat oven to 325°. Drain chicken and place in shallow baking dish. Discard marinade.

☐ Cover and bake for 1 hour. Serves 4 to 5.

MUSHROOM CHICKEN WITH WINE

6 - 8 boneless, skinless chicken breast halves
1 (10 ounce) can cream of mushroom soup
1 (10 ounce) can cream of onion soup
1 cup white wine

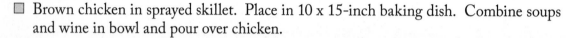

☐ Preheat oven to 325°.

☐ Brown chicken in sprayed skillet. Place in 10 x 15-inch baking dish. Combine soups and wine in bowl and pour over chicken.

☐ Cover and bake for 35 minutes. Uncover and bake for additional 25 minutes. Serves 6 to 8.

OVEN-GLAZED CHICKEN

4 boneless, skinless chicken breast halves
1 (10 ounce) can tomato soup
2 tablespoons marinade for chicken
2 tablespoons packed brown sugar

☐ Preheat oven to 350°.

☐ Place chicken breasts in sprayed 7 x 11-inch baking dish.

☐ Combine soup, marinade for chicken and brown sugar in small bowl and mix well. Spoon over chicken.

☐ Bake for 1 hour. Serves 4.

ROSEMARY CHICKEN

½ cup flour
1 tablespoon dried rosemary, divided
Italian dressing
3 - 5 boneless, skinless chicken breast halves

☐ Preheat oven to 350°.

☐ Combine flour and half rosemary in bowl. In separate shallow bowl, pour a little Italian dressing and dip chicken breasts in dressing.

☐ Dredge chicken in flour mixture. Place in sprayed 9 x 13-inch shallow baking dish.

☐ Bake for 40 minutes. Remove from oven and sprinkle remaining rosemary over breasts and cook for an additional 10 minutes. Serves 3 to 5.

BACON-WRAPPED CREAMY CHICKEN

1 (2.5 ounce) jar dried beef
6 boneless, skinless chicken breast halves
6 slices bacon
2 (10 ounce) cans mushroom soup
1 (6 ounce) package parmesan-butter rice, cooked

☐ Place dried beef slices in 5-quart slow cooker. Roll each chicken breast in slice of bacon and place over dried beef.

☐ Pour soup and ⅓ cup water in saucepan, heat just enough to mix and pour over chicken.

☐ Cover and cook on LOW for 7 to 8 hours. Serve over rice. Serves 6.

CREAMED CHICKEN

4 large boneless, skinless chicken breast halves
Lemon juice
1 red bell pepper, seeded, chopped
2 ribs celery, sliced diagonally
1 (10 ounce) can cream of chicken soup
1 (10 ounce) can cream of celery soup
⅓ cup dry white wine
1 (5 ounce) package grated parmesan cheese
Rice, cooked

☐ Rub a little lemon juice over chicken and sprinkle with salt and pepper.

☐ Place in slow cooker and top with bell pepper and celery. Combine soups and wine in saucepan and heat just enough to mix thoroughly.

☐ Pour over chicken breasts and sprinkle with parmesan cheese. Cover and cook on LOW for 6 to 7 hours. Serve over rice. Serves 4.

Here's some ideas for using leftovers:

- *Soups and stews*

- *Casseroles*

- *One-dish meals*

- *Meatloaf*

- *Open-face hot sandwiches with gravy*

- *Chopped meats over rice, noodles, mashed potatoes with gravy*

- *Meat pies*

HONEY-GLAZED CHICKEN

4 boneless, skinless chicken breast halves
Oil
1 (20 ounce) can pineapple chunks with liquid
½ cup refrigerated honey-mustard salad dressing
1 green bell pepper, julienned
1 red bell pepper, julienned
1 (10 ounce) box original couscous

☐ Cut chicken breasts into strips and sprinkle with a little salt and pepper.

☐ Brown in large skillet with a little oil. Add liquid from pineapple, cover and simmer for 15 minutes.

☐ Add honey-mustard dressing, julienned peppers and pineapple chunks to chicken and bring to a boil.

☐ Reduce heat, cover and simmer for additional 15 minutes.

☐ Cook couscous according to package directions and serve chicken over hot, cooked couscous. Serves 4.

Superfoods, said to have the most nutrients, include berries, chicken, garlic, grains, nuts, oats and soy, raisins, yogurt, apples, spinach, to name a few. These superfoods help to fight disease, boost the immune system, slow aging and increase energy.

ASPARAGUS-CHEESE CHICKEN

1 tablespoon butter
4 boneless, skinless chicken breast halves
1 (10 ounce) can broccoli-cheese soup
1 (10 ounce) package frozen cut asparagus
⅓ cup milk
1 (3.5 ounce) box boil-in-bag rice

☐ Heat butter in skillet and cook chicken for 10 to 15 minutes or until brown on both sides. Remove chicken.

☐ In same skillet, combine soup, asparagus and milk. Bring to a boil, return chicken to skillet and reduce heat to low.

☐ Cover and cook another 25 minutes until chicken is no longer pink and asparagus is tender.

☐ Cook rice according to package directions and serve chicken over rice. Serves 4.

Asparagus is low in calories and a good source of folic acid, vitamins C and A, phytonutrients, and fiber.

BROCCOLI-RICE CHICKEN

1¼ cups rice
2 pounds boneless, skinless chicken breast halves
1 teaspoon dried parsley
1 (1.8 ounce) packet cream of broccoli soup mix
1 (14 ounce) can chicken broth

☐ Place rice in lightly sprayed slow cooker. Cut chicken into slices and put over rice.

☐ Sprinkle with parsley.

☐ Combine soup mix, chicken broth and 1 cup water in saucepan. Heat just enough to mix well. Pour over chicken and rice.

☐ Cover and cook on LOW for 6 to 8 hours. Serves 8.

CHICKEN NOODLE DELIGHT

5 - 6 boneless, skinless chicken breast halves
1 teaspoon chicken seasoning
1 (10 ounce) can cream of chicken soup
1 (10 ounce) can broccoli-cheese soup
½ cup white cooking wine
1 (12 ounce) package medium noodles, cooked

☐ Cut chicken breasts in half if they are unusually large. Sprinkle breast halves with pepper and chicken seasoning and place in sprayed slow cooker.

☐ Combine soups and wine in saucepan and heat enough to mix well. Pour over chicken.

☐ Cover and cook on LOW for 5 to 6 hours. Serve chicken and sauce over noodles. Serves 5 to 6.

CHOW MEIN CHICKEN

4 boneless, skinless chicken breast halves
2 - 3 cups sliced celery
1 onion, coarsely chopped
¼ cup soy sauce
¼ teaspoon cayenne pepper
1 (14 ounce) can chicken broth
1 (15 ounce) can bean sprouts, drained
1 (8 ounce) can water chestnuts, drained
1 (15 ounce) can bamboo shoots
¼ cup flour
1 (6 ounce) package chow mein noodles

☐ Combine chicken, celery, onion, soy sauce, cayenne pepper and chicken broth in sprayed slow cooker.

☐ Cover and cook on LOW for 3 to 4 hours.

☐ Add bean sprouts, water chestnuts and bamboo shoots to chicken. Mix flour and ¼ cup water and stir into chicken and vegetables.

☐ Cook for additional 1 hour. Serve over chow mein noodles. Serves 4.

Chop up leftover meats and veggies and add them to fried rice recipes. Not only will you add flavor, but you add volume as well.

CRANBERRY CHICKEN

1 (10 ounce) jar sweet-and-sour sauce
1 (1 ounce) packet onion soup mix
1 (14 ounce) can whole cranberry sauce
6 - 8 boneless, skinless chicken breast halves

☐ Preheat oven to 325°.

☐ Combine sweet-and-sour sauce, onion soup mix and cranberry sauce in bowl.

☐ Place chicken breasts in sprayed 10 x 15-inch shallow baking dish. Pour cranberry mixture over chicken breasts.

☐ Cover and bake for 30 minutes. Uncover and bake for additional 25 minutes. Serves 6 to 8.

STIR-FRY CASHEW CHICKEN

1 pound chicken tenders, cut into strips
Oil
1 (16 ounce) package frozen broccoli, cauliflower and carrots
1 (8 ounce) jar stir-fry sauce
⅓ cup cashew halves
1 (12 ounce) package chow mein noodles

☐ Stir-fry chicken tenders in a little oil in 12-inch wok or skillet over high heat for about 4 minutes.

☐ Add vegetables and stir-fry another 4 minutes or until vegetables are tender.

☐ Stir in stir-fry sauce and cashews; cook just until mixture is hot. Serve over chow mein noodles. Serves 4.

SWEET-SPICY CHICKEN THIGHS

3 tablespoons chili powder
3 tablespoons honey
2 tablespoons lemon juice
10 - 12 boneless, skinless chicken thighs

☐ Preheat oven to 425°.

☐ Line 10 x 15-inch shallow baking pan with heavy foil. Combine chili powder, honey, lemon juice, and a little salt and pepper.

☐ Brush mixture over chicken thighs and turn thighs to coat completely. Bake, turning over once, for about 35 minutes or until at least 165°. Serves 5 to 6.

North Carolina State University recently posted as article outlining the health benefits of eating eggs. According to research there's no link between consumption of eggs and heart disease. In fact, health benefits from the high quality protein and nine essential amino acids found in eggs help prevent or lessen some diseases. Nutrients in eggs work against macular degeneration, cataracts, strokes, and heart attacks; and help regulate cardiovascular and nervous systems.

CHICKEN ALFREDO

1½ pounds boneless chicken thighs
2 ribs celery, sliced diagonally
1 red bell pepper, seeded, julienned
1 (16 ounce) jar alfredo sauce
3 cups fresh broccoli florets
1 (8 ounce) package fettuccini or linguine
1 (5 ounce) package grated parmesan cheese

☐ Cut chicken into strips. Layer chicken, celery and bell pepper in 4 to 5-quart slow cooker.

☐ Pour alfredo sauce evenly over vegetables. Cover and cook on LOW for 5 to 6 hours.

☐ About 30 minutes before serving, turn heat to HIGH and add broccoli florets to chicken-alfredo mixture. Cover and cook for additional 30 minutes.

☐ Cook pasta according to package directions and drain.

☐ Just before serving pour pasta into cooker and mix. Sprinkle parmesan cheese on top. Serves 4 to 6.

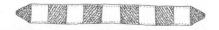

Egg Equivalents:

¼ cup egg substitute is equal to one egg

1 cup egg substitute is equal to 4 eggs

1 pint egg substitute is equal to 8 eggs

ARTICHOKE-CHICKEN PASTA

1½ pounds boneless chicken breast tenders
1 (15 ounce) can artichoke hearts, quartered
¾ cup roasted red peppers, chopped
1 (8 ounce) package shredded American cheese
1 tablespoon marinade for chicken
1 (10 ounce) can cream of chicken soup
1 (8 ounce) package shredded cheddar cheese
4 cups hot, cooked bow-tie pasta

▢ Combine chicken, artichokes, peppers, American cheese, marinade for chicken and soup in large slow cooker and mix well.

▢ Cover and cook on LOW for 6 to 8 hours. About 20 minutes before serving, fold in cheddar cheese, hot pasta, and a little salt and pepper. Serves 6 to 8.

All out of fresh herbs? Substitute one-third to one-half of amount of dried herbs for fresh herbs. If a recipe calls for 1 tablespoon (3 teaspoons) of fresh herbs, substitute 1 teaspoon dried herbs.

DELICIOUS CHICKEN PASTA

1 pound chicken tenders
Lemon-herb chicken seasoning
3 tablespoons butter
1 onion, coarsely chopped
1 (15 ounce) can diced tomatoes
1 (10 ounce) can cream of mushroom soup
1 (8 ounce) box angel hair pasta

☐ Sprinkle chicken tenders generously with chicken seasoning.

☐ Melt butter in large skillet, brown chicken and place in slow cooker.

☐ Pour remaining butter over chicken and cover with onion.

☐ In separate bowl, combine tomatoes and mushroom soup and pour over chicken and onions. Cover and cook on LOW for 4 to 5 hours.

☐ When ready to serve, cook pasta according to package directions. Serve chicken and sauce over pasta. Serves 4 to 6.

Simple Chicken Italian

4 boneless, skinless chicken breast halves
¼ cup lime juice
1 (1 ounce) packet Italian salad dressing mix
¼ cup (½ stick) butter, melted

☐ Preheat oven to 325°.

☐ Place chicken in shallow baking dish.

☐ Mix lime juice, salad dressing mix and melted butter in bowl and pour over chicken.

☐ Cover and bake for 45 minutes. Uncover and bake for additional 15 minutes. Serves 4.

Parmesan Chicken

1 (1 ounce) packet dry Italian salad dressing mix
½ cup grated parmesan cheese
¼ cup flour
¾ teaspoon garlic powder
4 - 5 boneless, skinless chicken breast halves

☐ Preheat oven to 375°.

☐ In shallow bowl, combine salad dressing mix, cheese, flour and garlic.

☐ Moisten chicken with a little water and coat with cheese mixture.

☐ Place in sprayed 9 x 13-inch baking pan. Bake for 25 minutes or until chicken is light brown and thoroughly cooked. Serves 4 to 5.

DELIGHTFUL CHICKEN AND VEGGIES

4 - 5 boneless skinless, chicken breast halves
Oil
1 (15 ounce) can whole kernel corn, drained
1 (10 ounce) box frozen green peas, thawed
1 (16 ounce) jar alfredo sauce
1 teaspoon chicken seasoning
1 teaspoon minced garlic
Pasta, cooked

☐ Brown chicken breasts in a little oil in skillet and place in sprayed slow cooker.

☐ Combine corn, peas, alfredo sauce, ¼ cup water, chicken seasoning and minced garlic in bowl and pour over chicken breasts.

☐ Cover and cook on LOW for 4 to 5 hours. Serve over pasta. Serves 4 to 5.

SLOW-COOK VEGGIE CHICKEN

4 boneless, skinless chicken breast halves
Oil
1 (15 ounce) can tomato sauce
2 (4 ounce) cans sliced mushrooms, drained
1 (10 ounce) package frozen seasoning blend onions and peppers, thawed
2 teaspoons Italian seasoning
1 teaspoon minced garlic

☐ Brown chicken breasts in a little oil in skillet and place in sprayed slow cooker.

☐ Combine tomato sauce, mushrooms, onions and peppers, Italian seasoning, minced garlic, and ¼ cup water in bowl and spoon over chicken breasts.

☐ Cover and cook on LOW for 4 to 5 hours. Serves 4.

BAKED MOZZARELLA CUTLETS

4 boneless, skinless chicken breast halves
1 cup Italian seasoned dry breadcrumbs, divided
1 cup prepared spaghetti sauce
4 slices mozzarella cheese

☐ Preheat oven to 350°.

☐ Pound each chicken breast to flatten slightly.

☐ Coat chicken well in breadcrumbs. Arrange chicken breasts in sprayed 9 x 13-inch
baking dish.

☐ Place one-fourth sauce over each breast. Place 1 slice cheese over each and garnish with
remaining breadcrumbs.

☐ Bake for 45 minutes. Serves 4.

TEMPTING CHICKEN

3 boneless, skinless chicken breast halves
3 boneless, skinless chicken thighs
Oil
1 (16 ounce) jar tomato-alfredo sauce
1 (10 ounce) can tomato bisque soup

☐ Brown chicken pieces in a little oil in large skillet.

☐ Combine tomato-alfredo sauce, soup and ½ cup water in bowl; pour over chicken pieces.

☐ Cover and simmer for about 30 minutes. Serves 6.

PEPPERED SQUASH AND CHICKEN

4 large boneless, skinless chicken breast halves
Oil
1 green bell pepper, julienned
1 red bell pepper, julienned
2 small yellow squash, seeded, julienned
1 (16 ounce) jar thick-and-chunky salsa
Rice, cooked

☐ Cut chicken breasts into thin strips. With a little oil in large skillet, saute chicken for about 5 minutes. Add peppers and squash and cook another 5 minutes or until peppers are tender-crisp.

☐ Stir in salsa and bring to a boil, lower heat and simmer for 10 minutes. Serve over hot rice. Serves 4.

SWEET 'N SPICY CHICKEN

1 pound boneless, skinless chicken breast halves
1 (1 ounce) packet taco seasoning
Oil
1 (16 ounce) jar chunky salsa
1 (12 ounce) jar peach preserves
Hot cooked rice

☐ Cut chicken into ½-inch cubes and place in large resealable plastic bag. Add taco seasoning and toss to coat.

☐ In skillet, brown chicken in a little oil. Combine salsa and preserves, stir into skillet and bring mixture to a boil.

☐ Reduce heat, cover and simmer about 15 minutes or until chicken is at least 165°. Serve over hot, cooked rice. Serves 4.

ENCORE CHICKEN

4 - 6 boneless, skinless chicken breast halves
1 (16 ounce) jar thick-and-chunky hot salsa
1 cup packed light brown sugar
1 tablespoon dijon-style mustard
Brown rice, cooked

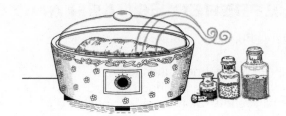

☐ Preheat oven to 325°.

☐ In large skillet with a little oil, brown chicken breasts and place in sprayed 9 x 13-inch baking dish.

☐ Combine salsa, brown sugar, mustard and ½ teaspoon salt and pour over chicken.

☐ Cover and bake 45 minutes. Serve over hot, cooked brown rice. Serves 4 to 6.

CREAMY SALSA CHICKEN

4 - 5 boneless, skinless chicken breast halves
1 (1 ounce) packet taco seasoning mix
1 cup salsa
½ cup sour cream

☐ Place chicken breasts in 5 to 6-quart oval slow cooker and add ¼ cup water.

☐ Sprinkle taco seasoning mix over chicken and top with salsa. Cover and cook on LOW for 5 to 6 hours.

☐ When ready to serve, remove chicken breasts and place on platter. Stir sour cream into juices and spoon over chicken breasts. Serves 4 to 5.

COMPANY CHICKEN

This is great served over cooked rice.

8 chicken quarters
2 (10 ounce) cans cream of mushroom soup
1 (1 pint) carton sour cream
1 cup sherry

☐ Preheat oven to 300°.

☐ Place chickens in large shallow baking dish. Combine soup, sour cream and sherry in saucepan.

☐ Pour mixture over chicken. Cover and bake for 1 hour 15 minutes. Serves 8.

LEMON SEASONED CHICKEN

1 (2½ - 3 pound) chicken, quartered
1 teaspoon dried oregano
2 teaspoons minced garlic
2 tablespoons butter
¼ cup lemon juice

☐ Season chicken quarters with salt, pepper and oregano and rub garlic on chicken.

☐ Brown chicken quarters on all sides in butter in skillet and transfer to sprayed oval slow cooker.

☐ Add ⅓ cup water to skillet, scrape bottom and pour over chicken. Cover and cook on LOW for 5 to 7 hours.

☐ Pour lemon juice over chicken and cook for additional 1 hour. Serves 6.

SUNSHINE CHICKEN

4 chicken quarters
Flour
Oil
1 cup barbecue sauce
½ cup orange juice

☐ Preheat oven to 350°.

☐ Place chicken in bowl of flour and coat well. Brown chicken in a little oil in skillet and place in sprayed shallow baking pan.

☐ Combine barbecue sauce and orange juice in bowl. Pour over chicken. Cover and bake for 45 minutes.

☐ Spoon sauce over chicken and bake uncovered for additional 20 minutes. Serves 4.

The shelf life for eggs is about three to five weeks from the time you take them home. If eggs are beyond the expiration date, crack one open to see if it smells okay. If there is an unusual smell, throw it away. Otherwise, it's probably fine to be cooked.

OVEN-FRIED CHICKEN

1 (1 ounce) packet ranch buttermilk salad dressing mix
1 cup buttermilk*
½ cup mayonnaise
1 (3 - 4 pounds) medium fryer chicken, cut into serving pieces
2 - 3 cups crushed corn flakes

☐ Preheat oven to 350°.

☐ Combine ranch dressing mix, buttermilk and mayonnaise in shallow bowl and mix well.

☐ Dip chicken pieces in mixture and cover well. Roll each piece in corn flakes and coat all sides well.

☐ Arrange pieces so they do not touch in sprayed 9 x 13-inch baking dish. Bake for 1 hour.

☐ If chicken pieces are not brown, cook for additional 15 minutes. Serves 6 to 8.

*TIP: *To make buttermilk, mix 1 cup milk with 1 tablespoon lemon juice or vinegar and let milk stand for about 10 minutes.*

Never eat more than you can lift.

– Miss Piggy

RUSSIAN CHICKEN

1 (8 ounce) bottle Russian salad dressing
1 (14 ounce) can whole cranberry sauce
1 (1 ounce) packet onion soup mix
1 whole chicken, skinned, quartered
Rice, cooked

☐ Combine dressing, cranberry sauce, ½ cup water and soup mix in bowl. Stir well.

☐ Place chicken quarters in 6-quart slow cooker and spoon dressing-cranberry mixture over chicken.

☐ Cover and cook on LOW for 4 to 5 hours. Serve sauce and chicken over rice. Serves 4 to 6.

TIP: If you don't want to cut up a chicken, use 4 to 6 chicken breasts.

ORANGEY BAKED CHICKEN

2 - 3 pounds chicken pieces
Olive oil
1 (1 ounce) packet onion soup mix
1 (6 ounce) can frozen orange juice concentrate, thawed

☐ Preheat oven to 350°.

☐ Brown chicken in little oil in skillet. Place in sprayed 10 x 15-inch baking dish.

☐ Combine onion soup mix, orange juice and ⅔ cup water in small bowl and stir well. Pour over chicken. Bake for 50 minutes. Serves 6 to 8.

TURKEY-BROCCOLI BAKE

Great dish for leftovers and no one will know it came from leftovers!

1 (16 ounce) package frozen broccoli spears, thawed
2 cups cooked, diced turkey

☐ Preheat oven to 350°.

☐ Arrange broccoli spears in bottom of sprayed 9 x 13-inch baking dish and sprinkle with diced turkey.

SAUCE:

1 (10 ounce) can cream of chicken soup
½ cup mayonnaise
2 tablespoons lemon juice
⅓ cup grated parmesan cheese

☐ In saucepan, combine soup, mayonnaise, lemon juice, cheese and ¼ cup water. Heat just enough to mix well.

☐ Pour over broccoli and turkey.

☐ Cover and bake for 20 minutes, uncover and continue baking for additional 15 minutes. Serves 4.

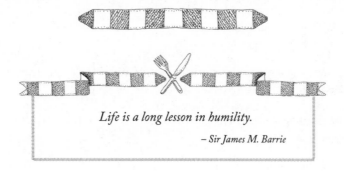

Life is a long lesson in humility.

– *Sir James M. Barrie*

TURKEY AND RICE BAKE

¾ pound cooked, sliced turkey
2 cups cooked instant brown rice
1 (10 ounce) can cream of chicken soup
1 (10 ounce) can diced tomatoes and green chilies
1½ cups crushed tortilla chips

☐ Preheat oven to 350°.

☐ Place turkey slices in bottom of sprayed 7 x 11-inch baking dish.

☐ In bowl, combine rice, soup, and tomatoes and green chilies; mix well. Pour over turkey slices.

☐ Sprinkle crushed tortilla chips over top of casserole.

☐ Bake uncovered for 40 minutes. Serves 4.

TURKEY-RICE OLÉ

This may be served as a main course or as a sandwich wrap in flour tortillas.

1 pound ground turkey
1 (5.5 ounce) package Mexican rice mix
2 (15 ounce) cans black beans, rinsed, drained
1½ cups thick-and-chunky salsa

☐ In large skillet, brown turkey and break up chunks with fork. Add rice mix and 2 cups water, bring to a boil and reduce heat.

☐ Simmer about 20 minutes or until rice is tender. Stir in beans and salsa and cook just until mixture is hot. Serves 4.

TURKEY WITH HONEY-GINGER GLAZE

⅔ cup honey
2 teaspoons grated, peeled fresh ginger
1 tablespoon soy sauce
1 tablespoon lemon juice
1 pound turkey tenders
Oil
1 (6 ounce) package roasted-garlic long grain-wild rice

☐ In small bowl combine honey, ginger, soy sauce and lemon juice; mix well.

☐ Cook turkey tenders in a little oil in heavy skillet for about 5 minutes on each side or until brown.

☐ Pour honey mixture into skillet with turkey and bring to a boil. Reduce heat and simmer for 15 minutes.

☐ Cook rice according to package directions.

☐ Serve turkey tenders with sauce over hot cooked rice. Serves 4.

WINTER TURKEY BAKE

1 (6 ounce) package stuffing mix for chicken, divided
1½ pounds turkey, cut into 1-inch strips
1 (10 ounce) can cream of chicken soup
½ cup sour cream
1 (16 ounce) package frozen mixed vegetables, thawed, drained

☐ Preheat oven to 375°.

☐ Sprinkle ½ cup dry stuffing mix evenly over bottom of sprayed 9 x 13-inch baking dish.

☐ In bowl, combine remaining stuffing and 1 cup water and stir just until moist.

☐ Place turkey strips over dry stuffing mix in baking dish.

☐ In bowl, mix soup, sour cream and vegetables; spoon over turkey strips. Top with prepared stuffing.

☐ Bake uncovered for 25 minutes. Serves 4 to 6.

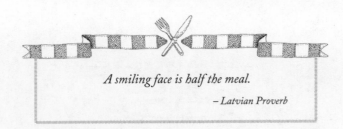

A smiling face is half the meal.

– Latvian Proverb

TURKEY PIZZA POCKETS

½ pound bulk turkey sausage
⅔ cup prepared pizza sauce
1 (10 ounce) package refrigerated pizza dough
½ cup shredded mozzarella cheese

☐ Preheat oven to 400°.

☐ In skillet, brown sausage and stir to break up pieces of meat. Drain sausage and add pizza sauce. Heat to a boil and then reduce to a simmer.

☐ Unroll pizza dough, place on flat surface and pat into 8 x 12-inch rectangle. Carefully cut dough into 6 squares.

☐ Divide sausage mixture evenly among squares and sprinkle with cheese.

☐ Lift 1 corner of each square and fold over filling to make triangle. Press edges together with fork to seal.

☐ Bake about 12 minutes or until light golden brown. Serve immediately. Serves 4.

Time and Tide wait for no man,
but Time always stands still for a woman of thirty.

– Robert Frost

STUFFED BROCCOLI-TURKEY POTATOES

4 large baking potatoes, baked
¼ cup (½ stick) butter, softened
¼ cup sour cream
1 cup finely chopped deli turkey
1 (10 ounce) package frozen broccoli florets, chopped, cooked
1 cup shredded sharp cheddar cheese

☐ Preheat oven to 400°.

☐ Cut potatoes down center, but not through to bottom. Create a well in middle of potatoes by pushing contents of potato to outside with a spoon. Place in sprayed baking dish.

☐ In bowl combine butter, sour cream, turkey, broccoli and cheese; mix well.

☐ Add heaping spoonfuls of broccoli-turkey mixture to each potato.

☐ Cook potatoes for 10 minutes or until heated through. Serves 4.

The most interesting information comes from children, for they tell all they know and then stop.

– Mark Twain

PORK PLATES

**Easy prep makes delicious
meals even better.**

PORK PLATES CONTENTS

PORK PLATES CONTENTS

You can always tell a real friend: when you've made a fool of yourself he doesn't feel you've done a permanent job.

— Laurence J. Peter

HAM-IT-UP WILD RICE

This is really simple to put together and the kids will be ready to eat their vegetables when they have ham and cheese with them.

1 (6 ounce) package instant long grain-wild rice
1 (10 ounce) package frozen broccoli spears, thawed
1 (8 ounce) can whole kernel corn, drained
3 cups cooked, cubed ham
1 (10 ounce) can cream of mushroom soup
1 cup mayonnaise
1 teaspoon mustard
1 cup shredded cheddar cheese
1 (3 ounce) can french-fried onions

☐ Preheat oven to 350°.

☐ Prepare rice according to package directions.

☐ Spoon rice into sprayed 3-quart baking dish. Top with broccoli, corn and ham.

☐ Combine soup, mayonnaise, mustard, shredded cheese, and ½ teaspoon each of salt and pepper in bowl and mix well. Spread over top of rice-ham mixture.

☐ Cover and bake for about 30 minutes. Sprinkle fried onions over top and bake uncovered for additional 15 minutes or until casserole bubbles around edges and fried onions are light brown. Serves 6.

HAM AND POTATOES OLÉ!

1 (24 ounce) package frozen hash browns with onion and peppers, thawed
3 cups cooked, cubed ham
1 (10 ounce) can cream of chicken soup
1 (10 ounce) can fiesta nacho cheese soup
1 cup hot salsa
1 (8 ounce) package shredded cheddar-Jack cheese

☐ Preheat oven to 350°.

☐ Combine hash browns, ham, soups and salsa in large bowl and mix well.

☐ Spoon into sprayed 9 x 13-inch baking dish.

☐ Cover and bake for 40 minutes.

☐ Sprinkle cheese over top and bake uncovered for additional 5 minutes. Serves 6 to 8.

Family meals help children learn the basics of good nutrition and how to take care of themselves. Family meals don't have to big deals, but can be simple meals with basic nutrition. Children learn how to strive for good health and how they are responsible for themselves. Family meals provide a time for family traditions and family memories to grow.

Noodles-Ham-Veggie Mix

1 (8 ounce) package medium egg noodles
1 (10 ounce) can cream of celery soup
1 (10 ounce) can cream of broccoli soup
1 teaspoon chicken bouillon granules
1½ cups half-and-half cream
1 (8 ounce) can whole kernel corn, drained
1 (16 ounce) package frozen broccoli, cauliflower and carrots, thawed
3 cups cooked, cubed ham
1 (8 ounce) package shredded cheddar-Monterey Jack cheese, divided

☐ Preheat oven to 350°.

☐ Cook noodles according to package directions and drain.

☐ In large bowl combine soups, bouillon granules, half-and-half cream, corn, broccoli-carrot mixture, ham, and ½ teaspoon each of salt and pepper. Mix well.

☐ Fold in egg noodles and half cheese.

☐ Spoon into sprayed 9 x 13-inch baking dish. Cover and bake for 45 minutes.

☐ Sprinkle remaining cheese on top and bake uncovered for additional 10 minutes or until cheese bubbles. Serves 6 to 8.

When you look at your life, the greatest happinesses are family happinesses.

— Joyce Brothers

WALNUT-HAM LINGUINE

2 teaspoons minced garlic
½ cup coarsely chopped walnuts
1 red bell pepper, seeded, thinly sliced
Oil
½ pound cooked ham, cut in strips
1 (16 ounce) jar creamy alfredo sauce
¼ cup grated parmesan cheese
1 (12 ounce) package linguine, cooked al dente
1 cup seasoned breadcrumbs

☐ Preheat oven to 350°.

☐ Saute garlic, walnuts and bell pepper in a little oil in skillet for 2 to 3 minutes.

☐ In large bowl combine garlic-bell pepper mixture, ham, alfredo sauce, parmesan cheese and linguine; mix well.

☐ Spoon into sprayed 3-quart baking dish. Sprinkle breadcrumbs over top.

☐ Bake for 35 minutes or until breadcrumbs are light brown. Serves 6.

Eating about one ounce of almonds, roasted, toasted or baked, instead of foods higher in saturated fat can lower cholesterol. Almonds are high in vitamin E and cholesterol-free.

SPECTACULAR HAM-ASPARAGUS CASSEROLE

½ cup slivered almonds
2 tablespoons butter, melted
½ cup seasoned breadcrumbs
1 pound fresh asparagus, trimmed
2 cups cooked, cubed ham
½ cup shredded cheddar cheese
3 green onions, chopped
½ cup chopped fresh mushrooms
3 tablespoons minced red bell pepper
1 tablespoon lemon juice
4 eggs, hard-boiled, divided
½ cup milk
1 (10 ounce) cream of mushroom soup

☐ Preheat oven to 250°.

☐ Toast almonds on baking sheet for 15 minutes.

☐ Increase oven to 350°.

☐ Combine butter and breadcrumbs in bowl and toss.

☐ Arrange fresh asparagus in steamer basket and steam for 3 minutes. Drain, arrange asparagus in sprayed 1½-quart baking dish.

☐ Combine ham, cheese, green onions, mushrooms, almonds, bell pepper and lemon juice in bowl. Mix well.

☐ Carefully slice eggs into thin, diagonal pieces.

☐ Layer half ham mixture over asparagus and top with half egg slices. Repeat layers.

☐ Combine milk and mushroom soup in bowl; blend well. Pour over ham mixture. Top with breadcrumb mixture. Bake for 25 to 30 minutes. Serves 4 to 6.

HAM AND POTATO CASSEROLE

2 - 3 large potatoes, peeled, thinly sliced
1 (8 ounce) package shredded cheddar cheese
½ cup chopped onion
½ cup chopped green bell pepper
2 ribs celery, sliced
2 cups cooked, chopped ham
1 (10 ounce) can cream of chicken soup
⅔ cup milk
1 teaspoon seasoned salt

☐ Place potatoes, cheese, onion, bell pepper, celery and ham in sprayed slow cooker and mix well.

☐ Combine soup, milk and seasoned salt in bowl and pour evenly over potato-vegetable mixture.

☐ Cover and cook on HIGH for 4 hours. Serves 6 to 8.

Say what you want about aging, it's still the only way to have old friends.

— Robert Brault

TORTELLINI-HAM SUPPER

This is a great recipe for leftover ham.

2 (9 ounce) packages fresh tortellini
1 (10 ounce) package frozen green peas, thawed
1 (16 ounce) jar alfredo sauce
2 - 3 cups cubed cooked ham

☐ Cook tortellini according to package directions.

☐ Add green peas about 5 minutes before tortellini is done; drain.

☐ In saucepan, combine alfredo sauce and ham. Heat until thoroughly hot.

☐ Toss with tortellini and peas. Serve immediately. Serves 4.

*Mankind has not only valued apples for their taste
but also for their shelf life. For centuries, so-called
winter apples prevalent in Asia and Europe could be
picked in late autumn and stored at temperatures as
low as just above freezing, and therefore serve as an
important food source during winter. Europeans who
settled America and Argentina repeated that pattern.*

CREAMY POTATOES AND HAM

1 pint half-and-half cream
1 cup milk
1 (10 ounce) can fiesta nacho cheese soup
2 (5 ounce) boxes scalloped potatoes mix
2 - 3 cups cooked, diced ham
2 (11 ounce) cans Mexicorn®, drained
1 cup shredded cheddar cheese

☐ Combine half-and-half cream, milk, soup and contents of seasoning packets from potatoes in large bowl; mix until blended well.

☐ Add potatoes, ham and corn and mix well. Pour mixture into sprayed 4-quart slow cooker.

☐ Pour 2 cups boiling water over mixture and stir to mix well.

☐ Cover and cook on LOW for 7 to 8 hours. Sprinkle 1 tablespoon cheese over each serving. Serves 8 to 10.

It is not the horse that draws the cart, but the oats.

– Russian Proverb

SLOW-COOK HAM-POTATO CASSEROLE

4 medium potatoes, peeled, sliced
2 cups cooked, cubed ham
1 (15 ounce) can whole kernel corn, drained
1 (10 ounce) package frozen chopped bell peppers and onions, thawed
2 tablespoons flour
½ cup milk, divided
2 (10 ounce) cans cheddar cheese soup

☐ In large bowl combine sliced potatoes, ham, corn, and bell peppers and onions; mix well. Pour into sprayed slow cooker.

☐ Mix flour and 2 tablespoons milk in bowl until smooth. Add remaining milk and soup and mix. Spoon mixture over potato-ham mixture.

☐ Cover and cook on LOW for 7 to 8 hours or until potatoes are tender. Serves 6.

According to the National Geographic, *scientists have settled the old dispute over which came first – the chicken or the egg. They say that reptiles were laying eggs thousands of years before chickens appeared, and the first chicken came from an egg laid by a bird that was not quite a chicken. Clearly, the egg came first.*

HAM AND SAUSAGE OVER RICE

1 cup cooked, cubed ham
1 onion, chopped
1 bell pepper, seeded, chopped
1 (15 ounce) can kidney beans, rinsed, drained
1 (15 ounce) can pinto beans, drained
1 (15 ounce) can tomato sauce
1 (10 ounce) can diced tomatoes and green chilies
3 cups instant rice
2 teaspoons Cajun seasoning
1 pound cooked smoked sausage, cut in ½-inch pieces.

☐ In large bowl combine ham, onion, bell pepper, kidney beans, pinto beans, tomato sauce, and tomatoes and green chilies. Mix well and pour into sprayed 4 to 6-quart slow cooker.

☐ Cover and cook on LOW for 8 to 9 hours.

☐ About 20 minutes before serving, heat 3 cups water to boiling in large saucepan. Remove from heat and stir in rice. Cover and let stand for about 5 minutes. Fluff rice with fork before serving.

☐ Increase heat to HIGH on slow cooker and stir in Cajun seasoning and smoked sausage. Cover and cook about 15 minutes or until sausage is thoroughly hot.

☐ Place ½ cup rice in each bowl and top with ¾ cup ham-sausage mixture. Serves 8.

SPECIAL HAM SUPPER

2½ cups cooked, ground ham
⅔ cup finely crushed cheese crackers
1 egg, slightly beaten
⅓ cup hot-and-spicy ketchup
¼ cup (½ stick) butter
1 (18 ounce) package frozen hash-brown potatoes, thawed
1 onion, coarsely chopped
1 (5 ounce) can evaporated milk
1½ cups shredded Monterey Jack cheese
½ teaspoon paprika

☐ Combine ground ham (you can also use leftover ham), crackers, egg and ketchup in bowl and shape into 6 patties.

☐ Melt butter in skillet and cook potatoes and onion on medium heat for about 10 minutes, turning frequently to prevent browning. Drain and transfer to sprayed slow cooker.

☐ Combine evaporated milk, cheese, paprika, and a little salt and pepper in bowl. Pour over potatoes and onions. Place ham patties on top; cover and cook on LOW for 3 to 5 hours. Serves 6.

HOME-STYLE HAM LOAF

3 cups cooked, ground ham
½ pound ground beef
½ pound hot sausage
½ cup finely chopped onion
¾ cup cracker crumbs
1 egg, slightly beaten
1 teaspoon sugar
1 tablespoon dijon-style mustard
¼ cup chili sauce

☐ Combine all ingredients in large bowl; mix well.

☐ Form into 9 x 5-inch loaf and place in sprayed, oblong slow cooker.

☐ Cover and cook on LOW for 6 to 7 hours. Slice to serve. Slices are also good for making sandwiches. Serves 6.

TIP: If using leftover ham chunks, grind ham in food processor.

PORK CHOP-CHEDDAR BAKE

8 boneless pork chops
1 (10 ounce) can cream of mushroom soup
1 cup rice
1½ cups shredded cheddar cheese, divided
½ cup minced onion
⅓ cup chopped bell pepper
1 (4 ounce) can sliced mushrooms, drained
1 (6 ounce) can french-fried onions

☐ Preheat oven to 325°.

☐ Brown pork chops lightly in large skillet. Drain and place in sprayed 9 x 13-inch baking dish.

☐ In same skillet, combine soup, 1¼ cups water, rice, ½ cup cheese, onion, bell pepper and mushrooms and mix well. Pour over pork chops.

☐ Cover and bake for 1 hour 10 minutes.

☐ Top with remaining cheese and french-fried onions. Bake uncovered just until cheese melts. Serves 8.

Apricots are full of betacarotene, fiber and potassium.
Fresh apricots are loaded with vitamins A and C
and are available from May through August.

APRICOT-PORK CHOPS

1 (15 ounce) can apricot halves with juice
8 (½ inch thick) boneless pork chops
3 tablespoons butter
⅓ cup chopped celery
1 yellow bell pepper, seeded, chopped
2½ cups instant rice
1 teaspoon chicken bouillon granules
⅓ cup golden raisins
½ teaspoon ground ginger
½ cup slivered almonds

☐ Preheat oven to 350°.

☐ Place apricots in food processor, cover and process until smooth.

☐ Brown pork chops in butter in skillet. Reduce heat and cook for about 10 minutes. Remove pork chops to plate and keep warm.

☐ In same skillet, saute celery and bell pepper. Add rice, ¾ cup water, bouillon granules, raisins, ginger, ½ teaspoon salt and apricot puree and bring to a boil.

☐ Remove from heat and stir in almonds. Spoon into 9 x 13-inch baking dish.

☐ Place pork chops on top of rice mixture.

☐ Cover and bake for 20 minutes. Serves 8.

PORK CHOP CASSEROLE

6 (¾ inch thick) boneless pork chops
Canola oil
1 green bell pepper
1 yellow bell pepper, seeded, chopped
1 (15 ounce) can tomato sauce
1 (15 ounce) can Italian stewed tomatoes with liquid
1 teaspoon minced garlic
1½ cups rice

☐ Preheat oven to 350°.

☐ Sprinkle pork chops with ½ teaspoon each of salt and pepper. Brown pork chops in a little oil in skillet. Remove chops from skillet and set aside.

☐ Cut top off green bell pepper, remove seeds and cut 6 rings.

☐ In separate bowl, combine yellow bell pepper, tomato sauce, Italian stewed tomatoes, 1 cup water, garlic and ½ teaspoon salt and stir well.

☐ Spread rice in sprayed 9 x 13-inch baking dish and slowly pour tomato mixture over rice.

☐ Arrange pork chops over rice and place green bell pepper ring over each chop. Cover and bake for 1 hour or until chops and rice are tender. Serves 6.

You can't change the past, but you can ruin the present by worrying over the future.

— *Anonymous*

ORANGE PORK CHOPS

6 (½ inch thick) boneless pork chops
2 tablespoons canola oil
1⅓ cups instant rice
1 cup orange juice
¼ teaspoon ground ginger
1 (10 ounce) can chicken with rice soup
½ cup chopped walnuts

☐ Preheat oven to 350°.

☐ Sprinkle a little salt and pepper over pork chops and brown with oil in skillet.

☐ Sprinkle rice in sprayed 7 x 11-inch baking dish. Add orange juice and arrange pork chops over rice.

☐ Add ginger to soup and stir right in can. Pour soup over pork chops.

☐ Sprinkle walnuts over top.

☐ Cover and bake for 25 minutes.

☐ Uncover and bake additional 10 minutes or until rice is tender. Serves 6.

QUICK TOMATO CHOPS

4 - 6 pork chops
Oil
1 large onion
1 bell pepper, seeded
1 (10 ounce) can diced tomatoes and green chilies

☐ Preheat oven to 350°.

☐ Brown pork chops in sprayed skillet in a little oil. Place chops in sprayed baking dish.

☐ Cut onion and bell pepper into large chunks and place on chops. Pour tomatoes and green chilies over chops.

☐ Cover and bake for 45 minutes. Serves 4 to 6.

LEMON-BAKED PORK CHOPS

¾ cup ketchup
¾ cup packed brown sugar
¼ cup lemon juice
4 butterflied pork chops

☐ Preheat oven to 325°.

☐ Combine ketchup, ½ cup water, brown sugar and lemon juice in bowl.

☐ Place pork chops in sprayed 7 x 11-inch baking dish and pour sauce over pork chops.

☐ Cover and bake for 50 minutes. Serves 4.

EASY BAKED CHOPS

4 (½ - 1-inch thick) pork chops
Oil
1 - 2 tablespoons onion soup mix
2 tablespoons French salad dressing

☐ Preheat oven to 350°.

☐ Brown pork chops on both sides in large skillet with a little oil. Remove and place in baking dish.

☐ In small bowl combine onion soup mix, salad dressing and ¼ cup water. Mix well and pour over pork chops.

☐ Cover and bake for about 1 hour. Serves 4.

Maybe the little things, like having a meal at the table, are more important than we realize. Maybe these little things are the things we never forget... our memories and family traditions.

CURRIED-ORANGE PORK CHOPS

¾ teaspoon curry powder, divided
½ teaspoon paprika
4 (½ inch thick) center-cut boneless pork chops
Oil
½ cup orange marmalade
1 heaping teaspoon horseradish
1 teaspoon balsamic vinegar
2 cups rice or couscous, cooked

☐ Combine ¼ teaspoon curry powder, paprika and ½ teaspoon salt and sprinkle over pork chops.

☐ Cook chops in a little oil in skillet on medium-high heat and cook 5 minutes on each side. Transfer chops to plate.

☐ In same skillet, combine remaining ½ teaspoon curry, marmalade, horseradish and vinegar. Cook for 1 minute, stirring continuously.

☐ When serving, place pork chops on bed of rice or couscous. Spoon sauce over pork chops. Serves 4.

An excellent health tip:
Try to Make Someone Smile at Least Once a Day.

STUFFED PORK CHOPS

4 (¾ inch thick) boneless center-cut pork chops
2 slices rye bread, diced
⅓ cup chopped onion
⅓ cup chopped celery
⅓ cup dried apples, diced
⅓ cup chicken broth
Oil

☐ Preheat oven to 400°.

☐ Make 1-inch wide slit on side of each chop and insert knife blade to other side, but not through pork chop. Sweep knife back and forth and carefully cut pocket opening larger.

☐ In bowl, combine rye bread pieces, onion, celery, apples and broth and mix well.

☐ Stuff chops with all the stuffing mixture.

☐ Place chops in heavy skillet with a little oil and saute about 3 minutes on each side.

☐ Transfer to non-stick baking dish and bake uncovered for 10 minutes. Serves 4.

Americans eat about 19 pounds of fresh apples per person every year. Europeans eat an average of 46 pounds annually.

SMOKY GRILLED PORK CHOPS

1 cup mayonnaise (not light)
2 tablespoons lime juice
1 teaspoon ground cilantro
1 teaspoon chili powder
2 teaspoons minced garlic
8 (1 inch thick) bone-in, pork chops

☐ Combine mayonnaise, lime juice, cilantro, chili powder and garlic and mix.
   Set aside ½ cup.

☐ Grill or broil pork chops while repeatedly basting with remaining sauce.

☐ Serve the set aside ½ cup sauce with chops. Serves 8.

PORK-POTATO CHOPS

6 boneless or loin pork chops
1 (14 ounce) can chicken broth
2 (1 ounce) packets onion soup mix
6 new (red) potatoes, sliced

☐ Brown pork chops in large sprayed skillet.

☐ Combine chicken broth and soup mix.

☐ Place potatoes with pork chops and pour soup mixture over pork chops and potatoes.

☐ Heat to boiling, reduce heat; cover and simmer for about 45 minutes or until pork chops
   and potatoes are fork-tender. Serves 6.

CHOPS WITH SOY-GINGER SAUCE

¾ cup chili sauce
2 teaspoons minced garlic
1 tablespoon minced fresh ginger
2 tablespoons Worcestershire sauce
1 large egg, beaten
½ cup seasoned breadcrumbs
2 tablespoons oil
4 (¾ inch thick) boneless pork chops

☐ In small bowl, combine chili sauce, garlic, ginger and Worcestershire and set aside for flavors to blend.

☐ Mix egg with 1 tablespoon water in shallow bowl.

☐ Place breadcrumbs in another shallow bowl.

☐ In skillet on medium heat, add oil. Dip each chop in beaten egg and dredge in breadcrumbs to coat well. Cook in skillet for 5 minutes on each side.

☐ Serve with ginger-soy sauce. Serves 4.

A jumper cable walks into a bar and sits down.
The bartender says, "Okay, I'll serve you, but don't
start anything."

PORK CHOPS WITH BLACK BEAN SALSA

2 teaspoons chili powder
½ teaspoon seasoned salt
2 tablespoons vegetable oil
6 thin-cut boneless pork chops

☐ Combine chili powder and seasoned salt. Rub oil over pork chops, sprinkle chili powder mixture over chops and rub into meat.

☐ Place in skillet over medium heat and cook pork chops about 5 minutes on both sides or until at least 145°.

BLACK BEAN SALSA:

1 (15 ounce) can black beans, rinsed, drained
1 (24 ounce) refrigerated citrus fruit, drained
1 ripe avocado, sliced
⅔ cup Italian salad dressing

☐ Combine beans, fruit and avocado and toss with salad dressing. Serve with pork chops. Serves 6.

A group of chess players were checking into a hotel and talked to each other in the lobby about a tournament. After some time, the hotel manager asked them to leave the lobby.

"Why?" said one of the players. "Because", he said, "I don't like a bunch of chess nuts boasting in an open foyer."

PARMESAN-TOPPED PORK CHOPS

½ cup grated parmesan cheese
⅔ cup Italian-seasoned dried breadcrumbs
1 egg
4 - 6 thin-cut pork chops
Oil

☐ In shallow bowl, combine cheese and dried breadcrumbs. Beat egg with 1 teaspoon water on shallow plate.

☐ Dip each pork chop in beaten egg and then breadcrumb mixture. Cook over medium-high heat in skillet with a little oil for about 5 minutes on each side or until light golden brown. Serves 4 to 6.

SWEET AND SAVORY PORK CHOPS

4 - 6 (1 inch thick) boneless pork chops, trimmed
Oil
½ cup grape, apple or plum jelly
½ cup chili sauce or hot ketchup
Soy sauce or teriyaki sauce

☐ Preheat oven to 325°.

☐ Brown pork chops in skillet in a little oil. Transfer browned pork chops to sprayed baking dish.

☐ Combine jelly and chili sauce or ketchup in bowl and spread over pork chops. Cook for 20 minutes.

☐ Baste with sauce and cook for additional 20 to 30 minutes or until pork chops are tender. Serve with soy sauce or teriyaki sauce. Serves 4 to 6.

TANGY PORK CHOPS

4 - 6 pork chops
Oil
¼ cup Worcestershire sauce
¼ cup ketchup
½ cup honey

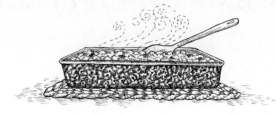

☐ Preheat oven to 325°.

☐ Brown pork chops in skillet in a little oil. Place in sprayed baking dish.

☐ Combine Worcestershire sauce, ketchup and honey in bowl. Pour over pork chops.

☐ Cover and bake for 45 minutes. Serves 4 to 6.

SUNNY ORANGE PORK CHOPS

6 - 8 medium thick pork chops
¼ cup (½ stick) butter
2¼ cups orange juice
⅓ cup orange marmalade

☐ Brown both sides of pork chops in butter in hot skillet and season with a little salt and pepper.

☐ Pour orange juice over chops. Cover and simmer until done, about 1 hour. (Time will vary with thickness of pork chops.)

☐ Add more orange juice, if necessary. During last few minutes of cooking, spread orange marmalade on pork chops. Serves 6 to 8.

TIP: This makes delicious gravy to serve over rice.

ITALIAN-STYLE PORK CHOPS

6 (¾ inch thick) bone-in pork chops
Oil
2 green bell peppers
1 (15 ounce) can tomato sauce
1 (15 ounce) can Italian stewed tomatoes with liquid
½ onion, chopped
1 teaspoon Italian seasoning
1 clove garlic, minced
1 tablespoon Worcestershire sauce
½ cup brown rice

☐ Preheat oven to 350°.

☐ Sprinkle pork chops with a little salt and pepper. Brown chops on both sides in a little oil in skillet. Remove chops from skillet, drain and set aside.

☐ Cut top off 1 bell pepper and remove seeds. Cut into 6 (¼-inch thick) rings and set aside. Core, seed and chop remaining bell pepper.

☐ Combine chopped bell pepper, tomato sauce, stewed tomatoes, 1 cup water, onion, Italian seasoning, garlic, Worcestershire, and ½ teaspoon each of salt and pepper in bowl and mix well.

☐ Spread rice evenly in lightly sprayed 9 x 13-inch baking dish. Slowly pour tomato mixture over rice.

☐ Arrange pork chops over rice mixture and top each pork chop with bell pepper ring.

☐ Cover and bake for 1 hour or until rice is tender. Serves 6.

APPLE PORK CHOPS

4 butterflied pork chops
2 apples, peeled, cored, halved
2 teaspoons butter
2 tablespoons brown sugar

☐ Preheat oven to 350°.

☐ Place pork chops in sprayed shallow baking dish.

☐ Cover and bake for 30 minutes. Uncover and place apple halves on top of pork chops. Add a little butter and a little brown sugar on each apple.

☐ Bake for additional 15 minutes. Serves 4.

TIP: Seasoning is always up to you, but salt and pepper are plenty for these pork chops.

I fear not the man who has practiced 10,000 kicks once, but I fear the man who has practiced one kick 10,000 times.

– Bruce Lee

PORK CHOPS IN CREAM GRAVY

4 (¼ inch thick) pork chops
1 cup flour
Olive oil
2¼ cups milk

☐ Dip pork chops in flour. Brown chops on both sides in a little oil in skillet over medium-high heat. Remove chops from skillet.

☐ Add about 2 tablespoons flour to skillet over medium-low heat, brown lightly while stirring constantly. Season with a little salt and pepper.

☐ Slowly stir in milk to make gravy. Return chops to skillet with gravy.

☐ Cover and simmer on low for about 40 minutes. Serves 4.

TIP: This is a great recipe to serve over noodles or rice.

If you want succulent chops, choose those that are about 1 inch thick. Thinner chops will tend to dry out no matter how careful you are about cooking them.

PROMISING PORK CHOPS

6 boneless pork chops
1 (4 ounce) can sliced mushrooms
1 (10 ounce) can diced tomatoes and green chilies
1 (10 ounce) can cream of mushroom soup
1 (8 ounce) carton sour cream
1 (8 ounce) package penne pasta

☐ Place pork chops in sprayed 5-quart slow cooker and layer mushrooms and tomatoes and green chilies over top. Spread mushroom soup over top with large spoon.

☐ Cover and cook on LOW for 6 to 8 hours. Transfer pork chops to container that can be kept warm in oven. Stir sour cream into sauce in slow cooker and cook on HIGH for about 10 minutes while you cook pasta according to package directions.

☐ Stir pasta into sauce and place pork chops on top, or if you prefer, place pasta and sauce on serving platter and top with warm pork chops. Serves 6.

Lives of great men all remind us
We can make our lives sublime,
And, departing, leave behind us
Footprints on the sands of time.

– *Henry Wadsworth Longfellow: "A Psalm of Life"*

ALOHA PORK CHOPS

1 green bell pepper, seeded, julienned
1 red bell pepper, seeded, julienned
1 onion, sliced
6 - 8 (½ inch thick) boneless pork chops
1 (15 ounce) can pineapple chunks with juice
1 tablespoon mustard
2 tablespoons white wine vinegar
1 tablespoon brown sugar
1 papaya, peeled, seeded, sliced
Macadamia nuts

☐ Place bell peppers and onion in sprayed slow cooker and place pork chops on top.

☐ Combine juice from pineapple, mustard, vinegar, brown sugar and ½ teaspoon salt in bowl; mix and pour over pork chops.

☐ Cover and cook on LOW for 5 to 6 hours.

☐ Place pork chops on serving plate; increase heat to HIGH and stir in pineapple and papaya and cook for additional 10 minutes. Pour sauce over pork chops and sprinkle with macadamia nuts. Serves 6 to 8.

Christopher Columbus discovered pineapple in 1493 on the island of Guadeloupe. James Cook introduced pineapple to Hawaii in 1770, but commercial harvesting of pineapple did not begin until the development of the steam engine. By 1903 James Dole began canning pineapples in Hawaii and business boomed by the 1920s. The last pineapple crop in Hawaii was harvested in 2008, freeing the land to make room for Hawaii's expanding tourist industry.

SALSA PORK CHOPS

6 boneless pork chops
½ cup salsa
½ cup honey or packed brown sugar
1 teaspoon soy sauce

☐ Preheat oven to 325°.

☐ Place pork chops in baking dish.

☐ Combine salsa, honey or brown sugar, and soy sauce in microwave-safe bowl and heat for 20 to 30 seconds in microwave; mix well.

☐ Pour salsa mixture over pork chops; cover and bake about 45 minutes or until pork chops are tender. Serves 6.

TIP: You can add an interesting "giddy-up" with ¼ teaspoon crushed red pepper flakes. It's not necessary, however, for a delicious dish.

Soften brown sugar in the bag by adding a few drops of water to the bag and microwaving it on 50% power for 20 to 30 seconds.

GINGER PORK CHOPS

6 (1 inch thick) pork chops
⅓ cup teriyaki sauce
1 (10 ounce) can tomato bisque soup
⅓ cup packed brown sugar
1 teaspoon ground ginger
2 cups instant rice

☐ Trim excess fat off pork chops, sprinkle with a little salt and pepper, and place in sprayed slow cooker.

☐ Combine teriyaki sauce, soup, brown sugar and ginger in bowl; mix until they blend well. Pour mixture over pork chops.

☐ Cover and cook on LOW for 4 hours 30 minutes to 6 hours.

☐ Cook rice according to package directions and place in serving plate. Top with pork chops and sauce. Serves 6.

Use leftover meats in salads. Chicken, steak, roast, pork or seafood make great toppings for salads and turns them into hearty meals.

GOOD OL' STANDBY CHOPS

6 - 8 (½ inch thick) boneless pork chops
Oil
1 cup orange juice
2 tablespoons dijon-style mustard
2 tablespoons lemon juice
¾ cup packed brown sugar
⅓ cup Craisins®
¼ cup (½ stick) butter
2 cups instant rice

☐ Cut off any fat on pork chops.

☐ Brown pork chops on both sides in skillet in a little oil on medium-high heat and place in sprayed slow cooker.

☐ Combine orange juice, mustard, lemon juice, brown sugar, Craisins® and butter in saucepan on medium heat. Cook while stirring until mixture is hot and blends well. Pour sauce over pork chops.

☐ Cover and cook on LOW for 6 to 8 hours.

☐ Cook rice according to package directions and place on serving plate. Top with pork chops and sauce. Serves 6 to 8.

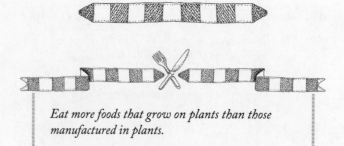

Eat more foods that grow on plants than those manufactured in plants.

SMOTHERED PORK CHOPS

1 (10 ounce) can cream of mushroom soup
1 (4 ounce) can sliced mushrooms
5 - 6 boneless pork chops
Oil
Lemon pepper
2 (15 ounce) cans whole new potatoes, drained
1 (10 ounce) package frozen green peas, thawed

☐ Combine soup, mushrooms and ¼ cup water in sprayed slow cooker; stir to mix well.

☐ Brown chops in skillet with a little oil over medium-high heat. Season each pork chop with lemon pepper and place in slow cooker. Cover and cook on LOW for 6 hours.

☐ Remove lid and place potatoes and peas around pork chops; turn heat to HIGH and cook for additional 1 hour to 1 hour 30 minutes. Serves 5.

The ornaments of a house are the friends who frequent it.

– Ralph Waldo Emerson

PERFECT PORK CHOPS AND POTATOES

2 tablespoons canola oil
6 - 8 boneless pork chops
1 (10 ounce) can cream of chicken soup
1 tablespoon mustard
½ cup chicken broth
1 teaspoon minced garlic
6 - 8 new (red) potatoes with peels, sliced
2 - 3 onions, sliced

☐ Heat oil in skillet on medium-high heat and brown pork chops on both sides.

☐ Combine soup, mustard, broth, garlic, and a little salt and pepper in sprayed slow cooker. Layer potatoes and onions in cooker; place browned pork chops on top.

☐ Cover and cook on LOW for 8 to 10 hours or on HIGH for 4 to 5 hours. Serves 6 to 8.

The round white potato and the round red potato are both best suited for boiling. The round white potato has a speckled brown skin and the red round has a red skin. Both have less starch than baking potatoes and more moisture. They are well suited to boiling and are used for mashed potatoes.

PORK, POTATOES AND KRAUT SUPPER

6 (¾ inch thick) pork chops
Oil
1 (16 ounce) bag sauerkraut, rinsed, drained
1 pound small new (red) potatoes, scrubbed
1 cup apple juice
½ (16 ounce) package baby carrots
½ onion, chopped
1 teaspoon dried thyme

- Brown pork chops in skillet with a little oil over medium heat. Lay pork chops in sprayed, 6-quart oblong slow cooker, without overlapping, if possible.

- Add sauerkraut, potatoes, juice, carrots, onion, thyme and 1 teaspoon pepper.

- Cover and cook on LOW for 8 hours or on HIGH for 4 hours. Serves 6.

The long white potato is very similar to the baking potato with a long, elliptical shape, but its skin is much thinner and has fewer eyes. It is sometimes called the California long white after the state in which it was developed. These are very good when fried, boiled or baked. The finger-size potatoes in the same group are called fingerling potatoes.

SLOW-COOK PORK CHOP DINNER

4 medium potatoes, peeled, sliced
2 onions, sliced
2 green bell peppers, seeded, sliced in strips
2 ribs celery, cut in 1-inch pieces
6 (½ inch thick) boneless pork chops
2 (10 ounce) cans cream of onion soup
½ cup milk

- Place potatoes, onions, bell peppers and celery in sprayed 4-quart slow cooker. Top with pork chops.

- Heat onion soup and milk in saucepan, mix until it blends well and pour over pork chops. Cover and cook on LOW for 6 to 8 hours. Serves 6.

Money-Saving Tip:

Buy only the quantity you need. Just because an item is "2 for $4" doesn't mean you have to buy 2. You can buy one for $2. (Some specials require a specific quantity so to be sure to check the fine print.)

PRALINE HAM

2 (½ inch thick) ham slices, cooked
½ cup maple syrup
3 tablespoons brown sugar
1 tablespoon butter
⅓ cup chopped pecans

- ☐ Preheat oven to 325°.

- ☐ Bake ham slices in sprayed, shallow pan for 10 minutes.

- ☐ Bring syrup, brown sugar and butter in to a boil in small saucepan and stir often.

- ☐ Stir in pecans and spoon over ham.

- ☐ Bake additional 20 minutes. Serves 4.

Money-Saving Tip:

Be aware of portion sizes. This will not only help your waistline, but also stretch your budget.

SWEET MUSTARD HAM

1 (1 inch) slice cooked ham
2 teaspoons dry mustard
⅓ cup honey
⅓ cup cooking wine

☐ Preheat oven to 350°.

☐ Rub ham slice with 1 teaspoon mustard on each side. Place in shallow baking pan.

☐ Combine honey and wine in bowl and pour over ham. Bake for about 35 minutes. Serves 4.

SMOTHERED HAM SUPPER

6 - 8 slices cooked ham
1 onion, sliced
2 ribs celery, cut in 1-inch pieces
4 medium potatoes, peeled, sliced
1 (11 ounce) can Mexicorn®, drained
1 (10 ounce) can cream of mushroom soup
1½ cups shredded mozzarella cheese
1 tablespoon marinade for chicken

☐ In sprayed 4-quart slow cooker layer ham slices, onion, celery, potatoes and corn.

☐ Combine mushroom soup, cheese and marinade for chicken in bowl and spoon over ham-corn layers.

☐ Cover and cook on LOW for 8 hours. Serves 6 to 8.

BROWN SUGAR GLAZED HAM

1 (1 pound) cooked smoked ½-inch thick center cut ham slice
⅓ cup orange juice
⅓ cup packed brown sugar
2 teaspoons dijon-style mustard

☐ Place ham slice in sprayed slow cooker.

☐ Combine juice, brown sugar and mustard in small bowl. Spread over ham slice.

☐ Cover and cook on LOW for 3 to 4 hours or until ham has glossy glaze. Cut into individual servings. Serves 4.

FRUIT-COVERED HAM

2 (15 ounce) cans fruit cocktail with juice
½ cup packed brown sugar
2 tablespoons cornstarch
1 (½ inch thick) cooked center-cut ham slice

☐ In saucepan, combine fruit cocktail, brown sugar and cornstarch; mix well. Cook and stir on medium heat until sauce thickens.

☐ Place ham slice in large non-stick skillet on medium heat. Cook about 5 minutes or just until ham heats thoroughly.

☐ Place on serving platter and spoon fruit sauce over ham. Serves 4.

CHERRY BEST HAM

1 (½ inch thick) cooked center-cut ham slice
⅔ cup cherry preserves
½ teaspoon ground cinnamon
⅓ cup chopped walnuts

☐ Preheat oven to 325°.

☐ Place ham slice in foil-lined 9 x 13-inch glass baking dish. Spread preserves over ham and sprinkle cinnamon and walnuts on top.

☐ Bake uncovered for 20 minutes. Serve right from baking dish. Serves 2.

SWEET POTATO HAM

1 (16 ounce/1½ inch thick) cooked ham slice
1 (18 ounce) can sweet potatoes, drained
½ cup packed brown sugar
⅓ cup chopped pecans

☐ Preheat oven to 350°.

☐ Slice outer edge of fat on ham slice at 1-inch intervals to prevent curling, but do not cut into ham.

☐ Place on 10-inch glass pie pan and broil for 5 minutes.

☐ In bowl, mash sweet potatoes with fork just once (not totally mashed). Add brown sugar and chopped pecans and mix well.

☐ Spoon mixture over ham slice and bake about 15 minutes. Serve right from pie pan. Serves 2.

HONEY-HAM SLICE

⅓ cup orange juice
⅓ cup honey
1 teaspoon mustard
1 (1 inch thick) cooked ham slice

☐ Combine orange juice, honey and mustard in small saucepan. Cook slowly for 10 minutes and stir occasionally. Brush ham with orange glaze.

☐ Place in broiling pan about 3 inches from heat. Broil 8 minutes on first side.

☐ Turn ham slice over. Brush with glaze again and broil for additional 6 to 8 minutes. Serves 4.

CRAN-APPLE HAM

1 cup apple juice, divided
1 tablespoon cornstarch
1 cup whole cranberry sauce
1 cooked center-cut ham slice or 1 (2 - 3 pound) smoked boneless ham

☐ Preheat oven to 350°.

☐ Combine ¼ cup apple juice and cornstarch in medium saucepan over low heat and stir constantly until cornstarch is smooth.

☐ Add remaining apple juice. Bring to a boil and cook on medium heat, stirring constantly until mixture thickens. Stir in cranberry sauce and heat for 2 to 3 minutes.

☐ Place ham slice in sprayed shallow baking pan. Spread sauce over ham slice, bake for 20 to 30 minutes and baste ham with sauce 2 to 3 times. Serve warmed sauce with ham. (If you use smoked boneless ham, cook 1 hour to 1 hour 15 minutes.) Serves 4.

HAM AND SWEET POTATO REWARD

3 tablespoons dijon-style mustard, divided
1 (3 - 4 pound) boneless smoked ham
½ cup honey or packed brown sugar
1 (29 ounce) can sweet potatoes

☐ Preheat oven at 325°.

☐ Spread 2 tablespoons mustard on ham. Place ham in sprayed, shallow baking pan and bake for 20 minutes.

☐ Combine remaining mustard with honey or brown sugar in bowl and spread over ham. Add sweet potatoes, baste with sauce and bake for 20 minutes. Serves 6 to 8.

PEACH-PINEAPPLE BAKED HAM

4 tablespoons dijon-style mustard, divided
1 (3 - 4) pound boneless smoked ham
1 cup peach preserves
1 cup pineapple preserves

☐ Preheat oven to 325°.

☐ Spread 2 tablespoons mustard on ham. Place ham in sprayed, shallow baking pan and bake for 20 minutes.

☐ Combine remaining 2 tablespoons mustard and preserves; heat in microwave for 20 seconds and mix well. (If you cook on stove, place sauce in small saucepan on low heat for 2 to 3 minutes.)

☐ Pour over ham and bake additional 15 minutes. Serves 8 to 10.

PINEAPPLE-GLAZED HAM

1 (3 pound) cooked ham
1 (15 ounce) can crushed pineapple, divided
⅔ cup packed brown sugar
⅓ cup orange marmalade, divided
1 teaspoon mustard

☐ Place ham in sprayed 5-quart slow cooker. Drain pineapple liquid from can into slow cooker. Refrigerate pineapple until ham is ready to serve.

☐ Combine brown sugar, 1 tablespoon marmalade and mustard in bowl and mix well; spread over ham. Cover and cook on LOW for 6 to 8 hours.

☐ When ready to serve, combine refrigerated pineapple and remaining orange marmalade in bowl and microwave on HIGH for about 1 minute or until thoroughly hot, stirring once halfway through cooking.

☐ Slice ham and serve with pineapple mixture. Serves 8.

HAM WITH A SPICY SAUCE

1 (6 - 7 pound) cooked ham butt or shank
Whole cloves
1 cup apricot jam
1 tablespoon vinegar
1 teaspoon dry mustard
¼ teaspoon ground cinnamon
Dash of hot sauce

☐ Place metal rack in sprayed slow cooker and position ham in center of cooker.

☐ Cover and cook on LOW for 5 to 6 hours. Remove ham and pour off juices; then remove fat and skin. Score ham and stud with whole cloves.

☐ Melt jam with vinegar, mustard, cinnamon and dash of hot sauce in small saucepan.

☐ Remove metal rack and return ham to slow cooker. Spoon sauce over ham

☐ Increase heat to HIGH; cover and cook for additional 30 minutes, brushing with sauce several times. Serve hot or cold. Serves 8 to 10.

Home can be any place in which we create our own sense of rest and peace as we tend to the spaces in which we eat and sleep and play. It is a place that we create and re-create in every moment, at every stage of our lives, a place where the plain and common becomes cherished and the ordinary becomes sacred.

– Katrina Kenison
The Gift of an Ordinary Day: A Mother's Memoir

DINNER PARTY HAM

1 (3 pound) fully cooked boneless ham
2 onions, quartered
2 (6 ounce) jars mango chutney
1 tablespoon balsamic vinegar
2 (15 ounce) cans sweet potatoes, drained

☐ Trim any excess fat off ham and place in sprayed 6-quart slow cooker. Spoon onions around ham.

☐ Combine chutney and balsamic vinegar in small bowl and pour over ham.

☐ Cover and cook on LOW for 7 hours. Place sweet potato chunks around ham and continue cooking for additional 1 hour or until sweet potatoes are thoroughly hot.

☐ Let ham stand for about 10 minutes before slicing. Serves 8.

Murphy's Law: *Your repairman will have never seen a model quite like yours.*

OUR BEST PORK ROAST

1 (14 ounce) can whole berry cranberry sauce
½ cup quartered dried apricots
½ teaspoon grated orange peel
⅓ cup orange juice
1 large shallot, chopped
1 tablespoon cider vinegar
1 teaspoon mustard
2 tablespoons brown sugar
¼ teaspoon dried ginger
2 - 3 pound pork loin roast

☐ Combine cranberry sauce, apricots, orange peel, orange juice, shallot, vinegar, mustard, brown sugar, ginger and 1 teaspoon salt in bowl. Stir mixture until well blended and spoon into sprayed slow cooker.

☐ Trim roast of any fat and add pork roast to slow cooker. Spoon a little cranberry mixture on top.

☐ Cover and cook on LOW for 7 to 9 hours or until pork is tender.

☐ Spoon off any fat from top of cranberry mixture; place roast on cutting board. Slice pork and serve with sauce. Serves 6 to 8.

I fear the day that technology will surpass our human interaction. The world will have a generation of idiots.

—Albert Einstein

(How many people around you interact more with cell phones than people?)

PORK ROAST, APRICOTS AND STUFFING

2 (6 ounce) boxes corn bread stuffing mix
2 ribs celery, sliced
1 onion, finely chopped
1 egg
1 (14 ounce) can chicken broth
¾ cup dried apricots, chopped
1 (3 pound) boneless pork loin roast
½ cup apricot preserves

☐ Combine stuffing mix, celery, onion, egg, broth, apricots and 1 cup water in bowl. (Using kitchen scissors is the easiest way to chop apricots.)

☐ Transfer to sprayed 4-quart slow cooker and place roast on top of stuffing mixture. Brush preserves over roast.

☐ Cover and cook on LOW for 7 to 8 hours. Slice roast and serve with stuffing. Serves 8.

PORK LOIN WITH FRUIT SAUCE

1 (4 pound) pork loin roast
1 teaspoon dried rosemary
2 tablespoons butter
1 cup orange juice
1 (14 ounce) can whole cranberry sauce
1 cup apricot preserves
1 (14 ounce) can chicken broth
1 teaspoon red wine vinegar
1 teaspoon sugar
1 tablespoon marinade for chicken
Rice, cooked

☐ Preheat oven to 350˚.

☐ Place roast in shallow roasting pan. Sprinkle with rosemary and 1 teaspoon pepper.

☐ Bake for 1 hour.

☐ Combine remaining ingredients except rice and 1 teaspoon salt in large saucepan. Bring to a boil, reduce heat and simmer for 20 minutes.

☐ Remove roast from oven and spoon about 1 cup sauce over roast. Return to oven and bake for additional 1 hour or until meat thermometer reads 165˚. Let roast stand for several minutes before slicing. Place on bed of rice on large platter.

☐ Spoon meat juices from roast into remaining fruit sauce. Heat and serve with pork roast and rice. Serves 8 to 10.

FIESTA PORK CASSEROLE

This zesty casserole is so easy to put together and it really gets your attention! It is specially nice for a change of pace from the usual Mexican dish with ground beef.

2 pounds boneless pork tenderloin
1 onion, chopped
1 green bell pepper, seeded, chopped
3 tablespoons canola oil
1 (15 ounce) can black beans, rinsed, drained
1 (10 ounce) can fiesta nacho cheese soup
1 (15 ounce) can stewed tomatoes
1 (4 ounce) can diced green chilies
1 cup cooked instant brown rice
¾ cup salsa
2 teaspoons ground cumin
½ teaspoon garlic powder
¾ cup shredded Mexican 3-cheese blend

☐ Preheat oven to 350°.

☐ Cut pork into 1-inch cubes. Brown and cook pork, onion and bell pepper in oil in large skillet or roasting pan until pork is no longer pink. Drain.

☐ Add beans, soup, stewed tomatoes, green chilies, rice, salsa, cumin, ½ teaspoon salt and garlic powder. Cook on medium heat, stirring occasionally, until mixture bubbles.

☐ Spoon into sprayed 4-quart baking dish. Bake for 30 minutes or until it bubbles around edges.

☐ Remove from oven and sprinkle with cheese. Let stand for a few minutes before serving. Serves 8 to 10.

One-Dish Pork and Peas

1 - 1½ pounds pork tenderloin, cut into ½-inch cubes
Canola oil
1 cup sliced celery
1 onion, chopped
1 red bell pepper, seeded, chopped
1 (8 ounce) package small egg noodles, cooked, drained
1 (10 ounce) can cream of chicken soup
½ cup half-and-half cream
1 (10 ounce) package frozen green peas, thawed
1 cup seasoned breadcrumbs
⅓ cup chopped walnuts

☐ Preheat oven to 350°.

☐ Brown cubed pork in a little oil in large skillet. Reduce heat and cook for about 20 minutes. Remove pork to separate dish.

☐ Saute celery, onion and bell pepper in a little oil in same skillet.

☐ Add pork, noodles, soup, half-and-half cream, peas, and ½ teaspoon each of salt and pepper.

☐ Spoon into sprayed 3-quart baking dish. Sprinkle with breadcrumbs and walnuts.

☐ Bake for about 25 minutes or until bubbly. Serves 6 to 8.

PEPPERED TENDERLOIN

1 pork tenderloin, thinly sliced
Olive oil
1 green bell pepper, seeded, thinly sliced
1 red bell pepper, seeded, thinly sliced
½ pound fresh mushrooms, quartered
1 onion, coarsely chopped
1 teaspoon minced garlic
½ cup beef broth
2 tablespoons ketchup
1 teaspoon lemon juice
1 teaspoon dried tarragon
1 tablespoon flour
½ cup sour cream
Noodles, cooked

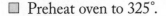

☐ Preheat oven to 325°.

☐ Brown pork slices in a little olive oil in skillet. Remove and keep warm.

☐ In same skillet, saute bell peppers, mushrooms, onion and garlic in a little more oil.

☐ Add broth, ketchup, lemon juice, tarragon and ½ teaspoon pepper. Simmer for 3 minutes. Return pork to skillet.

☐ Combine flour with sour cream and stir into pork mixture. Spoon into sprayed 7 x 11-inch baking dish.

☐ Cover and bake for 20 minutes. Serve over noodles. Serves 6.

Pork-Noodles Supreme

Canola oil
2 pounds pork tenderloin, cut into 1 inch cubes
2 ribs celery, chopped
1 red bell pepper, seeded, chopped
1 green bell pepper, seeded, chopped
1 onion, chopped
1 (12 ounce) package medium egg noodles, cooked, drained
1 (10 ounce) can cream of celery soup
1 (10 ounce) can cream of chicken soup
1 (15 ounce) can cream-style corn
¾ cup half-and-half cream
1½ cups corn flakes, crushed
3 tablespoons butter, melted

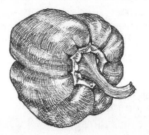

☐ Preheat oven to 350°.

☐ Heat a little oil in skillet, brown and cook pork for about 15 minutes. Spoon pork into large bowl.

☐ With a little oil in skillet, saute celery, bell peppers and onion. Spoon into bowl with pork. Add noodles, soups, corn, half-and-half cream, and a little salt and pepper.

☐ Mix well and pour into sprayed 9 x 13-inch baking dish.

☐ Combine crushed corn flakes and butter in bowl and sprinkle over casserole.

☐ Cover and bake for about 30 minutes. Serves 4 to 6.

CHOICE PORK LOIN SLICES

1 (3 - 4 pound) pork loin
1 (16 ounce) jar apricot preserves
⅓ cup lemon juice
⅓ cup ketchup
⅓ cup packed brown sugar
1 tablespoon light soy sauce
2 cups instant rice

☐ Place pork loin in sprayed slow cooker.

☐ Combine preserves, lemon juice, ketchup, brown sugar and soy sauce in bowl and pour over pork loin.

☐ Cover and cook on LOW for 7 to 9 hours.

☐ Cook rice according to package directions and place on serving plate. Let pork loin stand for about 15 minutes before slicing. Serve pork slices and sauce over rice. Serves 8.

Remember that limp vegetables like carrots and potatoes regain much of their crispness if soaked in ice water for at least 1 hour.

PORK LOIN TOPPED WITH PECANS

½ cup finely ground pecans
1 teaspoon mustard
1 tablespoon brown sugar
1 (3 pound) pork loin
1 (14 ounce) can beef broth
2 tablespoons chili sauce
2 tablespoons lemon juice
1 (10 ounce) box plain couscous

☐ Place ground pecans, mustard and brown sugar in small bowl and mix well.

☐ Press pecan mixture into pork roast and place in sprayed 4-quart slow cooker.

☐ Combine broth, chili sauce and lemon juice in bowl and pour into slow cooker.

☐ Cover and cook on LOW for 8 to 10 hours. Let stand for 10 minutes before slicing
to serve.

☐ Cook couscous according to package directions and place in serving bowl. Serve with
sliced pork roast. Serves 8 to 10.

*Cooking with love means never having to feel
chained to your stove, never feeling that getting
dinner on the table is a teeth-gritting experience
rather a charming interlude.*

– Francis Anthony

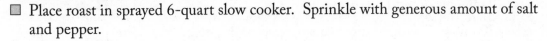

PORK ROAST WITH A PEACH TREAT

1 (4 pound) pork loin
1 (15 ounce) can sliced peaches in heavy syrup
½ cup chili sauce
½ cup packed light brown sugar
3 tablespoons apple cider vinegar
1 teaspoon pumpkin pie spice
1 tablespoon cornstarch
1 (16 ounce) package rotini (corkscrew) pasta
1 tablespoon dried parsley

- ☐ Place roast in sprayed 6-quart slow cooker. Sprinkle with generous amount of salt and pepper.

- ☐ Drain peaches. Whisk peach syrup, chili sauce, brown sugar, vinegar and pumpkin pie spice in bowl; pour over roast. Scatter peach slices on top.

- ☐ Cover and cook on HIGH for 3 hours or on LOW for 6 hours. Remove roast to serving platter and let stand for about 10 minutes. Spoon out peach slices and set aside.

- ☐ Place liquid from the slow cooker in small saucepan and bring to a boil.

- ☐ In small bowl stir 2 tablespoons water into cornstarch. Add to saucepan, stirring constantly and cook until sauce thickens.

- ☐ Cook pasta according to package directions, drain and toss with parsley.

- ☐ Slice roast, place peach slices on roast and pasta on each side of roast. Serve sauce on the side. Serves 8 to 10.

South of the Border Supper

1½ pounds boneless pork loin, cut into 1-inch pieces
1 (16 ounce) jar salsa
1 (10 ounce) can diced tomatoes and green chilies, drained
2 (15 ounce) cans pinto beans, rinsed, drained
2 cups instant rice
1 cup shredded Mexican Velveeta® cheese

- ☐ Combine pork pieces, salsa, and tomatoes and green chilies in sprayed 4-quart slow cooker.

- ☐ Cover and cook on LOW for 6 to 8 hours. Stir in beans; cover and continue cooking for additional 20 minutes or until mixture is hot.

- ☐ During last 20 minutes cooking time, cook rice according to package directions and place in large serving bowl. Spoon pork mixture over rice and sprinkle with shredded cheese. Serves 4.

Spicy Peach Pork Loin

1 (3 - 4 pound) pork loin
2 tablespoons light soy sauce
3 tablespoons dijon-style mustard
1 (16 ounce) jar peach preserves
1 (16 ounce) jar thick-and-chunky salsa
½ cup packed brown sugar

- ☐ Sprinkle pork loin with a little salt and pepper and place in sprayed slow cooker.

- ☐ Combine soy sauce, mustard, preserves, salsa and brown sugar in saucepan and cook on medium heat, stirring constantly until mixture blends well. Pour sauce over pork loin.

- ☐ Cover and cook on LOW for 5 to 7 hours.

- ☐ Uncover and spoon sauce over pork several times before slicing. Serves 8 to 10.

HAWAIIAN PORK TENDERLOIN

1 (2 pound) lean pork tenderloin, cut in 1-inch cubes
Oil
1 (15 ounce) can pineapple chunks with juice
1 (12 ounce) bottle chili sauce
1 teaspoon ground ginger

☐ Season pork cubes with salt and pepper and brown in skillet with a little oil. Add pineapple with juice, chili sauce and ginger. Cover and simmer for 1 hour 30 minutes. Serves 8.

HEARTY PORK TENDERLOIN

1 (3 pound) pork tenderloin
1 (15 ounce) can stewed tomatoes
1 (1 ounce) packet savory herb with garlic soup mix
2 tablespoons Worcestershire sauce

☐ Preheat oven to 325°.

☐ Cut tenderloin into ½-inch slices and place in sprayed roasting pan. Mix remaining ingredients in bowl and spread over meat.

☐ Cover and bake for 1 hour 20 minutes. Serves 6.

SAVORY PORK

1 - 2 pounds pork tenderloin
1 (12 ounce) bottle chili sauce
1 (14 ounce) can jellied cranberry sauce
¼ cup packed brown sugar
¼ teaspoon garlic powder
½ teaspoon seasoned salt
3 cups instant brown rice
2 tablespoons butter

☐ Trim pork tenderloin of any fat and place in sprayed 4-quart slow cooker.

☐ Combine chili sauce, cranberry sauce, brown sugar, garlic powder and seasoned salt in saucepan and bring to a boil, stirring constantly and cook just until mixture is blended. Pour over tenderloin.

☐ Cover and cook on HIGH for 4 to 5 hours, reduce to LOW and cook for additional 3 to 4 hours.

☐ Cook brown rice with 2½ cups water as directed on package, adding butter when rice has cooked. Place rice on serving platter, slice pork tenderloin and place on top of rice. Pour sauce over tenderloin or serve on the side. Serves 6 to 8.

If using fresh herbs in a recipe, the general rule is to add the herbs at the end, since long cooking can destroy color and flavor.

ON-THE-BORDER PORK CASSEROLE

2 - 2½ pounds pork tenderloin, cut into 1-inch cubes
1 (10 ounce) package frozen chopped bell peppers and onions, thawed
2 (15 ounce) can black beans, rinsed, drained
1 (10 ounce) can fiesta nacho cheese soup
1 (15 ounce) can Mexican-style stewed tomatoes
1 (16 ounce) jar mild salsa
2 teaspoons ground cumin
½ teaspoon garlic powder
1 (16 ounce) package shredded Mexican Velveeta® cheese, divided
2 cups cooked brown rice

☐ Combine pork cubes, bell peppers and onions, beans, fiesta nacho soup, tomatoes, salsa, cumin, garlic powder and half cheese in sprayed slow cooker.

☐ Cover and cook on LOW for 7 to 9 hours.

☐ Stir in rice, cover and cook for additional 15 minutes or until rice is thoroughly hot. Sprinkle with remaining cheese before serving. Serves 6 to 8.

It is incumbent upon every generation to pay its own debts as it goes. A principle which if acted on would save one-half the wars of the world.

– Thomas Jefferson

GOLDEN SWEET POTATOES AND PORK

4 - 5 medium sweet potatoes, peeled, cut into ½-inch slices
1 (4 pound) pork tenderloin
1 cup packed brown sugar
½ teaspoon cayenne pepper
2 teaspoons seasoned salt
½ teaspoon garlic powder

☐ Place sliced sweet potatoes in sprayed 5-quart slow cooker; place tenderloin on top.

☐ Combine brown sugar, cayenne pepper, seasoned salt and garlic in small bowl and sprinkle over pork and potatoes.

☐ Cover and cook on LOW for 8 to 10 hours. Remove pork from cooker and place on serving platter. Slice pork and spread sweet potatoes around pork. Spoon juices over top. Serves 8.

Everything comes to him who hustles while he waits.

– *Thomas A. Edison*

APPLE-TOPPED TENDERLOIN

1½ cups hickory marinade, divided
1 (3 - 4 pound) pork tenderloin
1 (20 ounce) can apple pie filling
¾ teaspoon ground cinnamon

☐ Combine 1 cup marinade and tenderloin in resealable plastic bag. Marinate in refrigerator for 4 to 8 hours.

☐ Remove tenderloin and discard used marinade.

☐ When ready to cook, preheat oven to 325°.

☐ Cook tenderloin for 1 hour and baste twice with ¼ cup marinade. Let stand for 10 or 15 minutes before slicing.

☐ Combine pie filling, remaining ¼ cup marinade and cinnamon in saucepan and bring to boil. Serve sauce over sliced tenderloin. Serves 6 to 8.

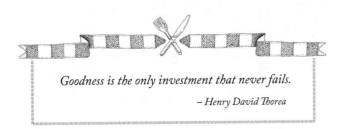

Goodness is the only investment that never fails.

– Henry David Thorea

PORK WITH A CRANBERRY GLAZE

1 (3 - 4 pound) pork shoulder roast
1 (16 ounce) package frozen stew vegetables, thawed
1 (14 ounce) can whole cranberry sauce
¾ cup chili sauce
1 teaspoon dijon-style mustard
2 tablespoons brown sugar

☐ Brown roast on all sides in sprayed skillet over medium heat. Place roast in sprayed slow cooker and top with stew vegetables.

☐ Combine cranberry sauce, chili sauce, mustard and brown sugar in saucepan; heat just enough to blend ingredients. Pour over roast and vegetables.

☐ Cover and cook on LOW for 8 to 9 hours or on HIGH for 4 hours to 4 hours 30 minutes. Transfer roast and vegetables to serving platter and keep warm.

☐ Strain cooking juices and skim off fat. Bring juices to a boil in medium saucepan; reduce heat and simmer uncovered for about 25 minutes or until mixture thickens. Serve sauce with sliced pork roast. Serves 6 to 8.

Let us have faith that right makes might; and in that faith let us to the end dare to do our duty as we understand it.

– Abraham Lincoln

HONEY-B PORK ROAST

1 (3 pound) boneless pork roast
1 (16 ounce) package baby carrots
6 - 8 small onions, halved
½ cup barbecue sauce
½ cup honey
¼ teaspoon ground nutmeg

☐ Place pork roast, carrots and onions in sprayed 4-quart slow cooker.

☐ Combine barbecue sauce, honey, nutmeg and ½ teaspoon pepper in small bowl. Spoon over roast.

☐ Cover and cook on LOW for 8 to 10 hours. Remove roast from cooker and let stand for about 10 to 15 minutes before slicing. Serves 6.

HONEY GOOD SPARERIBS

4 - 4½ pounds baby back pork ribs
1 (16 ounce) jar salsa
⅔ cup honey
2 tablespoons brown sugar
1 teaspoon ground ginger
1 tablespoon cornstarch

☐ Cut ribs into 1-rib portions and place on broiler pan. Broil for about 10 minutes on each side. Place ribs in sprayed slow cooker.

☐ Combine salsa, honey, brown sugar, ginger and cornstarch in bowl and pour over ribs.

☐ Cover and cook on LOW for 6 to 7 hours or on HIGH for 3 hours to 3 hours and 30 minutes. Skim off fat from sauce and serve sauce on side. Serves 6.

Glazed Country Ribs

2 pounds boneless country-style pork loin ribs
1 small onion, sliced, separated into rings
1 teaspoon minced garlic
½ cup chopped bell pepper
⅔ cup orange marmalade
2 tablespoons soy sauce
2 tablespoons cornstarch
½ teaspoon ground ginger

☐ Place ribs, onion and garlic in sprayed 4-quart slow cooker.

☐ Cover and cook on LOW for 8 to 9 hours.

☐ Five minutes before serving, remove ribs from slow cooker and place on serving platter; cover to keep warm.

☐ Combine bell pepper, marmalade, soy sauce, cornstarch and ground ginger in medium saucepan. Stir in ¾ cup juices from slow cooker (discard remaining juices). Cook on high, stirring constantly, until mixture has thickened. Pour sauce over ribs. Serves 6.

Slow cookers depend on cooking with steam. When you take the lid off a slow cooker, you release a lot of heat and it will take about 30 minutes to bring it back to its original cooking temperature.

SWEET AND SPICY RIBS

1 (10 ounce) package frozen chopped bell peppers and onions, thawed
2 teaspoons minced garlic
2 tablespoons canola oil
2 tablespoons tomato paste
1 (6 ounce) can frozen pineapple juice concentrate, thawed
½ cup packed brown sugar
¼ cup plus 2 tablespoons soy sauce, divided
2 tablespoons rice vinegar
¼ teaspoon cayenne pepper
3 pounds baby back pork ribs
1 tablespoon cornstarch

☐ Pulse bell peppers and onions, and garlic in food processor until finely chopped. Heat oil in skillet and cook on medium-high heat for about 5 minutes.

☐ Transfer to bowl and stir in tomato paste, pineapple juice concentrate, brown sugar, ¼ cup soy sauce, rice vinegar and cayenne pepper; mix well

☐ Season ribs with salt and pepper. Arrange in sprayed slow cooker and spoon sauce over top. Cover and cook on LOW for 4 to 6 hours.

☐ Set ribs aside and cover to keep warm. Place liquid from slow cooker in saucepan, skim off fat, and simmer over medium heat until reduced by half.

☐ Whisk cornstarch in remaining soy sauce in bowl and stir into saucepan. Cook until sauce is glossy and thickened. Slice ribs between bones and pour sauce over ribs and toss until well coated. Serves 6.

PARTY RIBS

1 (14 ounce) can beef broth
¼ cup soy sauce
¼ cup honey
⅓ cup maple syrup
⅓ cup barbecue sauce
3 pounds lean baby back pork ribs

☐ Combine broth, soy sauce, honey, maple syrup and barbecue sauce in bowl, mix well.

☐ Place ribs in shallow pan and broil for about 10 minutes to melt excess fat, then place ribs in sprayed 4-quart slow cooker. Sprinkle ribs with a little salt and pepper. Pour broth-honey mixture over ribs.

☐ Cover and cook on LOW for 6 to 8 hours or on HIGH for 3 to 4 hours. Serves 5 to 6.

GROOVY BABY BACKS

3 pounds baby back pork ribs
¾ cup hot-and-spicy ketchup
½ cup teriyaki marinade and sauce
½ cup apricot preserves
⅓ cup packed brown sugar
1 teaspoon minced garlic
¼ teaspoon liquid smoke

☐ Cut ribs between bones, making individual ribs and place in sprayed 4-quart slow cooker.

☐ Combine ketchup, teriyaki marinade, preserves, brown sugar, garlic, liquid smoke and ½ teaspoon salt; mix well and pour over ribs.

☐ Cover and cook on LOW for 6 to 8 hours. Skim fat off ribs. Cooked ribs can be held in slow cooker for 1 to 2 hours. Serves 4 to 6.

GERMAN-STYLE RIBS AND KRAUT

3 - 4 pounds baby back pork ribs or country-style pork ribs, trimmed
3 potatoes, peeled, sliced
1 (32 ounce) jar refrigerated sauerkraut, drained
¼ cup pine nuts, toasted

☐ Brown ribs in sprayed, large heavy pan on all sides. Add 1 cup water.

☐ Bring to a boil, turn down heat and simmer for about 2 hours or until ribs are very tender.

☐ Add potatoes and cook on low heat for 20 minutes. Add sauerkraut and continue cooking until potatoes are done.

☐ Sprinkle pine nuts on ribs and sauerkraut immediately before serving. Serves 4.

BARBECUED SPARERIBS

3 - 4 pounds pork spareribs or country-style pork ribs, trimmed
1 cup hot ketchup or chili sauce
½ cup honey or packed brown sugar
1 teaspoon liquid smoke

☐ Preheat oven to 350°.

☐ Place spareribs on sprayed broiler pan and bake for 1 hour 30 minutes

☐ Combine ketchup, honey or brown sugar and liquid smoke in small saucepan and simmer for 2 to 3 minutes. Baste spareribs generously on both sides with ketchup mixture.

☐ Reduce heat to 300°. Bake for additional 1 hour 30 minutes or until tender and baste generously every 15 to 20 minutes. Serves 4.

ITALIAN SAUSAGE AND RAVIOLI

1 pound sweet Italian pork sausage, casing removed
1 (26 ounce) jar extra chunky mushroom and green pepper spaghetti sauce
1 (24 ounce) package frozen cheese-filled ravioli, cooked, drained
Grated parmesan cheese

☐ Cook sausage according to package directions in roasting pan over medium heat or until brown and no longer pink; stir to separate meat.

☐ Stir in spaghetti sauce. Heat to boiling. Add ravioli, heat through and stir occasionally.

☐ Pour into serving dish and sprinkle with parmesan cheese. Serves 8.

PORK-STUFFED EGGPLANT

1 large eggplant
¾ pound ground pork
½ pound pork sausage
1 egg
½ cup breadcrumbs
½ cup grated romano cheese
1 tablespoon dried parsley flakes
1 tablespoon dried onion flakes
1 teaspoon dried oregano
1 (15 ounce) can stewed tomatoes
1 (8 ounce) can tomato sauce

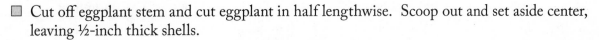

☐ Preheat oven to 350°.

☐ Cut off eggplant stem and cut eggplant in half lengthwise. Scoop out and set aside center, leaving ½-inch thick shells.

☐ Steam shell halves for about 5 minutes or just until tender. Drain well.

☐ Cube set aside eggplant and cook in saucepan with boiling salted water for about 6 minutes; drain well.

☐ Cook ground pork and sausage in skillet over medium heat until no longer pink and drain.

☐ In large bowl combine pork and sausage with eggplant cubes, egg, breadcrumbs, cheese, parsley flakes, onion flakes, oregano, and ½ teaspoon each of salt and pepper; mix well.

☐ Fill eggplant shells and place in sprayed 7 x 11-inch baking dish. Combine stewed tomatoes and tomato sauce and pour over eggplant.

☐ Cover and bake for 30 minutes. Serves 4 to 6.

ZESTY ZITI

1 (16 ounce) package ziti pasta
1 pound Italian sausage links, cut into ½-inch pieces
1 onion, coarsely chopped
1 green bell pepper, seeded, sliced
Canola oil
1 (15 ounce) can diced tomatoes
1 (15 ounce) can Italian stewed tomatoes
2 tablespoons ketchup
1 cup shredded mozzarella cheese

☐ Cook ziti according to package directions and drain.

☐ Preheat oven to 350°.

☐ Cook sausage, onion and bell pepper in a little oil in large skillet over medium heat and drain.

☐ Add diced tomatoes, stewed tomatoes and ketchup and mix well. Stir in pasta and cheese.

☐ Spoon into sprayed 3-quart baking dish. Cover and bake for 20 minutes. Serves 6.

It's easier to cook vegetables in the microwave than it is to wait for water to boil. Cook soft vegetables, such as peas, spinach and mushrooms, in microwave for 30 seconds to 1 minute with plastic wrap over vegetables, sealed but vented. Cook firm vegetables, such as potatoes, carrots and broccoli stems, in microwave for 2 to 3 minutes on high instead of steaming.

PEPPERONI TWIRLS

2 cups tomato-spinach macaroni twirls (rotini)
1 pound bulk Italian sausage
1 onion, chopped
1 green bell pepper, seeded, chopped
1 (15 ounce) can pizza sauce
1 (8 ounce) can tomato sauce
⅓ cup milk
1 (3 ounce) package sliced pepperoni, halved
1 (4 ounce) jar sliced mushrooms, drained
1 (2 ounce) can sliced ripe olives, drained
1 (8 ounce) package shredded mozzarella cheese, divided

☐ Preheat oven to 350°.

☐ Cook macaroni twirls according to package directions and drain.

☐ Cook sausage, onion and bell pepper in skillet over medium heat until sausage is no longer pink and drain.

☐ Combine pizza sauce, tomato sauce and milk in large bowl. Stir in sausage mixture, macaroni twirls, pepperoni, mushrooms, olives and half cheese and mix well.

☐ Spoon into sprayed 9 x 13-inch baking dish. Cover and bake for 30 minutes.

☐ Sprinkle remaining cheese over top of casserole and bake uncovered for 5 to 10 minutes or just until cheese melts. Serves 6 to 8.

CRANBERRY SAUCE EXTRA

This is great with any pork dish.

1 (14 ounce) carton strawberry glaze
1 (12 ounce) package frozen cranberries
½ cup orange juice
¼ cup sugar

☐ Combine glaze, cranberries, juice and sugar in saucepan. Heat to a boil and stir constantly.

☐ Reduce heat and simmer for 10 minutes or until cranberries pop; stir often.

☐ Refrigerate for several hours before serving. Serve with pork or ham. Makes 1½ pints.

SEAFOOD DISHES

**Fresh seafood is
a treat anytime.**

SEAFOOD DISHES CONTENTS

ROUGHY FLORENTINE

6 tablespoons butter, divided
2 (10 ounce) packages frozen spinach, thawed, drained
⅛ teaspoon ground nutmeg
2 pounds orange roughy fillets
⅓ cup minced onion
1 (1 ounce) packet cream of spinach soup mix
1 (16 ounce) carton half-and half-cream
2 cups shredded Swiss cheese

☐ Preheat oven to 350°.

☐ Heat 3 tablespoons butter in large skillet and cook spinach for about 2 minutes. Season with nutmeg and ½ teaspoon each of salt and pepper.

☐ Spread spinach in sprayed 9 x 13-inch baking dish.

☐ Lay orange roughy over spinach.

☐ Heat remaining butter in saucepan and saute onion. Add soup mix, half-and-half cream and cheese and mix well. Heat just until cheese melts.

☐ Pour sauce over fillets and spinach.

☐ Cover and bake for 20 to 25 minutes or until fillets flake easily and sauce is bubbly. Serves 6.

CREAMY ORANGE ROUGHY

½ cup (1 stick) butter, divided
1 red bell pepper, seeded, chopped
1 onion, chopped
¼ cup flour
1 teaspoon dried basil
1 (16 ounce) carton half-and-half cream
1 (3 ounce) package grated parmesan cheese
1 tablespoon marinade for chicken
1½ pounds orange roughy fillets
3 eggs, hard-boiled, sliced
1½ cups round buttery cracker crumbs

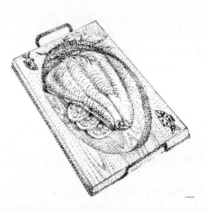

☐ Preheat oven to 350°.

☐ Melt half butter in skillet and saute bell pepper and onion.

☐ Add flour, basil, and ½ teaspoon each of salt and pepper to skillet and cook on medium heat for about 2 minutes. Slowly add half-and-half cream, stirring constantly, until mixture thickens.

☐ Stir in parmesan cheese and marinade for chicken.

☐ In separate skillet, melt 2 tablespoons butter and quickly brown orange roughy fillets. Transfer to sprayed 9 x 13-inch baking dish and place egg slices over fish.

☐ Pour cream sauce over eggs and fillets.

☐ Bake for 15 minutes.

☐ Melt remaining butter and combine with cracker crumbs in bowl.

☐ Sprinkle crumbs over casserole and bake for additional 10 to 15 minutes or until crumbs are light brown. Serves 6.

TIP: You may substitute any white fish for the orange roughy.

SPICY CATFISH AMANDINE

¼ cup (½ stick) butter, melted
3 tablespoons lemon juice
6 - 8 catfish fillets
1½ teaspoons Creole seasoning
½ cup sliced almonds

☐ Preheat oven to 375°.

☐ Combine butter and lemon juice and dip each fillet in butter mixture. Arrange in sprayed 9 x 13-inch baking dish. Sprinkle fish with Creole seasoning.

☐ Bake for 20 to 25 minutes or until fish flakes easily with fork. Sprinkle almonds over fish for last 5 minutes of baking. Serves 6 to 8.

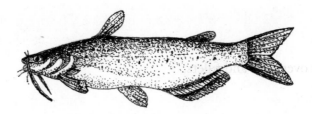

FRIED HADDOCK FILLETS

1½ cups lemon-lime soda
1 pound haddock fillets
2 cups biscuit mix
Olive oil

☐ Pour soda in shallow bowl, add fillets and marinate for 15 minutes.

☐ In separate shallow bowl, place biscuit mix. Remove fish from soda and coat with biscuit mix.

☐ Heat about ¼-inch oil in large skillet. Fry fish about 3 minutes on each side or until fish is golden and flakes with fork. Drain on paper towels. Serve 6.

BAKED HALIBUT SUPREME

2 (1 inch thick) halibut steaks
1 (8 ounce) carton sour cream
½ cup grated parmesan cheese
¾ teaspoon dill weed

☐ Preheat oven to 325°.

☐ Place halibut in sprayed 9 x 13-inch baking dish.

☐ Combine sour cream, parmesan cheese and dill weed. Spoon over halibut. Cover and bake for about 20 minutes.

☐ Uncover and bake for additional 10 minutes or until fish flakes easily with fork. Serves 2 to 4.

LEMON-BAKED FISH

1 pound sole or halibut fillets
¼ cup (½ stick) butter, melted, divided
2 teaspoons Italian seasoning
2 tablespoons lemon juice

☐ Preheat oven to 375°.

☐ Place fish fillets in sprayed, shallow pan. Sprinkle with 1 teaspoon butter and seasoning. Bake for 8 to 10 minutes.

☐ Turn and bake for additional 6 minutes or until fish flakes.

☐ Combine remaining butter with seasoning and lemon juice. Serve over warm fish fillets. Serves 2 to 4.

CRISPY FLOUNDER

⅓ cup mayonnaise
1 pound flounder fillets
1 cup seasoned breadcrumbs
¼ cup grated parmesan cheese

☐ Preheat oven to 375°.

☐ Place mayonnaise in small dish. Coat fish with mayonnaise and dip in breadcrumbs to coat well.

☐ Arrange in sprayed 9 x 13-inch baking dish and cover with parmesan cheese. Bake for 25 minutes. Serves 2 to 4.

ALFREDO SALMON AND NOODLES

3 cups uncooked medium egg noodles
1 (16 ounce) package frozen broccoli florets, thawed
1 cup prepared alfredo sauce
1 (15 ounce) can salmon, drained, boned, flaked

☐ In large saucepan, cook noodles according to package directions and add broccoli last 5 minutes of cooking. (Discard some of broccoli stems.) Drain well.

☐ Stir in alfredo sauce and salmon and cook on low heat, stirring occasionally, until mixture heats thoroughly. Spoon into serving bowl. Serves 4.

SCRUMPTIOUS SALMON BITES

1 (15 ounce) can pink salmon with liquid
1 egg
½ cup cracker crumbs
1 teaspoon baking powder

☐ Drain liquid from salmon into small bowl and set aside. Remove any bones and skin from salmon.

☐ Stir in egg and cracker crumbs with salmon in bowl.

☐ In separate bowl, combine baking powder with ¼ cup salmon liquid. Mixture will foam. After foaming, add to salmon mixture.

☐ Drop teaspoonfuls of mixture on hot greased skillet. Brown lightly on both sides. Sprinkle with a little salt and serve hot. Serves 4.

SALMON CASSEROLE

6 ounces dried egg noodles
1 (10 ounce) can cream of celery soup
1 (5 ounce) can evaporated milk
1 tablespoon lemon juice
½ onion, chopped
1 (15 ounce) can salmon, skinned, boned
1 cup shredded cheddar cheese
1 (8 ounce) can small green peas, drained
1 teaspoon Creole seasoning
1 cup crushed cheese crackers
2 tablespoons butter, melted

☐ Preheat oven to 350°.

☐ Cook noodles according to package directions and drain.

☐ Stir in soup, evaporated milk, lemon juice, onion, salmon, cheese, peas, Creole seasoning and 1 teaspoon salt.

☐ Spoon into sprayed 7 x 11-inch baking dish.

☐ Cover and bake for 25 minutes.

☐ Combine cheese crackers and butter in bowl and sprinkle over casserole. Bake uncovered for 10 minutes or until crumbs are light brown. Serves 4.

NO-NOODLE TUNA CASSEROLE

1 (8 ounce) tube refrigerated crescent rolls
1 cup shredded white cheddar cheese
1 (10 ounce) box frozen chopped broccoli, thawed, drained
4 eggs, beaten
1 (2 ounce) packet cream of broccoli soup mix
1 (8 ounce) carton sour cream
1 cup milk
½ cup mayonnaise
2 tablespoons dried onion flakes
½ teaspoon dill weed
2 (6 ounce) cans white meat tuna, drained
1 (2 ounce) jar diced pimentos, drained

☐ Preheat oven to 350°.

☐ Unroll crescent dough into 1 long rectangle and place in 9 x 13-inch baking dish. Seal seams and press onto bottom and ½ inch up sides.

☐ Sprinkle with cheese and chopped broccoli.

☐ Combine eggs, broccoli soup mix, sour cream, milk, mayonnaise, onion flakes and dill weed in bowl and mix well.

☐ Stir in tuna and pimentos. Pour over broccoli-cheese in baking dish.

☐ Cover and bake for 40 minutes or until knife inserted in center comes out clean. Cut in squares to serve. Serves 6 to 8.

TUNA-IN-THE-STRAW

1 (8 ounce) package egg noodles
2 (10 ounce) cans cream of chicken soup
1 (8 ounce) carton sour cream
1 teaspoon Creole seasoning
½ cup milk
2 (6 ounce) cans white meat tuna, drained
1 cup shredded Velveeta® cheese
1 (10 ounce) package green peas, thawed
1 (2 ounce) jar diced pimento
1 (2 ounce) can shoe-string potatoes

☐ Preheat oven to 350°.

☐ Cook noodles according to package directions and drain.

☐ Combine soup, sour cream, Creole seasoning and milk in bowl and mix well.

☐ Add noodles, tuna, cheese, peas and pimento.

☐ Pour into sprayed 9 x 13-inch baking dish. Sprinkle top with shoe-string potatoes.

☐ Bake for about 35 minutes or until shoe-string potatoes are light brown. Serves 6 to 8.

Os Guinness wrote in his book A Time For Truth *that "in a postmodern world, the question is no longer 'Is it true?' but rather 'Whose truth is it?' and 'Which power stands to gain?'*

HOT TUNA MELTS

1 (10 ounce) can refrigerated buttermilk biscuits
1 (12 ounce) can chunk light tuna packed in water, drained
¾ cup chopped celery
½ cup sweet pickle relish
½ cup mayonnaise
4 slices Swiss cheese

☐ Preheat oven to 350°.

☐ Bake biscuits according to package directions and cool slightly. Split biscuits and arrange cut-side up on same baking pan.

☐ In large bowl, combine tuna, celery, pickle relish and mayonnaise. Divide tuna mixture among split biscuits and place half slice cheese over top of tuna.

☐ Bake for 6 to 7 minutes or until filling is hot and cheese melts. Serves 4 to 6.

TUNA TEXAS TOAST

1 (10 ounce) can cream of chicken soup
1 (6 ounce) can tuna in water, drained
2 slices thick Texas toast
1 tomato, cubed

☐ Combine soup and tuna in saucepan over medium heat. Stir to break up chunks of tuna and heat thoroughly.

☐ Brown Texas toast on both sides. Pour soup mixture over toast.

☐ Sprinkle tomatoes and a little salt and pepper over soup mixture. Serve immediately. Serves 2.

CRESCENT TUNA BAKE

1 (8 ounce) package crescent rolls, divided
1 (6 ounce) can solid white tuna in water, drained, flaked
1 (15 ounce) can cut asparagus, drained
1 cup shredded cheddar cheese

☐ Preheat oven to 375°.

☐ Form 7-inch square using 4 crescent rolls. Pinch edges together to seal. Place in sprayed 8-inch square baking pan.

☐ Layer tuna, asparagus and cheese on top of dough. Form remaining 4 crescent rolls into 1 square. Place on top of cheese.

☐ Bake for about 20 minutes or until top is golden brown and cheese bubbles. Serves 6.

The next best thing to your own garden is a farmers' market. Find one near you and also look for farms where you can pick your own produce. Not only will kids like picking their own foods, but you'll save money and improve the quality of food you put on the table.

TUNA-TOMATO BOWL

2 tablespoons olive oil
1 teaspoon minced garlic
¼ teaspoon cayenne pepper
2 teaspoons dried basil
1 (15 ounce) can stewed tomatoes
1 (12 ounce) can water-packed tuna, drained
¾ cup sliced pitted green olives
¼ cup drained capers
1 cup favorite pasta, cooked

☐ Heat olive oil in saucepan and add garlic, cayenne pepper and basil; cook on low heat for 2 minutes.

☐ Add tomatoes and bring to a boil, reduce heat and simmer for 20 minutes.

☐ Combine tuna, olives, capers, pasta and a little salt in bowl. Stir in tomato sauce and toss. Serve immediately. Serves 4.

Instead of using salmon for salmon croquettes, try canned tuna or canned mackerel.

TUNA CASSEROLE

1 (7 ounce) package elbow macaroni
1 (8 ounce) package shredded Velveeta® cheese
2 (6 ounce) cans tuna, drained
1 (10 ounce) can cream of celery soup
1 cup milk

☐ Preheat oven to 350°.

☐ Cook macaroni according to package directions. Drain well, add cheese and stir until cheese melts.

☐ Add tuna, soup and milk and continue stirring.

☐ Spoon into sprayed 7 x 11-inch baking dish. Cover and bake 35 minutes or until bubbly. Serves 4.

TUNA-STUFFED TOMATOES

4 large tomatoes
2 (6 ounce) cans white meat tuna, drained
2 cups chopped celery
½ cup chopped cashews
1 small zucchini with peel, chopped
½ - ⅔ cup mayonnaise

☐ Cut thin slice off top of each tomato, scoop out pulp and discard. Turn tomatoes over on paper towels to drain.

☐ Combine tuna, celery, cashews and zucchini and mix well. Add ½ cup mayonnaise; add more if needed.

☐ Spoon into hollowed tomatoes and refrigerate. Serves 4.

FETTUCCINI OF THE SEA

¼ cup (½ stick) butter
¼ cup flour
1 teaspoon Creole seasoning
1 tablespoon minced garlic
1 (16 ounce) carton half-and-half cream
½ cup milk
½ cup red bell pepper, seeded, finely chopped
2 (6 ounce) cans tiny shrimp, picked, veined
2 (6 ounce) cans crabmeat, drained, flaked
1 (6 ounce) can chopped clams, drained
½ cup grated parmesan cheese
1 (12 ounce) package fettuccini, cooked al dente

☐ Preheat oven to 325°.

☐ Melt butter in saucepan and add flour, Creole seasoning, ¾ teaspoon pepper and garlic. Cook over medium heat and mix well.

☐ Gradually add half-and-half cream and milk and mix well. Cook, stirring constantly, until it thickens.

☐ Add bell pepper, shrimp, crabmeat, clams and parmesan cheese and heat thoroughly.

☐ Spoon half fettuccini in sprayed 9 x 13-inch baking dish and cover with half seafood sauce. Repeat layers.

☐ Cover and bake for 25 minutes or just until casserole bubbles. Serves 6 to 8.

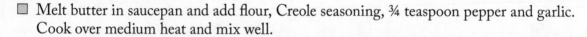

NEPTUNE LASAGNA

3 tablespoons butter
1 red bell pepper, seeded, chopped
1 onion, chopped
1 (8 ounce) package cream cheese, softened
1 (12 ounce) carton small curd cottage cheese
1 egg, beaten
2 teaspoons Creole seasoning
1 (10 ounce) can cream of shrimp soup
1 (10 ounce) can cream of celery soup
2 teaspoons dried basil
½ cup white wine
¾ cup milk
2 (8 ounce) packages imitation crabmeat
2 (6 ounce) packages small shrimp, rinsed, drained
9 lasagna noodles, cooked, drained
1 (3 ounce) package grated parmesan cheese
1 cup shredded white cheddar cheese

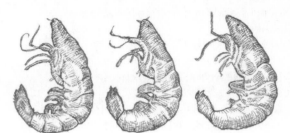

☐ Preheat oven to 350°.

☐ Heat butter in skillet and saute bell pepper and onion. Reduce heat and add cream cheese and stir until cream cheese melts. Remove from heat and add cottage cheese, egg, ½ teaspoon pepper and Creole seasoning.

☐ In bowl combine soups, basil, white wine, milk, crabmeat and shrimp; mix well.

☐ Arrange 3 noodles in sprayed 9 x 13-inch baking dish. Spread with one-third cottage cheese mixture and one-third seafood mixture. Repeat layers twice. Sprinkle with parmesan cheese.

☐ Cover and bake for about 40 minutes.

☐ Sprinkle with white cheddar cheese and bake uncovered for additional 10 minutes or until casserole bubbles. Let stand for about 10 minutes before serving. Serves 6 to 8.

SEAFOOD LASAGNA

2 tablespoons butter
1 onion, chopped
1 (8 ounce) package cream cheese, softened
1 (15 ounce) carton ricotta cheese
1 (4 ounce) jar diced pimentos, drained
1 egg, beaten
2 teaspoons dried basil
1 (10 ounce) can cream of shrimp soup
1 (10 ounce) can fiesta nacho cheese soup
½ cup milk
1 pound small, cooked shrimp, peeled, veined
2 (6 ounce) cans crabmeat, drained, flaked
8 lasagna noodles, cooked
1 cup shredded cheddar cheese

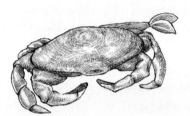

☐ Preheat oven to 350°.

☐ Melt butter in large saucepan and saute onion until tender. Stir in cream cheese, ricotta cheese, pimentos, egg, basil and a little salt.

☐ In separate saucepan, combine soups and milk; heat just to mix well. Add shrimp and crabmeat.

☐ Layer four noodles in sprayed 9 x 13-inch baking dish.

☐ Spread half of cheese-pimento mixture over noodles and top with half seafood mixture. Repeat layers with remaining four noodles, cheese-pimento mixture, then seafood mixture.

☐ Cover and bake for 45 minutes.

☐ Top with cheddar cheese and bake uncovered for additional 3 to 4 minutes. Serves 6 to 8.

SEAFOOD ROYALE

1 cup rice
2 (10 ounce) cans cream of shrimp soup
1 cup milk
⅔ cup mayonnaise
2 pounds small cooked, peeled shrimp
1 (6 ounce) can crabmeat, drained, flaked
1 onion, chopped
2 cups chopped celery
¼ cup snipped parsley
1 (8 ounce) can sliced water chestnuts, drained
1 teaspoon Creole seasoning
½ cup slivered almonds

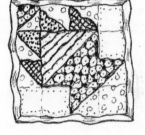

☐ Preheat oven to 325°.

☐ Cook rice according to package directions.

☐ Combine soup, milk and mayonnaise in bowl and mix well.

☐ Add shrimp, crabmeat, onion, celery, parsley, water chestnuts, Creole seasoning, and ½ teaspoon each of salt and pepper.

☐ Fold in rice and mix well.

☐ Pour into sprayed 3-quart baking dish and sprinkle almonds over top.

☐ Cover and bake for 25 minutes, uncover and bake for additional 10 minutes. Serves 6 to 8.

SEAFOOD IMPERIAL

10 slices white bread, crust removed, cubed, divided
1 (16 ounce) package imitation crabmeat
2 (6 ounce) cans tiny shrimp, drained, veined
1 cup mayonnaise
1 cup chopped celery, chopped
1 red bell pepper, seeded, chopped
1 teaspoon dried parsley flakes
1 teaspoon lemon juice
5 eggs, beaten
3½ cups milk, divided
1 (10 ounce) can cream of mushroom soup
¾ cup grated parmesan cheese

☐ Place half bread cubes in sprayed 10 x 15-inch baking dish.

☐ Combine crabmeat, shrimp, mayonnaise, celery, bell pepper, parsley flakes, lemon juice and ½ teaspoon pepper in bowl.

☐ Spread seafood mixture over bread cubes. Sprinkle remaining bread cubes over seafood mixture.

☐ Combine eggs and 3 cups milk in bowl and beat well. Slowly pour eggs and milk over bread cubes.

☐ Cover and refrigerate for 4 to 5 hours or overnight.

☐ When ready to bake, preheat oven to 325°. Bake for 1 hour.

☐ Combine mushroom soup, ½ cup milk and parmesan cheese in saucepan and heat just to mix well. Pour soup mixture over casserole.

☐ Increase oven to 400° and bake for 10 minutes. Serves 8 to 10.

NO ORDINARY SHRIMP

½ cup chopped onion
1 red bell pepper, seeded, thinly sliced
5 tablespoons butter, divided
2 tablespoons flour
¾ cup half-and-half cream
1 teaspoon marinade for chicken
3 cups cooked, peeled, veined shrimp
2 cups cooked rice
¾ cup shredded cheddar cheese
¾ cup round buttery cracker crumbs

☐ Preheat oven to 350°.

☐ Saute onion and bell pepper in 3 tablespoons butter in skillet, but do not brown.

☐ Blend in flour and ½ teaspoon each of salt and pepper; heat and mix well.

☐ Gradually add half-and-half cream and marinade for chicken over medium heat and stir until it thickens. Fold in shrimp.

☐ Place cooked rice in sprayed 7 x 11-inch baking dish and spread out. Pour shrimp mixture over rice.

☐ Sprinkle cheese over top and combine cracker crumbs and remaining butter in bowl. Sprinkle over casserole.

☐ Bake for about 20 to 25 minutes or until crumbs are light brown. Serves 4 to 6.

SHRIMP DELIGHT

1½ pounds raw shrimp
Shrimp boil
1 onion, chopped
1 red bell pepper, seeded, chopped
1 green bell pepper, seeded, chopped
1 teaspoon minced garlic
2 tablespoons butter
1 (10 ounce) can cream of shrimp soup
1 (10 ounce) can cream of celery soup
2 cups cooked rice
1 teaspoon Creole seasoning
1 cup crushed potato chips

☐ Preheat oven to 350°.

☐ Cook shrimp in shrimp boil according to package directions. Cool, peel and vein.

☐ Saute onion, bell peppers and garlic with butter in large skillet.

☐ In large bowl combine shrimp, onion-pepper mixture, soups, rice, ¾ teaspoon pepper and Creole seasoning; mix well.

☐ Spoon into sprayed 9 x 13-inch baking dish and sprinkle with potato chips. Bake for 30 minutes. Serves 6 to 8.

SHRIMP AND ARTICHOKES

1 onion, chopped
1 cup diagonally chopped celery
1 teaspoon minced garlic
2 red bell peppers, seeded, thinly sliced
1 green bell pepper, seeded, thinly sliced
½ cup (1 stick) butter
3 pounds shrimp, cooked, peeled, veined
3½ cups cooked rice
½ cup tomato sauce
1 (8 ounce) carton whipping cream
¼ teaspoon cayenne pepper
1 teaspoon Creole seasoning
2 (14 ounce) cans artichoke hearts, drained, halved
1 (8 ounce) package shredded cheddar cheese

☐ Preheat oven to 350°.

☐ Saute onion, celery, garlic and bell peppers in butter in large skillet, but be careful not to brown.

☐ Add cooked shrimp, rice, tomato sauce, cream, cayenne pepper and Creole seasoning and mix well. Fold in artichoke hearts.

☐ Spoon into sprayed 10 x 15-inch baking dish. Cover and bake for 20 minutes.

☐ Sprinkle cheese over top and bake uncovered for additional 10 minutes. Serves 8 to 10.

SAVORY SHRIMP FETTUCCINI

2 tablespoons butter
⅓ cup chopped onion
1 teaspoon seafood seasoning
½ pound small shrimp, peeled, veined
1 (10 ounce) can cream of shrimp soup
½ cup half-and-half cream
½ cup mayonnaise
2 teaspoons marinade for chicken
½ teaspoon horseradish
1 cup shredded white cheddar cheese, divided
2 cups cooked fettuccini
1 (16 ounce) package frozen broccoli florets, cooked

☐ Preheat oven to 350°.

☐ Melt butter in large saucepan and saute onion. Add seasoning and shrimp. Cook while stirring until shrimp turns pink, about 2 minutes.

☐ Add soup, half-and-half cream, mayonnaise, marinade for chicken, horseradish and half cheese. Heat just until cheese melts.

☐ Fold in fettuccini and broccoli (cut some broccoli stems away and discard).

☐ Spoon into sprayed 3-quart baking dish.

☐ Cover and bake for 30 minutes. Sprinkle remaining cheese on top. Bake uncovered for additional 5 minutes. Serves 6.

EASY SHRIMP NEWBURG

2 (10 ounce) cans cream of shrimp soup
1 teaspoon seafood seasoning
1 (1 pound) frozen cooked salad shrimp, thawed
Hot cooked rice

☐ Combine soup, ¼ cup water and seafood seasoning in saucepan. Bring to a boil, reduce heat and cook for 3 minutes.

☐ Stir in shrimp. Heat thoroughly and serve over rice. Serves 4.

SHRIMP AND CHICKEN CURRY

2 (10 ounce) cans cream of chicken soup
⅓ cup milk
1½ teaspoons curry powder
1 (12 ounce) can chicken breast, drained
2 (6 ounce) cans shrimp, drained
Hot cooked rice

☐ In saucepan, heat soup, milk and curry powder. Stir in chicken pieces and shrimp. Cook, stirring constantly, until mixture heats thoroughly.

☐ Serve over rice. Serves 4.

SHRIMP AND RICE CASSEROLE

2 cups instant rice
1½ pounds frozen cooked shrimp
1 (10 ounce) jar alfredo sauce
1 (4 ounce) can diced pimentos, drained
4 fresh green onions with tops, chopped
1 (8 ounce) package shredded cheddar cheese, divided

☐ Cook rice according to package directions and place in sprayed 9 x 13-inch baking dish.

☐ Thaw shrimp in colander under cold running water, drain well and remove tails.

☐ In saucepan on medium heat, combine alfredo sauce, pimentos and green onions. Stir in shrimp and spoon mixture over rice.

☐ Cover with half cheese and bake about 15 minutes.

☐ Sprinkle remaining cheese on top and bake uncovered for 5 minutes. Serves 4 to 6.

TIP: Thawing shrimp under running water is better than thawing in refrigerator.

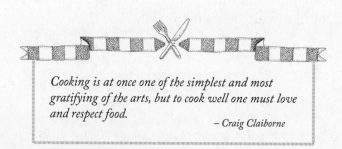

> *Cooking is at once one of the simplest and most gratifying of the arts, but to cook well one must love and respect food.*
>
> *– Craig Claiborne*

SKILLET SHRIMP MAGIC

2 teaspoons olive oil
2 pounds shrimp, peeled, veined
⅔ cup herb-garlic marinade with lemon juice
¼ cup finely chopped green onions with tops

☐ Heat oil in large non-stick skillet. Add shrimp and marinade.

☐ Cook, stirring often, until shrimp turn pink. Stir in green onions. Serves 4.

TIP: Serve as is or over rice or your favorite pasta.

BROILED LEMON-GARLIC SHRIMP

1 pound shrimp, peeled, veined
½ teaspoon garlic salt
2 tablespoons lemon juice
2 tablespoons butter, melted

☐ Place shrimp in resealable plastic bag.

☐ Combine garlic salt, lemon juice and butter; mix well. Pour over shrimp and marinate in refrigerator for 20 minutes.

☐ Preheat broiler.

☐ Pour onto baking dish. Broil on 1 side for 3 minutes. Turn and broil for additional 3 minutes. Serves 2.

TIP: If shrimp are large, split them down middle and spread them out like a butterfly before seasoning.

SUPER CRAB-POTATO SALAD

5 potatoes, peeled, cubed
2 (8 ounce) packages imitation crabmeat, chopped
1 cup finely chopped onion
2 cups mayonnaise

☐ Place potatoes in saucepan covered with water, bring to a boil and cook for about 20 minutes or until tender. Drain and cool.

☐ Combine potatoes, crabmeat and onion in large bowl. Toss with mayonnaise. Season to taste with salt and pepper.

☐ Refrigerate for about 3 hours before serving. Serves 4 to 6.

NO-PANIC CRAB CASSEROLE

1 (16 ounce) package imitation crabmeat, flaked
1 cup half-and-half cream
1½ cups mayonnaise
6 eggs, hard-boiled, finely chopped
1 cup seasoned breadcrumbs, divided
1 tablespoon dried parsley flakes
2 tablespoons butter, melted

☐ Preheat oven to 350°.

☐ Combine crabmeat, half-and-half cream, mayonnaise, hard-boiled eggs, ½ cup breadcrumbs, parsley and a little salt and mix well.

☐ Pour into sprayed 2-quart baking dish. Combine remaining breadcrumbs and butter and sprinkle over top of casserole. Bake uncovered for 40 minutes. Serves 6.

CRAB-STUFFED BAKED POTATOES

If you have been looking for a baked potato that is truly a meal in itself, this is it!

4 large baking potatoes
½ cup (1 stick) butter
½ cup whipping cream
1 bunch fresh green onions, chopped
2 (6 ounce) cans crabmeat, drained, flaked
¾ cup shredded cheddar cheese
2 tablespoons fresh minced parsley

☐ Preheat oven to 375°.

☐ Bake potatoes for 1 hour or until well done. Half each potato lengthwise and scoop out flesh but leave skins intact.

☐ Mash potatoes with butter in large bowl. Add whipping cream, green onions, ¾ teaspoon salt and ½ teaspoon pepper. Stir in crabmeat.

☐ Fill potato skins with potato mixture. Sprinkle with cheese.

☐ Bake at 350° for about 15 minutes.

☐ Sprinkle with fresh parsley. Serves 4.

CRABMEAT SPECIAL

½ cup chopped celery
1 cup chopped onion
½ cup chopped red bell pepper
¼ cup (½ stick) butter
2 tablespoons flour
1 (16 ounce) carton half-and-half cream
1 egg, beaten
2½ teaspoons Cajun seasoning
1 cup cooked rice
1 pound fresh crabmeat, flaked, shredded
1 cup shredded cheddar cheese

☐ Preheat oven to 325°.

☐ Saute celery, onion and bell pepper with butter in skillet, but do not brown. Blend in flour over low heat.

☐ Combine half-and-half cream, egg, Cajun seasoning, ½ teaspoon salt and ¼ teaspoon pepper in bowl. Gradually add to veggies in skillet and cook on medium heat, stirring constantly, until mixture thickens, about 5 minutes.

☐ Fold in rice and crabmeat and blend well. Spoon into sprayed 2-quart baking dish.

☐ Cover and bake for 20 minutes or until it bubbles. Sprinkle cheese over top and bake uncovered for about 5 minutes, just until cheese melts. Serves 6.

GEORGIA OYSTER CASSEROLE

3 whole green onions, chopped
1 cup chopped green bell pepper
½ cup (1 stick) butter, divided
1½ cups sliced fresh mushrooms
2 pints oysters, drained
¼ cup flour
1 (8 ounce) carton whipping cream
1 (3 ounce) package grated parmesan cheese
¾ cup seasoned breadcrumbs

☐ Saute green onions and bell pepper in 2 tablespoons butter in large skillet until tender.

☐ Add mushrooms and oysters and saute for 5 minutes.

☐ Melt 2 tablespoons butter in saucepan over medium-low heat. Add flour and stir well. Slowly add cream, stirring constantly, until sauce thickens.

☐ Fold in cheese, mix well and pour cheese sauce into oyster mixture. Season with ½ teaspoon each of salt and pepper. Simmer for 3 to 5 minutes.

☐ Spoon mixture into sprayed 9 x 13-inch baking dish. Sprinkle breadcrumbs over top and dot with remaining ¼ cup butter. Place under broiler and brown until casserole bubbles. Watch closely. Serves 6 to 8.

From morning till night, sounds drift from the kitchen, most of them familiar and comforting... On days when warmth is the most important need of the human heart, the kitchen is the place you can find it...

– E. B. White

CORN-OYSTER CASSEROLE

It tastes "hard to make", but it's easy.

1 quart oysters, drained, quartered
2 (15 ounce) cans cream-style corn
½ cup evaporated milk
⅛ teaspoon Tabasco sauce
3 cups crumbled saltine crackers
1 cup butter, melted

☐ Preheat oven at 350°.

☐ In a bowl mix oysters with corn, milk, 1 teaspoon salt, ½ teaspoon pepper and Tabasco.

☐ Add crackers to melted butter and put in a sprayed baking dish. Top with oyster mixture.

☐ Bake for 40 minutes. Serves 6 to 8.

Family meals reduce the risk of obesity and substance abuse. Family meals are more nutritious than fast food. You can control the foods and portions as well as use less fat, less salt, less sugar and fewer calories.

SCALLOPED OYSTERS

1⅓ cups breadcrumbs, divided
1 tablespoon butter, divided
24 oysters, divided
½ cup oyster liquor
½ cup milk

- ☐ Preheat oven to 350°.

- ☐ Spread bottom of sprayed baking dish with ⅓ cup crumbs. Layer with 8 oysters. Sprinkle with salt and pepper. Dot with 1 teaspoon butter.

- ☐ Repeat layers twice. Top with remaining ⅓ cup crumbs.

- ☐ Mix oyster liquor and milk and pour over casserole.

- ☐ Bake for 30 minutes. Serves 6.

TIP: Serve with crumbled crisp bacon.

It's amazing how quickly the kids learn to drive a car, yet are unable to understand the lawn mower, snow blower or vacuum cleaner.
— Ben Bergor

FETTUCCINI A LA SHRIMP

1 (12 ounce) package fettuccini
3 bell peppers, seeded, chopped
3 onions, chopped
6 ribs celery, chopped
1½ cups (3 sticks) butter
1 (8 - 10 ounce) package frozen shrimp, thawed, drained
2 tablespoons snipped parsley
4 - 5 cloves garlic, minced
1 (16 ounce) carton half-and-half cream
½ cup flour
1 (16 ounce) package cubed jalapeno cheese

☐ Preheat oven to 300°.

☐ Cook fettuccini according to package directions. Drain.

☐ Saute bell peppers, onions and celery in butter in skillet.

☐ Add shrimp, simmer for 8 to 10 minutes and stir occasionally.

☐ Add parsley, garlic, and half-and-half cream and mix well. Gradually stir in flour and mix well. Simmer for 30 minutes and stir occasionally.

☐ Add cheese and continue to stir until it melts and blends. Mix fettuccini with sauce.

☐ Pour into sprayed 4-quart baking dish. Bake for 15 to 20 minutes or until it is hot. Serves 8.

CAKES, COOKIES, PIES & DESSERTS

**We always remember
the sweets.**

CAKES, COOKIES, PIES & DESSERTS CONTENTS

CAKES, COOKIES, PIES & DESSERTS CONTENTS

PUMPKIN-PIE POUND CAKE

1 cup shortening
1¼ cups sugar
¾ cup packed brown sugar
5 eggs, room temperature
1 cup canned pumpkin
2½ cups flour
2 teaspoons ground cinnamon
1 teaspoon ground nutmeg
1 teaspoon baking soda
½ cup orange juice, room temperature
2 teaspoons vanilla
1½ cups chopped pecans

☐ Preheat oven to 325°.

☐ Cream shortening, sugar and brown sugar in bowl for about 4 minutes. Add eggs, one at a time and mix well after each addition. Blend in pumpkin.

☐ In separate bowl, mix flour, spices, ¼ teaspoon salt and baking soda and mix well. Gradually beat dry ingredients into sugar-pumpkin mixture until ingredients mix well.

☐ Fold in orange juice, vanilla and pecans. Pour into sprayed, floured bundt pan. Bake for 70 to 75 minutes or until toothpick inserted in center comes out clean. Allow cake to stand in pan for about 15 minutes. Turn cake out onto rack to cool completely before frosting.

FROSTING:

1 (1 pound) box powdered sugar
6 tablespoons (¾ stick) butter, melted
¼ teaspoon orange extract
2 - 3 tablespoons orange juice

☐ Thoroughly mix all ingredients in bowl using only 2 tablespoons orange juice. Add more orange juice if frosting seems too stiff. Serves 12 to 16.

A REALLY GREAT POUND CAKE

½ cup shortening
1 cup butter
3 cups sugar
5 eggs
3½ cups flour
½ teaspoon baking powder
1 cup milk
1 teaspoon rum flavoring
1 teaspoon coconut flavoring

☐ Preheat oven to 325°.

☐ Cream shortening, butter and sugar in bowl. Add eggs one at a time and beat well after each addition.

☐ In separate bowl, mix flour and baking powder. Add dry ingredients and milk alternately to butter-sugar mixture, beginning and ending with flour.

☐ Add rum and coconut flavorings. Pour into large sprayed, floured tube pan.

☐ Bake for 1 hour 30 minutes to 1 hour 45 minutes. (Do not open door during baking.)

☐ Cake is done when toothpick inserted in center comes out clean.

GLAZE:

⅓ cup sugar
½ teaspoon almond extract

☐ Right before cake is done, combine 1 cup water and sugar in saucepan and bring to a rolling boil. Remove from heat and add almond extract.

☐ While cake is still in pan and right out of the oven, pour glaze over cake and let stand for about 30 minutes before removing from pan. Serves 12 to 16.

NUTTY POUND CAKE

1 cup (2 sticks) butter, softened
2 cups sugar
5 large eggs
1 teaspoon vanilla
1 teaspoon butter flavoring
1 teaspoon almond extract
2 cups flour, divided
2 cups chopped pecans
Powdered sugar

☐ Preheat oven to 325°.

☐ Cream butter and sugar in bowl and beat in eggs, one at a time. Stir in vanilla, butter and almond flavorings.

☐ Add 1¾ cups flour and beat well. Combine remaining flour with pecans and fold into batter.

☐ Bake in sprayed, floured bundt pan for 70 to 75 minutes.

☐ Cool, remove cake from pan and dust with powdered sugar. Serves 12 to 16.

I feel a recipe is only a theme, which an intelligent cook can play each time with a variation.

– Madame Benoit

BRANDIED APPLE DESSERT

1 (10 ounce) loaf pound cake
1 (20 ounce) can apple pie filling
½ teaspoon ground allspice
2 tablespoons brandy

☐ Slice pound cake and place on individual dessert plates.

☐ Combine pie filling, allspice and brandy in saucepan. Heat and stir just until mixture heats thoroughly.

☐ Place several spoonfuls over each slice. Serves 8.

CHOCOLATE-ORANGE CAKE

1 (10 ounce) frozen loaf pound cake, thawed
1 (12 ounce) jar orange marmalade, divided
1 (16 ounce) container ready-to-spread chocolate fudge frosting

☐ Cut cake horizontally to make 3 layers.

☐ Place 1 layer on cake platter. Spread with half marmalade.

☐ Place second layer over first and spread with remaining marmalade.

☐ Top with third cake layer and spread frosting liberally on top and sides of cake. Refrigerate. Serves 8 to 10.

CHIFFON TORTE

1 bakery round orange chiffon cake
1 (20 ounce) can crushed pineapple with juice
1 (5 ounce) package vanilla instant pudding mix
1 (8 ounce) carton frozen whipped topping, thawed

☐ Slice cake horizontally to make 3 layers.

☐ Combine pineapple and pudding mix in bowl and beat with spoon until mixture begins to thicken. Fold in whipped topping.

☐ Spread on each layer and cover top of cake. Refrigerate overnight. Serves 12.

STRAWBERRY DELIGHT

1 (6 ounce) package strawberry gelatin
2 (10 ounce) packages frozen strawberries with juice
1 (8 ounce) carton frozen whipped topping, thawed
1 (12 ounce) prepared angel food cake

☐ Dissolve strawberry gelatin in 1 cup boiling water in bowl and mix well. Add strawberries.

☐ Refrigerate until partially set and fold in whipped topping.

☐ Break angel food cake into large bite-size pieces and layer cake and gelatin mixture in 9 x 13-inch shallow dish.

☐ Refrigerate. Cut in squares to serve. Serves 12.

PINK LADY CAKE

1 (18 ounce) box strawberry cake mix
3 eggs
1 teaspoon lemon extract
1 (20 ounce) can strawberry pie filling

☐ Preheat oven to 350°.

☐ Beat cake mix, eggs and lemon extract in bowl. Fold into pie filling.

☐ Pour in sprayed, floured 9 x 13-inch baking pan.

☐ Bake for 30 to 35 minutes. Cake is done when toothpick inserted in center comes out clean. Serves 12.

TIP: If you want an icing, try a prepared vanilla frosting or whipped topping. They are the quickest and easiest.

I am only one, but I am one. I cannot do everything, but I can do something. And because I cannot do everything, I will not refuse to do the something that I can do. What I can do, I should do. And what I should do, by the grace of God, I will do.

– Edward Everett Hale

EASY PINEAPPLE CAKE

2 cups sugar
2 cups flour
1 (20 ounce) can crushed pineapple with juice
1 teaspoon baking soda

☐ Preheat oven to 350°.

☐ Combine all ingredients in bowl and mix with spoon.

☐ Pour into sprayed, floured 9 x 13-inch baking pan. Bake for 30 to 35 minutes.

EASY PINEAPPLE CAKE ICING:

1 (8 ounce) package cream cheese, softened
½ cup (1 stick) butter, melted
1 cup powdered sugar
1 cup chopped pecans

☐ Beat cream cheese, butter and powdered sugar in bowl

☐ Add chopped pecans and spoon over hot cake. Serves 12.

FLUFFY ORANGE CAKE

1 (18 ounce) box orange cake mix
4 eggs
⅔ cup canola oil

☐ Preheat oven to 350°. Combine all ingredients and ½ cup water in bowl.

☐ Beat on low speed to blend and beat on medium speed for 2 minutes. Pour into sprayed, floured 9 x 13-inch baking pan.

☐ Bake for 30 minutes or until toothpick inserted in center comes out clean. Cool.

FLUFFY ORANGE CAKE TOPPING:

1 (14 ounce) can sweetened condensed milk
⅓ cup lemon juice
1 (8 ounce) carton frozen whipped topping, thawed
2 (11 ounce) cans mandarin oranges, drained, halved, chilled

☐ Blend sweetened condensed milk and lemon juice in large bowl and mix well.

☐ Fold in whipped topping until blended well. Fold in orange slices.

☐ Pour mixture over cooled cake. Cover and refrigerate. Serves 12.

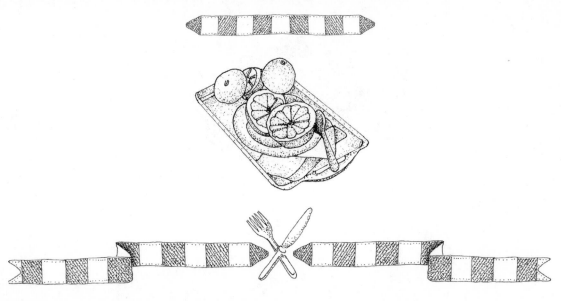

PINA COLADA CAKE

1 (18 ounce) box pineapple cake mix
3 eggs
⅓ cup canola oil
1 (14 ounce) can sweetened condensed milk
1 (15 ounce) can cream of coconut
1 cup flaked coconut
1 (8 ounce) can crushed pineapple, drained
1 (8 ounce) carton frozen whipped topping, thawed

☐ Preheat oven to 350°.

☐ Combine cake mix, eggs, 1¼ cups water and oil in bowl. Beat for 3 to 4 minutes and pour into sprayed, floured 10 x 15-inch baking pan. Bake for 35 minutes.

☐ When cake is done, punch holes in top with fork so frosting will soak into cake. Mix sweetened condensed milk, cream of coconut, coconut and pineapple in bowl.

☐ While cake is still warm, pour mixture over top of cake. Refrigerate for about 1 hour, spread whipped topping over cake, and return to refrigerator. Serves 12 to 14.

Baked goods freeze well and are very handy to have in the freezer for an emergency. Cookie dough is great to freeze. Baked cakes with buttercream icing and other frostings also freeze well. Avoid freezing cakes with cream cheese frosting or filling.

MOCKINGBIRD CAKE

3 cups flour
2 cups sugar
1 teaspoon baking soda
1 teaspoon ground cinnamon
3 eggs, beaten
1½ cups canola oil
1½ teaspoons vanilla
1 (8 ounce) can crushed pineapple with juice
1 cup chopped pecans
½ cup flaked coconut
2 bananas, mashed

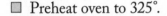

☐ Preheat oven to 325°.

☐ Combine flour, sugar, baking soda, ½ teaspoon salt and cinnamon in large bowl and stir well. Add eggs, oil and vanilla and stir only until dry ingredients are moist, but do not beat.

☐ Stir in pineapple, pecans, coconut and bananas. Spoon batter into sprayed, floured tube pan and bake for 1 hour 15 minutes. Cake is done when toothpick inserted in center comes out clean. Remove pan when slightly cool.

GLAZE:

1 cup sugar
½ cup buttermilk*
1 tablespoon corn syrup
¼ teaspoon baking soda
1 teaspoon vanilla
1 tablespoon butter

☐ Mix all ingredients and ¼ teaspoon salt in saucepan, bring to a boil and stir constantly. Remove from heat and cool for 4 to 5 minutes.

☐ Punch holes in cake with toothpicks so glaze will soak into cake. Pour glaze over cake slowly. Serves 12 to 18.

*TIP: To make buttermilk, mix 1 cup milk with 1 tablespoon lemon juice or vinegar and let milk stand for about 10 minutes.

COCONUT-ANGEL CAKE

1 (14 ounce/10 inch) round angel food cake
1 (20 ounce) can coconut pie filling
1 (12 ounce) carton frozen whipped topping, thawed
3 tablespoons flaked coconut

☐ Cut angel food cake horizontally to make 3 layers.

☐ Combine coconut pie filling and whipped topping. Spread one-third mixture on first layer. Top with second layer.

☐ Spread one-third mixture on second layer and top with third layer. Spread remaining whipped topping mixture on top of cake.

☐ Sprinkle coconut on top of cake. Refrigerate. Serves 8 to 12.

QUICK APPLE CAKE

1 (18 ounce) box spiced cake mix
1 (20 ounce) can apple pie filling
2 eggs
⅓ cup chopped walnuts

☐ Preheat oven to 350°.

☐ Combine all ingredients in bowl and mix very thoroughly with spoon. Make sure all lumps from cake mix break up.

☐ Pour into sprayed, floured bundt pan. Bake for 50 minutes or until toothpick inserted in center comes out clean. Serves 10 to 12.

TIP: You may substitute any other pie filling in this cake.

THE BEST FRESH APPLE CAKE

1½ cups canola oil
2 cups sugar
3 eggs
2½ cups flour
½ teaspoon baking soda
2 teaspoons baking powder
½ teaspoon ground cinnamon
1 teaspoon vanilla
3 cups peeled, grated apples
1 cup chopped pecans

☐ Preheat oven to 350°.

☐ Mix oil, sugar and eggs in bowl and beat well.

☐ In separate bowl, combine flour, ½ teaspoon salt, baking soda, baking powder and cinnamon. Gradually add flour mixture to creamed mixture.

☐ Add vanilla, fold in apples and pecans and pour into sprayed, floured tube pan.

☐ Bake for 1 hour. While cake is still warm, invert onto serving plate.

GLAZE:

2 tablespoons butter, melted
2 tablespoons milk
1 cup powdered sugar
1 teaspoon vanilla
¼ teaspoon lemon extract

☐ Mix all ingredients in bowl and drizzle over cake while cake is still warm. Serves 18 to 20.

CHOCOLATE-CHERRY CAKE

1 (18 ounce) box milk chocolate cake mix
1 (20 ounce) can cherry pie filling
3 eggs

☐ Preheat oven to 350°.

☐ Combine all ingredients in bowl and mix with spoon.

☐ Pour into sprayed, floured 9 x 13-inch baking pan.

☐ Bake for 35 to 40 minutes or until toothpick inserted in center comes out clean.

CHOCOLATE-CHERRY CAKE FROSTING:

5 tablespoons butter
1¼ cups sugar
½ cup milk
1 (6 ounce) package chocolate chips

☐ When cake is done, combine butter, sugar and milk in medium saucepan.

☐ Boil for 1 minute, stirring constantly. Add chocolate chips and stir until chips melt. Pour over hot cake. Serves 12.

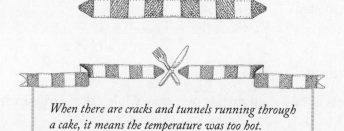

When there are cracks and tunnels running through a cake, it means the temperature was too hot.

CHOCOLATE PUDDING CAKE

1 (18 ounce) box milk chocolate cake mix
1¼ cups milk
⅓ cup canola oil
3 eggs

☐ Preheat oven to 350°.

☐ Combine all ingredients in bowl and beat well.

☐ Pour into sprayed, floured 9 x 13-inch baking pan.

☐ Bake for 35 minutes or when toothpick inserted in center comes out clean.

CHOCOLATE PUDDING CAKE FROSTING:

This is a very good, quick icing on any cake.

1 (14 ounce) can sweetened condensed milk
¾ (16 ounce) can chocolate syrup
1 (8 ounce) carton frozen whipped topping, thawed
⅓ cup chopped pecans

☐ Mix sweetened condensed milk and chocolate syrup in small bowl.

☐ Pour over cake and let soak into cake. Refrigerate for several hours.

☐ Spread whipped topping over top of cake and sprinkle with pecans. Refrigerate.
Serves 12.

OREO CAKE

1 (18 ounce) box white cake mix
⅓ cup canola oil
4 egg whites
2¼ cups coarsely chopped Oreo® cookies, divided

☐ Preheat oven to 350°.

☐ Combine cake mix, oil, 1¼ cups water and egg whites in bowl. Blend on low speed until moist. Beat for 2 minutes at high speed.

☐ Gently fold in 1¼ cups coarsely chopped cookies. Pour batter into 2 sprayed, floured 8-inch round cake pans.

☐ Bake for 25 to 30 minutes or until toothpick inserted in center comes out clean.

☐ Cool for 15 minutes and remove from pan. Cool completely and frost.

OREO CAKE FROSTING:

4¼ cups powdered sugar
1 cup (2 sticks) butter, softened
1 cup shortening (not butter-flavored)
1 teaspoon almond flavoring

☐ Combine all ingredients in bowl and beat until creamy.

☐ Frost first layer of cake and place second layer on top; frost top and sides.

☐ Sprinkle top with remaining crushed Oreo® cookies. Serves 12.

CHOCOLATE ROUND-UP CAKE

2 cups sugar
2 cups flour
½ cup (1 stick) butter, melted
½ cup canola oil
4 heaping tablespoons cocoa
½ cup buttermilk*
2 eggs, beaten
1 teaspoon baking soda
1 teaspoon ground cinnamon
1 teaspoon vanilla

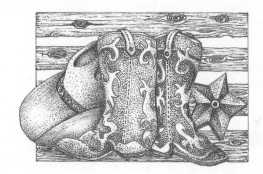

- ☐ Preheat oven to 350°.

- ☐ Blend sugar and flour in bowl and set aside.

- ☐ Combine butter, oil, cocoa and 1 cup water in saucepan and bring to a boil. Pour over flour-sugar mixture and beat well. Add buttermilk, eggs, baking soda, cinnamon, vanilla and ½ teaspoon salt.

- ☐ Mix well and pour in sprayed, floured 9 x 13-inch baking pan and bake for 40 to 45 minutes.

FROSTING:

½ cup (1 stick) butter, melted
¼ cup cocoa
6 tablespoons milk
1 (1 pound) box powdered sugar
1 teaspoon vanilla
1 cup chopped pecans
1 (10 ounce) can flaked coconut

- ☐ Five minutes before cake is done, combine butter, cocoa, milk, powdered sugar and vanilla in bowl and mix well. Add pecans and coconut, mix well and spread on hot cake. Serves 12.

TIP: To make buttermilk, mix 1 cup milk with 1 tablespoon lemon juice or vinegar and let milk stand for about 10 minutes.

Rich Turtle Cake

1 (18 ounce) box German chocolate cake mix
½ cup (1 stick) butter, softened
½ cup canola oil
1 (14 ounce) can sweetened condensed milk, divided
1 cup chopped pecans
1 (16 ounce) bag caramels

☐ Preheat oven to 350°.

☐ Combine cake mix, butter, 1½ cups water, oil and half can sweetened condensed milk in bowl and beat well.

☐ Fold in pecans and pour half batter into sprayed, floured 9 x 13-inch baking dish. Bake for 25 minutes.

☐ Combine caramels and remaining sweetened condensed milk in saucepan; cook and stir over medium heat until caramels melt. Spread evenly over baked cake and cover with remaining batter. Bake for additional 20 to 25 minutes.

Frosting:

½ cup (1 stick) butter
¼ cup cocoa
4 - 5 tablespoons milk
1 (1 pound) box powdered sugar
1 teaspoon vanilla

☐ Melt butter in saucepan, add cocoa and 4 tablespoons milk and mix well.

☐ Add powdered sugar and vanilla and stir well. (If frosting seems too stiff, add 1 tablespoon milk.) Spread over warm, but not hot, cake. Serves 12 to 14.

BUTTER-PECAN CAKE

1 (18 ounce) box butter-pecan cake mix
½ cup (1 stick) butter, melted
1 egg
1 cup chopped pecans

☐ Preheat oven to 350°.

☐ Combine cake mix, ¾ cup water, butter and egg in bowl; beat well. Stir in pecans.

☐ Pour into sprayed, floured 9 x 13-inch baking dish.

☐ Bake as is or add Pecan Cake Topping below before baking.

☐ Bake for 40 minutes or until toothpick inserted in center comes out clean. Serves 12.

PECAN CAKE TOPPING:

1 (8 ounce) package cream cheese, softened
2 eggs
1 (1 pound) box powdered sugar

☐ Beat cream cheese, eggs and powdered sugar in bowl. Pour over cake mixture before baking. Makes 1 pint.

To get more volume when beating eggs, allow eggs to reach room temperature.

BROWN SUGAR-RUM CAKE

1½ cups (3 sticks) butter, softened
1 (15 ounce) box light brown sugar
1 cup sugar
5 large eggs
¾ cup milk
¼ cup rum
2 teaspoons vanilla
3 cups flour
2 teaspoons baking powder
1½ cups chopped pecans
Powdered sugar, optional

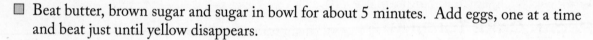

☐ Preheat oven to 325°.

☐ Beat butter, brown sugar and sugar in bowl for about 5 minutes. Add eggs, one at a time and beat just until yellow disappears.

☐ In separate bowl, combine milk, rum and vanilla. In separate bowl, combine flour, baking powder and ¼ teaspoon salt.

☐ Add half flour mixture to butter mixture and beat at low speed. Add milk mixture and mix.

☐ Add remaining flour mixture, beat at low speed and fold in pecans.

☐ Pour into sprayed, floured tube pan. Bake for 1 hour 20 minutes. Cake is done when toothpick inserted in center comes out clean.

☐ Cool in pan for 20 minutes. Remove from pan, sprinkle with powdered sugar, if desired, and continue to cool. Serves 18 to 20.

PUMPKIN-CHESS CAKE

1 (18 ounce) box yellow cake mix
¾ cup (1½ sticks) butter, softened, divided
4 eggs, divided
1 (15 ounce) can pumpkin
2 teaspoons ground cinnamon
½ cup packed brown sugar
⅔ cup milk
½ cup sugar
⅔ cup chopped pecans

☐ Preheat oven to 350°.

☐ Set aside 1 cup cake mix. Mix rest of cake mix, ½ cup butter and 1 egg and press into sprayed 9 x 13-inch baking pan.

☐ Mix pumpkin, 3 eggs, cinnamon, brown sugar and milk in bowl and pour over batter in pan.

☐ Mix set aside cake mix, sugar, remaining butter and pecans to make topping and crumble over cake. Bake for 1 hour. Serves 10 to 12.

The easiest way to "fancy up" a dessert is to add whipped cream. With a cherry or with chopped nuts or cinnamon sprinkled on top, you've made the dessert extra special.

POPPY SEED-STRAWBERRY CUPCAKES

2 cups flour
¾ cup sugar
1 tablespoon baking powder
1 tablespoon poppy seeds
½ teaspoon ground cinnamon
1 egg
¾ cup milk
¼ cup (½ stick) unsalted butter, melted
½ cup strawberry preserves

☐ Preheat oven to 350°.

☐ Place paper baking cups in 16 muffin cups. Combine flour, sugar, baking powder, poppy seeds and cinnamon in bowl.

☐ In separate bowl, beat egg, milk and butter and stir into dry ingredients just until moist.

☐ Fold in strawberry preserves and mix well. Fill muffin cups with batter two-thirds full.

☐ Bake for 20 to 25 minutes or until toothpick inserted in center comes out clean and muffins are golden brown.

☐ Cool for at least 5 minutes before removing from pan. Cool completely before frosting. Makes 16 cupcakes.

DECORATIONS:

1 (12 ounce) container ready-to-serve vanilla frosting
1 pint fresh strawberries, halved

☐ Spread frosting over all cupcakes with icing spatula or back of spoon. Top with strawberry half.

RASPBERRY-FILLED LEMON CUPCAKES

2 cups flour
2½ teaspoons baking powder
¼ teaspoon baking soda
¾ cup (1½ sticks) unsalted butter, softened
1¼ cups sugar
1 egg plus 3 egg yolks
1 tablespoon lemon juice, plus enough milk to equal ¾ cup
1 tablespoon grated lemon peel
½ cup seedless raspberry jam

☐ Preheat oven to 350°.

☐ Place paper baking cups in 16 muffin cups. Sift flour, baking powder, baking soda and ¼ teaspoon salt in bowl.

☐ In separate bowl, beat butter and sugar until mixture lightens. Beat in egg and egg yolks and mix well. Add flour mixture alternating with lemon juice-milk mixture, beginning and ending with flour. Stir in lemon peel.

☐ Fill muffin cups with batter two-thirds full and bake for 20 to 23 minutes or until dry to touch. Remove from pans and cool on rack for 25 minutes before frosting.

☐ Poke a hole in center of each cupcake with handle of wooden spoon. Go almost to the bottom while cupcakes are still hot.

☐ Place raspberry jam in plastic bag and snip off a small corner. Dip corner of bag into cupcake hole and pipe about 1½ teaspoons jam into centers of cupcakes. Makes 16 cupcakes.

DECORATIONS:

1 (12 ounce) container ready-to-serve white frosting
1 pint fresh raspberries

☐ Spread frosting over top of cupcakes using an icing spatula or the back of spoon. Top with fresh raspberries. Lemon icing is also amazing!

ZUCCHINI CUPCAKES

1½ cups self-rising flour
1 teaspoon baking soda
1½ teaspoons pumpkin pie spice
3 egg whites or ¾ cup egg substitute
¾ cup packed brown sugar
½ cup canola oil
2 cups peeled, grated zucchini

☐ Preheat oven to 350°.

☐ Place paper baking cups in 12 muffin cups. Combine flour, baking soda and pumpkin pie spice in small bowl.

☐ Beat eggs, brown sugar and oil in mixing bowl for about 3 minutes. Add zucchini and stir until they blend well. Add flour mixture and stir until ingredients combine thoroughly.

☐ Fill muffin cups with batter three-fourths full and bake for 20 to 25 minutes. Cool on wire rack. Makes 12 cupcakes.

DECORATIONS:

Cream cheese frosting, optional
1½ cups walnut pieces, optional

☐ These are delicious without a frosting, but if you want a frosting cream cheese is wonderful with these cupcakes. Frost each cupcake and top with walnut pieces for a special touch.

CARROT CAKE CUPCAKES

1 (18 ounce) box carrot cake mix
3 eggs
½ cup canola oil
1 (8 ounce) can crushed pineapple with juice
¾ cup chopped pecans
½ cup raisins, optional

☐ Preheat oven to 350°.

☐ Place paper baking cups in 24 muffin cups. Mix cake mix, eggs, oil, pineapple and ½ cup water in bowl and beat on low speed for 1 minute.

☐ Increase speed to medium and beat for 2 minutes. Fold in pecans and raisins and spoon into muffin cups.

☐ Bake for 20 to 24 minutes or until toothpick inserted in center comes out clean. Cool in pan for 5 minutes. Remove cupcakes from pan and cool completely before frosting. Makes 24 cupcakes.

DECORATIONS:

1 (16 ounce) container ready-to-serve cream cheese frosting
Powdered sugar, optional
Pecan pieces, optional

☐ Cream cheese frosting is a traditional favorite with carrot cake. But one of the easiest (and equally delicious) toppings is to sprinkle the cupcakes with powdered sugar and pecan pieces.

HARVEST PUMPKIN CUPCAKES

1 (15 ounce) can pumpkin
3 eggs, slightly beaten
½ cup oil
1½ teaspoons ground cinnamon
1 teaspoon baking soda
1 (18 ounce) box yellow cake mix
½ cup chopped walnuts
1 (16 ounce) container ready-to-serve buttercream frosting

☐ Preheat oven to 350°.

☐ Place paper baking cups in 24 muffin cups. Combine pumpkin, eggs, oil, cinnamon and baking soda in bowl and mix well.

☐ Add cake mix, ¼ cup water and beat for 1 minute on low speed. Increase speed to high and beat for 2 minutes. Fold in walnuts.

☐ Fill muffin cups two-thirds full and bake for 19 to 22 minutes or until toothpick inserted in center comes out clean. Cool for 10 minutes in pan; remove from pan and cool completely before frosting. Makes 24 cupcakes.

Decorate or garnish desserts with chocolate curls by scraping a vegetable peeler across a large piece of chocolate. Place the curls on top of dessert. To get chocolate shavings, move the vegetable peeler across chocolate in short strokes.

MAPLE CREAM CUPCAKES

1½ cups flour
⅓ cup sugar
3 teaspoons baking powder
1 teaspoon ground cinnamon
1 teaspoon ground nutmeg
¼ cup shortening
¾ cup quick-cooking oats
1 egg, beaten
½ cup milk
½ cup maple syrup

☐ Preheat oven to 350°.

☐ Place paper baking cups in 16 muffin cups. Sift flour, sugar, baking powder, ¼ teaspoon salt, cinnamon and nutmeg in bowl. Cut in shortening until mixture resembles coarse crumbs.

☐ Stir in oats; add egg, milk and maple syrup, stir only until dry ingredients are moist. Fill muffin cups one-half full.

☐ Bake for 18 to 21 minutes. Let stand in pan for about 5 minutes. Cool completely before frosting. Makes 16 cupcakes.

DECORATIONS:

1 (12 ounce) container ready-to-serve buttercream frosting
2 tablespoons maple syrup
1 tablespoon butter, melted
Ground cinnamon

☐ Place buttercream frosting in small bowl, stir in maple syrup and butter; blend well. Frost each cupcake and sprinkle with a little cinnamon.

TIP: *Prepared coconut–pecan frosting with a sprinkling of finely chopped pecans is also great with these.*

SPICY CUPCAKES

½ cup shortening
1 cup sugar
2 egg yolks
⅓ cup raisins, chopped
⅓ cup chopped walnuts
1 teaspoon baking soda
2½ cups flour
½ teaspoon ground cloves
½ teaspoon ground mace
1½ teaspoons ground cinnamon
¾ cup buttermilk*
1 egg white, stiffly beaten
Ready-to-serve cream cheese frosting

☐ Preheat oven to 350˚.

☐ Place paper baking cups in 18 muffin cups. Cream shortening, sugar and egg yolks in mixing bowl. Add raisins and walnuts. Dissolve baking soda in 1 tablespoon hot water and add to mixture.

☐ Mix and sift flour, ½ teaspoon salt and spices and add alternately with buttermilk to first mixture. Fold in stiffly beaten egg white.

☐ Spoon into muffin cups and bake for 15 to 20 minutes. Cool and top with cream cheese frosting. Makes 18 cupcakes.

TIP: To make buttermilk, mix 1 cup milk with 1 tablespoon lemon juice or vinegar and let milk stand for about 10 minutes.

SURPRISE CUPCAKES

1 (8 ounce) package cream cheese, softened
2 cups sugar, divided
1 egg, slightly beaten
1 cup white chocolate chips
2 cups flour
1 teaspoon baking soda
⅓ cup canola oil

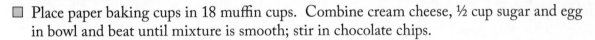

- Preheat oven to 350°.

- Place paper baking cups in 18 muffin cups. Combine cream cheese, ½ cup sugar and egg in bowl and beat until mixture is smooth; stir in chocolate chips.

- In separate bowl, combine 1½ cups sugar, flour, baking soda, oil and 1 cup water and stir with spoon. Mix well, but not too vigorously.

- Fill 18 muffin cups half full with batter and place 1 heaping tablespoon cream cheese mixture over each cupcake.

- Bake for 25 to 27 minutes or until toothpick inserted in batter comes out clean. Remove cupcake from pan while muffins are still hot. Cool on rack. These cupcakes need to be refrigerated. Makes 18 cupcakes.

TIP: These cupcakes really don't need a frosting, but you can dust them with powdered sugar and top with fruit if you like. Raspberries go great with white chocolate!

Sour Cream Cupcakes

1 tablespoon shortening
1 cup sugar
2 eggs
½ teaspoon baking soda
½ cup sour cream
1½ cups flour
½ teaspoon cream of tartar
⅛ teaspoon mace
1 (12 ounce) container ready-to-serve vanilla frosting

▢ Preheat oven to 350°.

▢ Place paper baking cups in 18 muffin cups. Cream shortening, sugar and eggs together until light and fluffy.

▢ In small bowl dissolve baking soda in sour cream.

▢ Sift flour, 1½ teaspoons salt, cream of tartar and mace together and add alternately with sour cream to shortening mixture. Beat thoroughly.

▢ Spoon batter into muffin cups about two-thirds full and bake for 18 to 22 minutes. Top with vanilla frosting. Makes 18 cupcakes.

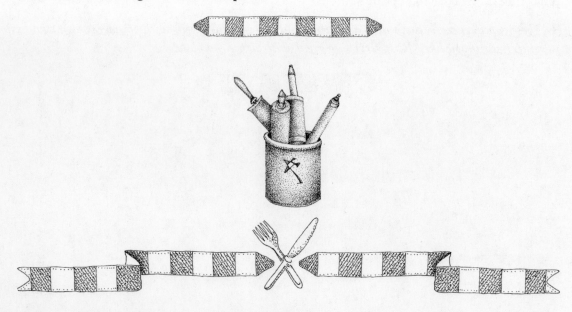

BUTTERSCOTCH SUPREME CUPCAKES

2 cups flour
1¼ cups sugar
1 (3.4 ounce) package instant butterscotch pudding mix
1 (3.4 ounce) package instant vanilla pudding mix
2 teaspoons baking powder
4 eggs, lightly beaten
¾ cup canola oil
1 teaspoon vanilla
1 (12 ounce) package butterscotch chips, divided
1 (12 ounce) container buttercream frosting

☐ Preheat oven to 350°.

☐ Place paper baking cups in 18 muffin cups. Combine flour, sugar, both pudding mixes, baking powder and ½ teaspoon salt in bowl.

☐ In separate bowl, combine 1 cup water, eggs, oil and vanilla; stir this mixture into dry ingredients and mix just until moist. Stir in 1 cup butterscotch chips and mix well.

☐ Spoon batter into muffin cups about two-thirds full. Bake for 16 to 20 minutes or until toothpick inserted in center comes out clean. Cool for 5 minutes before removing from pan. Cool completely before frosting.

☐ Spread buttercream frosting over tops of cupcakes and sprinkle with remaining butterscotch chips. Makes 18 cupcakes.

CINNAMON CHOCOLATE CHIP CUPCAKES

2½ cups flour
1 (3.4 ounce) package instant French vanilla pudding mix
2 teaspoons ground cinnamon
½ teaspoon baking powder
½ teaspoon baking soda
⅓ cup sugar
3 eggs
1 cup buttermilk*
½ cup canola oil
1 teaspoon vanilla
1 cup miniature semi-sweet chocolate chips

☐ Preheat oven to 350°.

☐ Place paper baking cups in 18 muffin cups. Combine flour, pudding mix, cinnamon, baking powder, baking soda, sugar and a little salt in bowl.

☐ In separate bowl, combine eggs, buttermilk, oil and vanilla; mix well and add mixture to dry ingredients. Whisk for 1 to 2 minutes and fold in chocolate chips.

☐ Fill muffin cups with batter about two-thirds full. Bake for 18 to 21 minutes or until a toothpick inserted in center comes out clean. Cool for about 5 minutes before removing from pan. Allow cupcakes to cool completely before frosting. Makes 18 cupcakes.

DECORATIONS:

1 (12 ounce) container ready-to-serve vanilla frosting
1 teaspoon vanilla
Ground cinnamon

☐ Combine frosting and 1 teaspoon vanilla. Spread frosting over all and sprinkle with cinnamon.

*TIP: To make buttermilk, mix 1 cup milk with 1 tablespoon lemon juice or vinegar and let milk stand for about 10 minutes.

DOUBLE RICH CHOCOLATE CUPCAKES

½ cup cocoa
1⅔ cups flour
1½ cups sugar
½ teaspoon baking soda
½ cup shortening
2 eggs
1 (6 ounce) package chocolate chips
1 (16 ounce) container ready-to-serve dark chocolate frosting

☐ Preheat oven to 350°.

☐ Place paper baking cups in 24 muffin cups. Mix cocoa and 1 cup hot water in bowl until mixture is smooth. Let mixture cool for about 10 minutes.

☐ Add flour, sugar, baking soda, shortening and eggs and beat on low speed for 2 minutes. Increase speed and beat for 2 minutes. Stir in chocolate chips and mix well. Fill muffin cups two-thirds full.

☐ Bake for 18 to 20 minutes or until toothpick inserted in center comes out clean. Cool completely for at least 30 minutes. Top with frosting. Makes 24 cupcakes.

TIP: Grab a Hershey's® chocolate bar and slice chocolate curls with a potato peeler to put on top of the dark chocolate frosting. You will have Triple Chocolate Chocolate Chocolate Cupcakes.

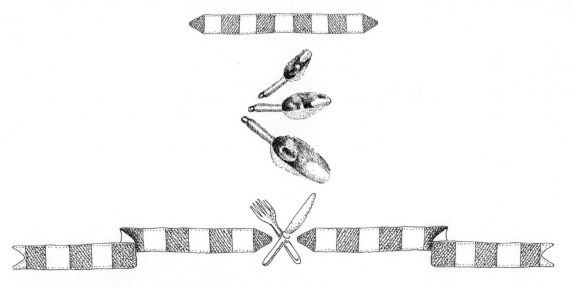

CHOCOLATE PEANUT BUTTER YUMMIES

1 (21 ounce) package double fudge brownie mix
2 eggs
2 (12 ounce) packages miniature peanut butter cups, divided
1 (16 ounce) container ready-to-serve buttercream frosting
½ cup creamy peanut butter

☐ Preheat oven to 350°.

☐ Place paper baking cups in 18 muffin cups. Prepare brownie mix according to package directions using 2 eggs. Spoon into muffin cups and fill two-thirds full.

☐ Place peanut butter cup in center of each and push into batter. Bake for 20 to 25 minutes or until toothpick inserted in center comes out clean.

☐ Place buttercream frosting in small bowl, stir in creamy peanut butter and mix well. Spread frosting generously over cupcakes. Top with peanut butter cup. Makes 18.

TIP: Use chocolate frosting for an extra chocolate rush!

Just about any cake recipe that starts out by creaming butter and sugar can be made into cupcakes. Bake at the same temperature as a cake, but cut the time by about half. A recipe for a two-layer cake will make about two dozen cupcakes.

CHOCOLATE-FILLED CUPCAKES

1 (18 ounce) box devil's food cake mix
1⅓ cups buttermilk*
4 eggs, divided
⅓ cup canola oil
1 cup mini semi-sweet chocolate chips, divided
1 (8 ounce) package cream cheese, softened
½ cup sugar

☐ Preheat oven to 350°.

☐ Place paper baking cups in 24 muffin cups. Combine cake mix, buttermilk, 3 eggs and oil in large bowl. Beat on low speed to blend, then beat on medium for 2 minutes. Stir ½ cup chocolate chips into batter.

☐ In separate bowl, beat cream cheese, sugar and remaining egg until mixture is smooth. Melt remaining chocolate chips in saucepan and add to cream cheese mixture. Beat mixture until blends well.

☐ Fill each muffin cup half full with batter. Drop 1 tablespoon chocolate-cream cheese mixture in center and spoon remaining batter evenly over filling.

☐ Bake for 25 minutes or until toothpick inserted in center comes out clean. Makes 24 cupcakes.

*TIP: *To make buttermilk, mix 1 cup milk with 1 tablespoon lemon juice or vinegar and let milk stand for about 10 minutes.*

NUTTY RED VELVET CUPCAKES

1 (18 ounce) box red velvet cake mix
3 eggs
⅓ cup canola oil
1 (6 ounce) package white chocolate chips
½ cup chopped walnuts
1 (16 ounce) container ready-to-serve buttercream or vanilla frosting

☐ Preheat oven to 350°.

☐ Place paper baking cups in 24 muffin cups. Blend cake mix, 1¼ cups water, eggs and oil in bowl on low speed for 30 seconds.

☐ Beat on medium speed for 2 minutes. Stir in white chocolate chips and walnuts and pour into muffin cups.

☐ Bake for 19 to 23 minutes or until toothpick inserted in center in center comes out clean. Let stand on wire rack for 30 minutes. Remove each cupcake from pan and cool completely before frosting. Top with frosting. Makes 24 cupcakes.

I totally take back all those times I didn't want to take a nap when I was younger.

WHITE VELVET DAZZLE

1 (18 ounce) box white cake mix
⅓ cup canola oil
1 teaspoon almond extract
3 large egg whites
1 cup white chocolate chips
1 (16 ounce) container ready-to-serve classic white frosting

☐ Preheat oven to 350°.

☐ Place paper baking cups in 24 muffin cups. Beat cake mix, 1¼ cups water, oil, almond extract and egg whites in bowl on low speed for 30 seconds.

☐ Increase speed to medium and beat for 2 minutes. Stir in white chocolate chips. Divide batter among muffin cups.

☐ Bake for 19 to 22 minutes or until toothpick inserted in center comes out clean. Cool for 10 minutes before removing from pan. Cool for 30 minutes before frosting. Top with frosting. Makes 24 cupcakes.

*Home gives us a sense of place
and a sense of who we are.*

TROPICAL CHEESECAKE

1¼ cups graham cracker crumbs
½ cup flaked coconut
½ cup chopped pecans
2 tablespoons light brown sugar
¼ cup (½ stick) butter, melted
2 (8 ounce) packages cream cheese, softened
1 (14 ounce) can sweetened condensed milk
3 eggs
¼ cup frozen orange juice concentrate, thawed
1 teaspoon pineapple extract
1 (20 ounce) can pineapple pie filling, divided
1 cup sour cream

☐ Preheat oven to 300°.

☐ Combine crumbs, coconut, pecans, brown sugar and butter. Press firmly into 9-inch springform pan and set aside.

☐ In large mixing bowl, beat cream cheese until fluffy. Gradually beat in sweetened condensed milk.

☐ Add eggs, juice concentrate and pineapple extract and mix well. Stir in ¾ cup pineapple pie filling.

☐ Pour into prepared springform pan. Bake 1 hour or until center sets.

☐ Spread top with sour cream and bake 5 minutes longer. Cool, spread remaining pineapple pie filling over cheesecake and refrigerate. Serves 8 to 12.

PRALINE CHEESECAKE

1¼ cups graham cracker crumbs
¼ cup sugar
¼ cup (½ stick) butter, melted
3 (8 ounce) packages cream cheese, softened
1¼ cups packed dark brown sugar
2 tablespoons flour
3 large eggs
2 teaspoons vanilla
½ cup finely chopped pecans
Pecan halves
Maple syrup

☐ Preheat oven to 350°. Combine crumbs, sugar and butter and press into 9-inch springform pan. Bake for 10 minutes.

☐ Beat cream cheese, brown sugar and flour in mixing bowl and blend at medium speed. Add eggs, one at a time, and mix well after each addition. Blend in vanilla, stir in chopped pecans, and pour mixture over crust. Bake for 50 to 55 minutes.

☐ Remove from oven and loosen cake from rim of pan. Let cake cool before removing from pan. Refrigerate. Place pecan halves around edge of cheesecake (about 1-inch from edge and 1 inch apart) and pour syrup over top. When you slice cheesecake, pour additional syrup over each slice so some will run down sides. Serves 8 to 12.

Take away the heritage of a people and they are easily persuaded.

— *Karl Marx*

EMERGENCY CHEESECAKE

1 (8 ounce) package cream cheese, softened
1 (14 ounce) can sweetened condensed milk
½ cup lemon juice
1 (6 ounce) ready graham cracker piecrust

☐ Beat cream cheese, condensed milk and lemon juice in bowl. Pour into piecrust and refrigerate at least 4 hours. Serves 8.

TIP: Serve with the pie filling of your choice.

EASY SUGAR COOKIES

1 (8 ounce) package cream cheese, softened
¾ cup sugar
1 cup (2 sticks) butter
½ teaspoon lemon extract
2½ cups flour

☐ Combine cream cheese with sugar, butter and lemon extract in medium bowl. Beat until ingredients blend well.

☐ Add flour and mix thoroughly. Cover and refrigerate several hours or overnight.

☐ When ready to bake, preheat oven to 375° and roll dough out on lightly floured surface to ⅛-inch thickness.

☐ Cut shapes with cookie cutter and place on unsprayed baking sheet.

☐ Bake for 6 to 8 minutes. Remove from oven, let cookies cool for 1 minute on cookie sheet and transfer to cooling rack. Makes 1 dozen.

SNAPPY ALMOND-SUGAR COOKIES

1 cup (2 sticks) butter
1 cup plus 2 tablespoons sugar
½ teaspoon almond extract
2 cups flour
1 cup chopped almonds

☐ Cream butter, 1 cup sugar and almond extract until light and fluffy. Slowly beat in flour and stir in almonds.

☐ Shape dough into roll, wrap and refrigerate for about 2 hours until thoroughly chilled.

☐ Preheat oven to 325°.

☐ Slice roll into ¼-inch pieces, place on unsprayed cookie sheet, and bake for 20 minutes.

☐ Sprinkle with remaining 2 tablespoons sugar while still hot. Makes 1 dozen.

EASY SAND TARTS

1 cup (2 sticks) butter, softened
¾ cup powdered sugar
2 cups sifted flour
1 cup chopped pecans
1 teaspoon vanilla

☐ Preheat oven to 325°.

☐ In mixing bowl, cream butter and powdered sugar. Slowly add flour, pecans and vanilla.

☐ Roll dough into balls or crescents and place on unsprayed cookie sheet. Bake for 20 minutes.

☐ Roll in extra powdered sugar after tarts have cooled. Makes 1 dozen.

BAYLOR COOKIES

The best "ice box" cookies around.

1 cup shortening
¼ cup packed brown sugar
1 cup sugar
1 egg
1½ teaspoons vanilla
2 cups flour
2 teaspoons baking powder
1 cup chopped pecans

☐ Combine shortening, brown sugar, sugar, egg, ¼ teaspoon salt and vanilla in bowl and mix well.

☐ Add flour and baking powder and mix until it blends well. Add pecans and mix.

☐ On floured wax paper divide dough in half and roll in log shapes. Wrap each roll in wax paper and refrigerate for several hours or until thoroughly chilled.

☐ Preheat oven to 350°.

☐ Slice dough into ½-inch slices.

☐ Bake on cookie sheet for 15 minutes or until slightly brown. Makes 3 dozen cookies.

LEMONADE COOKIES

1 cup (2 sticks) butter, softened
1½ cups sugar, divided
2 eggs
1 (6 ounce) can frozen lemonade concentrate, thawed, divided
3 cups flour
1 teaspoon baking soda

☐ Preheat oven to 350°.

☐ Cream butter and 1 cup sugar in bowl. Add eggs and beat.

☐ Add ½ cup lemonade concentrate and mix. Add flour, baking soda and ¼ teaspoon salt and mix.

☐ Drop tablespoonfuls of dough onto cookie sheet 2 inches apart. Bake for about 8 minutes or until cookies just begin to brown around edges.

☐ Brush hot cookies lightly with remaining lemonade concentrate and sprinkle with remaining sugar.

☐ Remove cookies to wire rack. Makes about 36 cookies.

When you are making cookies, double the recipe and freeze half the dough. The next time you want cookies, all you have to do is go to the freezer.

OLD-FASHIONED PEACH COOKIES

1 (20 ounce) can peach pie filling
1 (18 ounce) box yellow cake mix
2 eggs
1 cup finely chopped pecans
Sugar

☐ Preheat oven to 350°.

☐ In blender, process pie filling until smooth.

☐ In large bowl, combine pie filling, dry cake mix and eggs and blend well. Stir in pecans.

☐ Drop by tablespoonfuls onto sprayed cookie sheet. Sprinkle with sugar.

☐ Bake for 15 minutes or until cookies are light brown around edges. Makes about 2 dozen.

If cookies cool on the cookie sheet and stick, reheat cookie sheet in oven for about 1 minute to remove them easily.

CLASSIC SNICKERDOODLES

½ cup (1 stick) butter, softened
½ cup shortening
1¾ cups sugar, divided
2 eggs
2¼ cups flour
2 teaspoons cream of tartar
1 teaspoon baking soda
½ teaspoon ground cinnamon

☐ Preheat oven to 350°.

☐ Mix butter, shortening, 1½ cups sugar and eggs in medium bowl and beat well.

☐ Stir in flour, cream of tartar, baking soda and ¼ teaspoon salt.

☐ Shape rounded tablespoonfuls of dough into balls.

☐ Mix ¼ cup sugar and cinnamon in small bowl and roll dough balls in mixture to cover.

☐ Place balls on cookie sheet 2 inches apart.

☐ Bake for 8 to 10 minutes or until edges just begin to brown. Makes about 2 dozen.

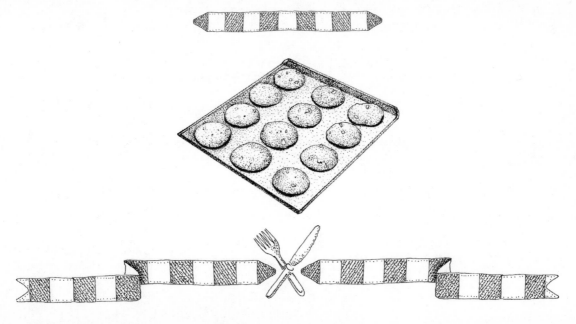

SOFT MOLASSES COOKIES

2¼ cups flour
1 teaspoon ground ginger
1 teaspoon ground cinnamon
2 teaspoons baking soda
½ cup shortening
½ cup sugar
½ cup molasses
1 egg

☐ Preheat oven to 400°.

☐ Combine flour, ginger, cinnamon and ¼ teaspoon salt in bowl. Dissolve baking soda in 2 tablespoons hot water.

☐ In separate bowl, mix shortening, sugar, molasses and egg until creamy. Mix in flour mixture a little at a time and alternate with 6 tablespoons cold water and dissolved baking soda.

☐ Drop rounded tablespoonfuls of dough about 2 inches apart onto sprayed cookie sheet.

☐ Bake about 12 minutes or until done. Makes about 24 cookies.

TIP: If you like nuts, add ½ cup chopped pecans or walnuts.

To get the best results when baking with eggs, milk and butter, allow ingredients to reach room temperature before combining them. If separating eggs, separate them while cold; then let the whites and yolks come to room temperature.

OMA'S GINGERBREAD COOKIES

¾ cup (1½ sticks) butter, softened
2 egg yolks
1 (18 ounce) box spice cake mix
1 teaspoon ginger

☐ Preheat oven to 375°.

☐ Combine butter and egg yolks in large bowl. Gradually blend in cake mix and ginger and mix well.

☐ Roll out to ⅛-inch thickness on lightly floured surface. Use gingerbread cookie cutter to cut out cookies and place 2 inches apart on cookie sheet.

☐ Bake for about 8 minutes or until edges are slightly brown. Cool cookies before transferring to cookie bowl. Makes 1 to 2 dozen.

CREAMY CHEESECAKE COOKIES

1 cup (2 sticks) butter, softened
2 (3 ounce) packages cream cheese, softened
2 cups sugar
2 cups flour

☐ Preheat oven to 325°.

☐ Beat butter and cream cheese in bowl. Add sugar and beat until light and fluffy. Add flour and beat well.

☐ Drop teaspoonfuls of dough onto cookie sheet and bake for 12 to 15 minutes or until edges are golden. Makes 3 dozen.

BUTTER COOKIE SPECIAL

1 (18 ounce) box butter cake mix
1 (3.4 ounce) package butterscotch instant pudding mix
1 cup canola oil
1 egg, beaten

☐ Preheat oven to 350°.

☐ Combine cake mix, pudding mix, oil and egg in bowl and mix with spoon. Beat thoroughly.

☐ Drop teaspoonfuls of dough onto cookie sheet about 2 inches apart.

☐ Bake for about 8 minutes. Do not overcook. Makes 3 dozen.

TIP: Add 1¼ cups chopped pecans to batter.

You can buy a bus load of cheap bananas if you get them when they are overripe at the grocery store. Bring them home, peel them and cut them in half. Put them in resealable plastic bags and freeze them for quick and easy smoothies, muffins, breads and cakes.

OLD-FASHIONED OATMEAL-RAISIN COOKIES

¾ cup (1½ sticks) butter, softened
¾ cup sugar
1 cup packed brown sugar
2 eggs
2 teaspoons vanilla
1¼ cups flour
1 teaspoon baking powder
¼ teaspoon baking soda
¾ teaspoon ground cinnamon
2 cups old-fashioned oats
1 cup golden raisins

☐ Preheat oven to 375°.

☐ Beat butter in bowl until creamy. Add sugar, brown sugar, eggs and vanilla and beat until they mix well.

☐ In separate bowl, combine flour, baking powder, baking soda and cinnamon. Stir flour mixture into butter-sugar mixture a little at a time.

☐ Stir in oats and raisins. Drop rounded tablespoonfuls of dough onto sprayed cookie sheet.

☐ Bake for 9 to 10 minutes or until edges are golden brown.

☐ Let cookies stand on cookie sheet for 1 minute and transfer to wire rack to cool. Makes about 36 cookies.

OATMEAL-CHOCOLATE CHIP COOKIES

1 (18 ounce) box yellow cake mix
1 cup quick-cook rolled oats
¾ cup (1½ sticks) butter, softened
2 eggs
1 cup semi-sweet chocolate chips

☐ Preheat oven to 350°.

☐ Combine cake mix, oats, butter and eggs in bowl and beat until they blend well.

☐ Stir in chocolate chips.

☐ Drop teaspoonfuls of dough onto unsprayed cookie sheet.

☐ Bake for 10 to 12 minutes or until light brown.

☐ Allow cookies to cool slightly, remove from cookie sheet and cool completely on wire rack. Makes about 2 dozen.

In 1930 Ruth and Kenneth Wakefield bought the Toll House Inn near Whitman, Massachusetts.

While making chocolate cookies for her guests, Ruth realized she did not have her standard baker's chocolate, so she grabbed a Nestlé® semi-sweet chocolate bar and broke it into small pieces, stirred them into the cookie dough and baked them. The chocolate pieces did not melt, but merely softened.

(Continued on next page.)

LAUREN'S CHOCOLATE CHIP COOKIES

½ cup (1 stick) butter, softened
¼ cup shortening
½ cup sugar
⅓ cup packed brown sugar
1 egg
1 teaspoon vanilla
1½ cups flour
½ teaspoon baking soda
1 (6 ounce) package semi-sweet chocolate chips

☐ Preheat oven to 350°.

☐ Combine butter, shortening, sugar, brown sugar, egg and vanilla in bowl and beat until smooth. Add flour, baking soda and ½ teaspoon salt and continue to beat. Stir in chocolate chips.

☐ Drop tablespoonfuls of dough onto sprayed cookie sheet and bake for 12 to 14 minutes. Store in airtight container. Makes about 30 cookies.

(Continued from previous page.)

Andrew Nestlé struck a deal with her to print her recipe on every Nestlé® semi-sweet chocolate bar wrapper. In return she was provided with chocolate for life. Nestlé began packaging chocolate morsels (chips) in 1939 similar to what we have today; the recipe is still printed on the packages.

Ruth Graves Wakefield died in 1977, but her Toll House Chocolate Chip Cookies live on. Originally built in 1709, the Toll House Inn burned to the ground in 1984 and was not rebuilt.

THE GREAT CHOCOLATE CHUNK COOKIES

¾ cup shortening
1¼ cups packed brown sugar
2 tablespoons milk
2 teaspoons vanilla
1 egg
1¾ cups flour
¾ teaspoon baking soda
1 (8 ounce) chocolate candy bar, broken in small chunks
1 cup chopped pecans

☐ Preheat oven to 375°.

☐ Cream shortening, brown sugar, milk and vanilla in large bowl and blend until creamy. Add egg and mix.

☐ Add flour, 1 teaspoon salt and baking soda to creamed mixture and stir well. Stir in chocolate chunks and pecans.

☐ Drop rounded tablespoonfuls of dough onto cookie sheet.

☐ Bake for 10 minutes for chewy cookies and 11 to 13 minutes for crispy cookies. Makes about 24 (2 inch) cookies.

NUTTY DEVIL'S FOOD COOKIES

1 (18 ounce) box devil's food cake mix
½ cup canola oil
2 eggs
¾ cup chopped pecans

☐ Preheat oven to 350°.

☐ Combine cake mix, oil, eggs and pecans in bowl and mix well.

☐ Drop teaspoonfuls of dough onto non-stick cookie sheet.

☐ Bake for 10 to 12 minutes. Cool and remove to wire rack. Makes 3 dozen.

PEANUTTY FUDGIES

1 (18 ounce) box fudge cake mix
1 (8 ounce) carton sour cream
⅔ cup peanut butter chips
½ cup chopped peanuts

☐ Preheat oven to 350°.

☐ Beat cake mix and sour cream in bowl until mixture blends and becomes smooth. Stir in peanut butter chips and peanuts.

☐ Drop teaspoonfuls of dough onto sprayed cookie sheet. Bake for 10 to 12 minutes. Remove from oven and cool. Makes 3 dozen.

CHOCOLATE-CRUNCH COOKIES

1 (18 ounce) box German chocolate cake mix with pudding
1 egg, slightly beaten
½ cup (1 stick) butter, melted
1 cup rice crispy cereal

☐ Preheat oven to 350°.

☐ Combine cake mix, egg and butter in bowl. Add cereal and stir until they blend well.

☐ Shape dough into 1-inch balls. Place onto sprayed cookie sheet.

☐ Dip fork in flour and flatten cookies in crisscross pattern. Bake for 10 to 12 minutes. Cool. Makes 3 dozen.

PEPPY PEANUT BUTTER CUPS

1 (18 ounce) roll refrigerated peanut butter cookie dough
48 miniature peanut butter cup candies

☐ Preheat oven to 350°.

☐ Slice cookie dough into ¾-inch slices. Cut each slice into quarters and place each quarter, pointed side up in sprayed miniature muffin cups.

☐ Bake for 10 minutes. Remove from oven and immediately press peanut butter cup candy gently and evenly into cookies. (Be sure you take paper wrapper off peanut butter cups.)

☐ Cool and remove from pan; refrigerate until firm. Makes 48.

COCONUT MACAROONS

2 (7 ounce) packages flaked coconut
1 (14 ounce) can sweetened condensed milk
2 teaspoons vanilla
½ teaspoon almond extract

☐ Preheat oven to 350°.

☐ Combine coconut, sweetened condensed milk, vanilla and almond extract in bowl and mix well.

☐ Drop rounded teaspoonfuls of dough onto foil-lined cookie sheet.

☐ Bake for 8 to 10 minutes or until light brown around edges. Immediately remove from foil. (Macaroons will stick if allowed to cool.)

☐ Store at room temperature. Makes 2 dozen.

NO-COOK LEMON BALLS

2½ cups graham cracker crumbs, divided
1 (6 ounce) can frozen lemonade concentrate, thawed
½ cup (1 stick) butter, softened
1 (16 ounce) box powdered sugar, sifted

☐ Combine 1½ cups graham cracker crumbs, lemonade concentrate, butter and powdered sugar in bowl. Shape into small balls.

☐ Roll in remaining graham cracker crumbs and put on wax paper.

☐ Refrigerate for 3 to 4 hours in airtight container or freeze to serve later. Makes 3 dozen.

TIP: You can substitute almond or pecan shortbread cookie crumbs for graham cracker crumbs.

Light Pecan Puffs

2 egg whites
¾ cup packed light brown sugar
1 teaspoon vanilla
1 cup chopped pecans

☐ Preheat oven to 250°.

☐ Beat egg whites in bowl until foamy. Gradually add brown sugar ¼ cup at a time
and add vanilla.

☐ Continue beating until stiff peaks form (about 3 or 4 minutes). Fold in pecans.

☐ Drop teaspoonfuls of mixture onto cookie sheet. Bake for 45 minutes. Makes 2 dozen.

Old-Fashioned Marshmallow Treats

¼ cup (½ stick) butter
4 cups miniature marshmallows
½ cup crunchy peanut butter
5 cups rice crispy cereal

☐ Melt butter in saucepan on medium heat and add marshmallows. Stir until they melt and
add peanut butter.

☐ Remove from heat. Add cereal and stir well. Press mixture into 9 x 13-inch pan. Cut in
squares when cool. Makes 1½ dozen.

MILLION-DOLLAR BARS

½ cup (1 stick) butter
2 cups graham cracker crumbs
1 (6 ounce) package chocolate chips
1 (6 ounce) package butterscotch chips
1 cup chopped pecans
1 (7 ounce) can flaked coconut
1 (14 ounce) can sweetened condensed milk

☐ Preheat oven to 325°.

☐ Melt butter in sprayed 9 x 13-inch baking dish.

☐ Sprinkle crumbs over butter and stir. Add layers of chocolate chips, butterscotch chips, pecans and coconut.

☐ Pour sweetened condensed milk over top and bake for about 30 minutes. Cool in pan and cut bars. Makes 12 to 14 bars.

The first cookbook written by an American was American Cookery *by Amelia Simmons. It was published in 1796 and included two recipes for cookies.*

Cookie recipes expanded in variety with modern transportation. Railroads provided quick shipment of coconuts, oranges and other perishable foods. When cornflakes were invented, it and other cereal products became cookie ingredients.

CHOCOLATE CHIP-CHEESE BARS

1 (18 ounce) package refrigerated chocolate chip cookie dough
1 (8 ounce) package cream cheese, softened
½ cup sugar
1 egg

☐ Preheat oven to 325°.

☐ Cut cookie dough in half. Press half dough onto bottom of sprayed 9-inch square baking pan or 7 x 11-inch baking pan.

☐ Beat cream cheese, sugar and egg in bowl until smooth. Spread over crust. Crumble remaining cookie dough over top.

☐ Bake for 35 to 40 minutes or until toothpick inserted in center comes out clean. Cool on wire rack. Cut into bars. Refrigerate leftovers. Serves 12.

SWEET WALNUT BARS

1⅔ cups graham cracker crumbs
1½ cups coarsely chopped walnuts
1 (14 ounce) can sweetened condensed milk
¼ cup flaked coconut, optional

☐ Preheat oven to 350°.

☐ Place graham cracker crumbs and walnuts in bowl. Slowly add sweetened condensed milk, coconut and pinch of salt. Mixture will be very thick.

☐ Pack into sprayed 9-inch square pan. Pack mixture down with back of spoon.

☐ Bake for 35 minutes. When cool cut into squares. Makes 16.

SPECIAL APRICOT BARS

1¼ cups flour
¾ cup packed brown sugar
6 tablespoons (¾ stick) butter
¾ cup apricot preserves

☐ Preheat oven to 350°.

☐ Combine flour, brown sugar and butter in bowl and mix well.

☐ Place half mixture in 9-inch square baking pan. Spread apricot preserves over top of mixture. Add remaining flour mixture over top.

☐ Bake for 30 minutes. Cut into squares. Makes 1 dozen.

Chocolate-Cherry Bars

1 (18 ounce) box devil's food cake mix
1 (20 ounce) can cherry pie filling
2 eggs
1 cup milk chocolate chips

☐ Preheat oven to 350°.

☐ Mix all ingredients in large bowl with spoon and blend well.

☐ Pour batter into sprayed, floured 9 x 13-inch baking dish.

☐ Bake for 25 to 30 minutes or until toothpick inserted in center comes out clean. Cool and frost.

Chocolate Cherry Bars Frosting:

3 (1 ounce) squares semi-sweet chocolate, melted
1 (3 ounce) package cream cheese, softened
½ teaspoon vanilla
1½ cups powdered sugar

☐ Beat chocolate, cream cheese and vanilla in medium bowl until smooth. Gradually beat in powdered sugar.

☐ Pour over chocolate-cherry bars. Makes 1½ dozen.

SHORTCUT BLONDE BROWNIES

1 (1 pound) box light brown sugar
4 eggs
2 cups biscuit mix
2 cups chopped pecans

☐ Preheat oven to 350°.

☐ Beat brown sugar, eggs and biscuit mix in bowl. Stir in pecans and pour into sprayed 9 x 13-inch baking pan.

☐ Bake for 35 minutes. Cool and cut into squares. Makes 1½ dozen.

SECRET SNICKERS BROWNIES

1 (18 ounce) box German chocolate cake mix
¾ cup (1½ sticks) butter, melted
½ cup evaporated milk
4 (3 ounce) Snickers® candy bars, cut in ⅛-inch slices

☐ Preheat oven to 350°.

☐ Combine cake mix, butter and evaporated milk in large bowl. Beat on low speed until mixture blends well.

☐ Place half batter in sprayed, floured 9 x 13-inch baking pan. Bake for 10 minutes.

☐ Place candy bar slices evenly over brownies. Drop spoonfuls of remaining batter over candy bars and spread as evenly as possible.

☐ Bake for additional 20 minutes. When cool, cut into squares. Makes 1½ dozen.

CHEERLEADER BROWNIES

Great, chewy, chocolaty brownies! They won't last long!

⅔ cup canola oil
2 cups sugar
4 eggs, beaten
⅓ cup corn syrup
½ cup cocoa
1½ cups flour
1 teaspoon baking powder
2 teaspoons vanilla
1 cup chopped pecans

☐ Preheat oven to 350°.

☐ Mix oil, sugar, eggs and corn syrup in large bowl.

☐ In separate bowl, mix cocoa, flour, 1 teaspoon salt and baking powder.

☐ Slowly pour cocoa-flour mixture into sugar mixture and mix thoroughly. Stir in vanilla and pecans.

☐ Pour into sprayed 9 x 13-inch baking pan and bake for about 50 minutes or until toothpick inserted in center comes out clean. Makes 12 to 14 brownies.

CHOCOLATE-PEANUT BUTTER CRISPS

1 (10 count) package 8-inch flour tortillas
1 (8 ounce) package semi-sweet chocolate chips
⅓ cup creamy or crunchy peanut butter
1 (14 ounce) can sweetened condensed milk

☐ Preheat oven to 350°.

☐ Cut each tortilla into 8 wedges and place on baking sheet. Bake for 10 minutes and cool on rack.

☐ Melt chocolate in heavy saucepan over low heat and stir constantly.

☐ Stir in peanut putter, sweetened condensed milk and 2 tablespoons water and heat thoroughly. (If sauce is too thick, add 1 teaspoon water at a time, until sauce smoothly drizzles on foil.)

☐ Drizzle warm chocolate sauce over wedges or serve immediately in chafing dish or fondue pot and dip with crisp tortilla wedges. Serves 6 to 8.

SURPRISE CHOCOLATES

2 pounds white chocolate or almond bark
2 cups Spanish peanuts
2 cups small pretzel sticks, broken

☐ Melt chocolate in double boiler. Stir in peanuts and pretzels.

☐ Drop by teaspoonfuls onto wax paper. Work fast because mixture hardens quickly.

☐ Place in freezer for 1 hour before storing at room temperature. Makes about 2 dozen.

SCOTCH CRUNCHIES

½ cup crunchy peanut butter
1 (6 ounce) package butterscotch chips
2½ cups frosted flakes cereal
½ cup peanuts

☐ Combine peanut butter and butterscotch chips in large saucepan over low heat. Stir until butterscotch chips melt. Stir in cereal and peanuts.

☐ Drop teaspoonfuls of mixture onto wax paper. Refrigerate until firm. Store in airtight container. Makes 2 dozen.

BEST BUTTERSCOTCH BITES

1 (12 ounce) and 1 (6 ounce) packages butterscotch chips
2¼ cups chow mein noodles
½ cup chopped walnuts
¼ cup flaked coconut

☐ Melt butterscotch chips in double boiler. Add noodles, walnuts and coconut.

☐ Drop tablespoonfuls of mixture onto wax paper. Makes 2 dozen.

PEANUTTY COCOA PUFFS

¾ cup light corn syrup
1¼ cups sugar
1¼ cups crunchy peanut butter
4½ cups cocoa puff cereal

☐ Bring syrup and sugar in large saucepan to a rolling boil. Stir in peanut butter and mix well. Stir in cocoa puffs.

☐ Drop teaspoonfuls of mixture onto wax paper. Makes 3 dozen.

In 1877 Quaker® Oats received the first trademark registered for a breakfast cereal. The logo had a man dressed in Quaker clothing.

In 1891 Quaker® introduced premium products inside boxes of Quaker® cereal. In the same year Quaker became the first company to put a recipe on the product box.

In 1908 the first oatmeal cookie recipe appeared on the Quaker® cereal box. The ingredients included butter, sugar, flour and 3 cups of Quaker® oats.

BANANA-VANILLA PIE

1 banana, sliced
1 (9 ounce) graham cracker piecrust
2 cups cold milk
⅓ cup sugar
2 (3.4 ounce) packages vanilla instant pudding mix
1 (8 ounce) carton French vanilla frozen whipped topping, thawed, divided

☐ Place banana slices in graham cracker piecrust.

☐ Pour milk in medium-size bowl and add sugar and pudding mixes; beat about 2 minutes. Mixture will be thick. Fold in half of whipped topping and spoon into piecrust.

☐ Refrigerate before serving. Top each serving with dabs of remaining whipped topping. Serves 8.

In the early 1900's the Corn Products Refining Company of New York introduced Karo® syrup made with corn and generically known as corn syrup. Until this syrup was introduced, housewives took syrup containers to the grocery store for the grocer to fill their containers from barrels.

Because of the development of corn syrup, the modern pecan pie came into its own. A corporate executive's wife made a Karo® Pie, which is the modern-day Pecan Pie. The recipe helped to propel Karo® syrup nationwide to make pecan pie's popularity go well beyond the South.

CLASSIC PEACH PIE

2 (9 inch) refrigerated piecrusts
5 cups peeled, sliced fresh peaches
¾ cup sugar
⅓ cup flour
1 tablespoon lemon juice
2 tablespoons butter

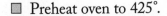

☐ Preheat oven to 425°.

☐ Place one piecrust into pie pan.

☐ In large bowl, gently mix peaches and sugar. (If peaches are tart, add a little more sugar.) Stir in flour and lemon juice. Spoon mixture into pie crust.

☐ Dot with butter and place remaining piecrust over filling.

☐ Fold edges of top crust under edges of bottom crust to seal. Flute edges with fingers and cut several slits in top crust.

☐ Bake for 15 minutes and remove pie from oven. Cover edges of piecrust with foil to prevent excessive browning.

☐ Return to oven and bake for 15 to 20 minutes or until pie is bubbly and crust is light, golden brown. Serves 8 to 10.

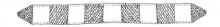

INDIVIDUAL APPLE PIES

2 tart baking apples
⅔ cup sugar
¾ teaspoon cinnamon
2 tablespoons flour
1 sheet of frozen or refrigerated piecrust (½ of 15 ounce package)

☐ Preheat oven to 425°.

☐ Peel, core and chop apples. In bowl, combine chopped apples, sugar, cinnamon and flour.

☐ Unroll piecrust flat and cut five circles. Place each circle inside a muffin cup. Evenly divide apple mixture. Using remaining piecrust, cut into strips and place on top of apple mixture.

☐ Place about ⅓ cup water in extra muffin cup(s). Bake for 18 minutes or until bubbling and remove from pan when cool. Serves 5.

MERRY BERRY PIE

1 (6 ounce) package strawberry gelatin mix
1 cup whole cranberry sauce
½ cup cranberry juice
1 (8 ounce) carton frozen whipped topping, thawed
1 (9 inch) baked piecrust

☐ Dissolve gelatin in 1 cup boiling water in bowl. Add cranberry sauce and juice and refrigerate until mixture begins to thicken.

☐ Fold in whipped topping, refrigerate again until mixture mounds and pour into piecrust.

☐ Refrigerate for several hours before serving. Serves 8.

OLD-FASHIONED BLUEBERRY PIE

2 (9 inch) refrigerated piecrusts
4 cups fresh blueberries
¾ cup sugar
¼ cup flour
2 tablespoons lemon juice
2 tablespoons butter

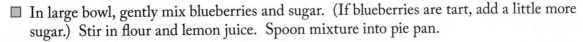

☐ Preheat oven to 425°.

☐ Place one piecrust in 9-inch pie pan.

☐ In large bowl, gently mix blueberries and sugar. (If blueberries are tart, add a little more sugar.) Stir in flour and lemon juice. Spoon mixture into pie pan.

☐ Dot with butter and place top crust over pie filling.

☐ Fold edges of top crust under edges of bottom crust to seal. Flute edges with fingers and cut several slits in top crust.

☐ Bake for 15 minutes and remove pie from oven. Cover edges of piecrust with strips of foil to prevent excessive browning.

☐ Return to oven and bake for 30 to 40 minutes or until pie is bubbly and crust is golden brown. Serves 8 to 10.

MAGIC CHERRY PIE

2 (6 ounce) cartons cherry yogurt
1 (3 ounce) package cherry gelatin
1 (8 ounce) carton frozen whipped topping, thawed
1 (6 ounce) ready shortbread piecrust

☐ Combine yogurt and dry gelatin in bowl and mix well.

☐ Fold in whipped topping and spoon into piecrust.

☐ Freeze. Take out of freezer 20 minutes before slicing. Serves 8.

TIP: *Add several spoonfuls of cherry pie filling on top of this pie and it will be even better.*

CHERRY-PECAN PIE

1 (14 ounce) can sweetened condensed milk
¼ cup lemon juice
1 (8 ounce) carton frozen whipped topping, thawed
1 cup chopped pecans
1 (20 ounce) can cherry pie filling
2 (6 ounce) ready graham cracker piecrusts

☐ Combine condensed milk and lemon juice in bowl. Stir well and fold in whipped topping.

☐ Fold in pecans and pie filling.

☐ Spoon into piecrusts. Refrigerate overnight. Serves 16.

STRAWBERRY-CREAM CHEESE PIE

2 (10 ounce) packages frozen sweetened strawberries, thawed
2 (8 ounce) packages cream cheese, softened
⅔ cup powdered sugar
1 (8 ounce) carton frozen whipped topping, thawed
1 (6 ounce) ready chocolate crumb piecrust
Fresh strawberries

☐ Drain strawberries and set aside ¼ cup liquid. Combine cream cheese, set aside liquid, strawberries and powdered sugar in bowl and beat well.

☐ Fold in whipped topping and spoon into piecrust. Refrigerate overnight and garnish with fresh strawberries. Serves 8.

The annual California Strawberry Festival is held in Oxnard. Strawberries are the big treats and are used in strawberry shortcake, strawberry tarts, strawberries dipped in chocolate, strawberry smoothies and strawberry pizza.

STRAWBERRY-MARGARITA PIE

60 vanilla wafers
½ cup (1 stick) butter, melted
1 (14 ounce) can sweetened condensed milk
2 tablespoons lime juice
¼ cup tequila
⅓ cup triple sec liqueur
2 (10 ounce) packages sweetened strawberries, thawed, drained
1 (8 ounce) carton frozen whipped topping, thawed
Fresh strawberries

☐ Crush vanilla wafers in food processor or in resealable plastic bag with rolling pin. Combine crumbs and melted butter and mix well. Pour into large springform pan and pat down.

☐ Combine sweetened condensed milk, lime juice, tequila and triple sec in large bowl and stir well. Add strawberries and whipped topping and fold in.

☐ Pour into springform pan and freeze. Leave in freezer until ready to serve. Garnish with fresh strawberries. Serves 12.

FROZEN LEMONADE PIE

½ gallon vanilla ice cream, softened
1 (6 ounce) can frozen pink lemonade concentrate, softened
1 (6 ounce) ready graham cracker piecrust
1 (8 ounce) carton frozen whipped topping, thawed

☐ Combine ice cream and pink lemonade in large bowl. Work quickly.

☐ Spread mixture into piecrust and freeze.

☐ Top with layer of whipped topping before serving. Serves 8.

CREAMY LIME-ALMOND PIE

2 cups almond shortbread cookie crumbs, divided
½ cup (1 stick) butter, softened
1 cup lime sherbet, softened
1 cup frozen whipped topping, thawed

☐ Preheat oven to 350°.

☐ Mix 1½ cups cookie crumbs with butter and pat evenly into 9-inch pie pan.

☐ Bake for 10 minutes, remove and cool.

☐ Combine sherbet and whipped topping in bowl. Place in crumb crust and sprinkle remaining cookie crumbs on top.

☐ Freeze for 6 to 8 hours or until firm. Remove from freezer 20 minutes before serving. Serves 8.

FIVE-CITRUS CREAM PIE

1 (14 ounce) can sweetened condensed milk
1 (6 ounce) can frozen five-citrus concentrate, partially thawed
1 (8 ounce) carton frozen whipped topping, thawed
1 (6 ounce) ready graham cracker piecrust

☐ Stir sweetened condensed milk and five-citrus concentrate in bowl until they mix well.

☐ Fold into whipped topping. Spoon mixture into piecrust. Refrigerate for 6 to 8 hours. Serves 8.

PINEAPPLE FLUFF PIE

1 (20 ounce) can crushed pineapple with juice
1 (3.4 ounce) package instant lemon pudding mix
1 (8 ounce) carton frozen whipped topping, thawed
1 (6 ounce) ready graham cracker piecrust

☐ Combine pineapple and pudding mix in bowl and beat until it thickens.

☐ Fold in whipped topping. Spoon into piecrust.

☐ Refrigerate for several hours before serving. Serves 8.

EASY PUMPKIN PIE

2 eggs
1 (30 ounce) can pumpkin pie mix
1 (5 ounce) can evaporated milk
1 (9 inch) deep-dish piecrust

☐ Preheat oven to 400°.

☐ Beat eggs lightly in large bowl. Stir in pumpkin pie mix and evaporated milk. Pour mixture into piecrust.

☐ Cut 2-inch strips of foil and cover crust edges to prevent excessive browning.

☐ Bake for 15 minutes. Reduce temperature to 325° and bake for additional 40 minutes or until knife inserted in center comes out clean. Cool. Serves 8.

COOL CHOCOLATE PIE

22 large marshmallows
3 (5 ounce) milk chocolate-almond candy bars
1 (8 ounce) carton frozen whipped topping, thawed
1 (6 ounce) ready graham cracker piecrust

☐ Melt marshmallows and chocolate bars in double boiler. Cool partially and fold in whipped topping.

☐ Pour into piecrust. Refrigerate for several hours before serving. Serves 6.

BROWNIE PIE

Really a special treat!

1 cup sugar
½ cup flour
2 eggs, beaten slightly
½ cup (1 stick) butter, melted
1 cup chopped pecans
1 cup chocolate chips
1 teaspoon vanilla
1 (9 inch) refrigerated piecrust
Frozen whipped topping, thawed

☐ Preheat oven to 350°.

☐ Combine sugar and flour in bowl; add eggs and mix.

☐ Add slightly cooled melted butter and mix well. Add pecans, chocolate chips and vanilla.

☐ Pour into piecrust and bake for 45 minutes. Top with whipped topping. Serves 6 to 8.

MINT-CHOCOLATE ICE CREAM PIE

1 cup mint-chocolate chip ice cream, softened
1 cup frozen whipped topping, thawed
¾ cup crushed chocolate sandwich cookies with mint filling, divided
1 (6 ounce) ready chocolate cookie piecrust

☐ Combine ice cream, whipping topping and ½ cup crushed cookies in bowl.

☐ Place in piecrust and sprinkle remaining cookie crumbs on top.

☐ Freeze for 3 to 4 hours or until firm. Serves 8.

EASY CHOCOLATE PIE

2 (5 ounce) milk chocolate candy bars
1 (16 ounce) carton frozen whipped topping, thawed, divided
¾ cup chopped pecans
1 (9 inch) frozen or refrigerated piecrust, cooked, cooled

☐ Break candy into small pieces and melt in saucepan over low heat. Remove and cool for several minutes.

☐ Fold in two-thirds whipped topping and mix well. Stir in chopped pecans and pour into piecrust.

☐ Spread remaining whipped topping over pie. Refrigerate for at least 8 hours. Serves 8.

IRRESISTIBLE CHOCOLATE-AMARETTO PIE

3 (5 ounce) milk chocolate-almond candy bars
⅓ cup amaretto liqueur
2 (8 ounce) cartons whipping cream, whipped
1 (6 ounce) ready shortbread piecrust

☐ Melt chocolate in double boiler on low heat. Remove from heat and pour in amaretto.

☐ Stir chocolate and amaretto for about 10 or 15 minutes until mixture reaches room temperature.

☐ Fold in whipped cream. Pour into piecrust. Refrigerate for several hours before serving. Serves 8.

CARAMEL ICE CREAM PIE

1 (18 ounce) roll refrigerated butterscotch cookie dough
½ gallon vanilla ice cream
1 (12 ounce) jar caramel ice cream topping

☐ Bake cookies according to package directions.

☐ When cookies cool, crumble and place in 10-inch deep-dish pie pan, but set aside about ½ cup crumbs to use for topping.

☐ Place ice cream in bowl to soften. Stir caramel sauce into ice cream (do not mix completely) and spoon mixture into pie pan.

☐ Sprinkle remaining crumbs over top of pie and freeze. Serves 8.

CREAM CHEESE CRUST

Use with any pie filling.

½ cup (1 stick) butter, softened
1 (3 ounce) package cream cheese, softened
1 cup flour

☐ Beat butter, cream cheese and flour in bowl.

☐ Blend with pastry blender or with fork until mixture can be made into ball. Refrigerate pastry for 1 hour.

☐ Roll out on floured surface to 9-inch round. Place in 9-inch pie pan and press down evenly. Makes 1 (9 inch) piecrust.

TIP: Fill crust with your favorite pie filling and top with whipped topping, nuts or fruit slices.

While trying to manufacture Neufchatel cheese in 1872, William Lawrence of Chester, New York accidentally invented cream cheese. He wrapped it in a foil package and gave it the name, Philadelphia Brand Cream Cheese in 1880. By 1928 the cheese was well known and James Kraft, who invented pasteurized cheese, bought the brand and began pasteurizing cream cheese. Today it is the most popular cream cheese used in cheesecakes.

BLUEBERRY BUCKLE

Excellent for brunch!

2 cups flour
¾ cups sugar
2 teaspoons baking powder
1 egg
¾ cup milk
¼ cup (½ stick) butter, softened
2 cups blueberries

☐ Preheat oven to 375°.

☐ Combine flour, sugar, baking powder, egg, ½ teaspoon salt, milk and butter in large bowl. Fold in blueberries carefully.

☐ Spread in sprayed 9-inch square pan.

TOPPING:

¼ cup (½ stick) butter, softened
⅓ cup flour
½ cup sugar
½ teaspoon ground cinnamon

☐ Combine butter, flour, sugar and cinnamon in bowl and sprinkle over blueberry mixture.

☐ Bake for 35 to 40 minutes. Serve warm. Serves 8 to 10.

CHOICE STRAWBERRY CRUNCH

2 (20 ounce) cans strawberry pie filling
1 (18 ounce) box white cake mix
1 cup slivered almonds
½ cup (1 stick) butter

☐ Preheat oven to 350°.

☐ Spread pie filling evenly in sprayed, floured 9 x 13-inch baking pan.

☐ Sprinkle dry cake mix evenly and smooth over top. Sprinkle almonds evenly over cake mix.

☐ Cut butter into ⅛-inch slices and place over entire surface.

☐ Bake for 40 to 45 minutes or until top is brown. Serves 12 to 14.

While some histories tell us that cobblers, crunches and crisps are probably derivatives of English pies, it is reasonable to assume their origins started in the northeast with the colonists. The place of origin is less important than the imagination of the people who settled America. They used only ingredients they could carry or find in the general area where they lived. They adapted the recipes from their home countries and came up with purely American originals.

SIMPLE APPLE CRISP

Peeling apples is the most difficult part of this recipe.

5 cups peeled, cored, sliced apples
½ cup (1 stick) butter, melted
1 cup quick-cooking oats
½ cup firmly packed brown sugar
⅓ cup flour

☐ Preheat oven to 375°.

☐ Place apple slices in sprayed, floured 8-inch or 9-inch square baking pan. Combine butter, oats, brown sugar and flour in bowl and sprinkle mixture over apples.

☐ Bake for 40 to 45 minutes or until apples are tender and topping is golden brown. Serves 9.

TIP: *For a change, add 1 teaspoon cinnamon and ½ cup raisins or dried cranberries (Craisins®) to apples before placing in baking pan.*

Cobbler-type dishes are called a variety of names: crisps, crumbles, Brown Bettys, grunts and slumps. They all are based on a fruit filling with biscuit or pastry on top. Crisps have crumbs on top and are called crumbles in England.

STRAWBERRY-FRUIT PIZZA

1 (18 ounce) package sugar cookie dough
1 (8 ounce) package cream cheese, softened
½ cup sugar
1 pint strawberries or raspberries
⅓ cup strawberry jelly for glaze

☐ Preheat oven to 350°.

☐ Spread cookie dough onto unsprayed pizza pan. Bake for 10 to 15 minutes or until dough is light brown around edges and cooked in middle.

☐ Remove from oven and cool.

☐ Blend cream cheese and sugar until light and fluffy. Spread mixture over cooled crust.

☐ Arrange strawberries on top. Warm strawberry jelly and brush over strawberries with pastry brush.

☐ Refrigerate before serving. Serves 10.

CARAMEL-APPLE DELIGHT

3 (2 ounce) Snickers® candy bars, frozen
2 Granny Smith apples, chopped
1 (12 ounce) carton frozen whipped topping, thawed
1 (3.4 ounce) package instant vanilla pudding mix

☐ Smash frozen candy bars in wrappers with hammer.

☐ Mix all ingredients in bowl and refrigerate. Serves 4 to 6.

TIP: Before smashing candy bars, place in resealable plastic bag to prevent any spills or flying pieces.

SWEET BLUEBERRY FLUFF

1 (20 ounce) can blueberry pie filling
1 (20 ounce) can crushed pineapple, drained
1 (14 ounce) can sweetened, condensed milk
1 (8 ounce) carton frozen whipped topping, thawed

☐ Mix pie filling, pineapple and sweetened condensed milk in bowl.

☐ Fold in whipped topping. Pour into parfait glasses. Refrigerate. Serves 6 to 8.

SPICED PEARS

1 (15 ounce) can pear halves
⅓ cup packed brown sugar
¾ teaspoon ground nutmeg
¾ teaspoon ground cinnamon

☐ Drain pears. Mix syrup from pears, brown sugar, nutmeg and cinnamon in saucepan and bring to a boil.

☐ Reduce heat and simmer uncovered for 5 to 8 minutes; stir often.

☐ Add pears and simmer 5 minutes longer or until thoroughly hot. Serves 4.

SPICED AMARETTO PEACHES

4½ cups peeled, sliced fresh peaches
½ cup amaretto liqueur
½ cup sour cream
½ cup packed brown sugar

☐ Lay peaches in 2-quart baking dish. Pour amaretto over peaches and spread sour cream over peaches. Sprinkle brown sugar evenly over all.

☐ Broil mixture until it heats thoroughly and sugar melts. Serves 6.

DIVINE STRAWBERRIES

This is wonderful served over pound cake or just served in sherbet glasses.

1 quart fresh strawberries
1 (20 ounce) can pineapple chunks, well drained
2 bananas, sliced
2 (16 ounce) cartons strawberry glaze

☐ Cut strawberries in half (or in quarters if strawberries are very large).

☐ Combine strawberries, pineapple chunks and bananas in bowl.

☐ Fold in strawberry glaze and refrigerate. Serves 6 to 8.

CARAMEL-AMARETTO DESSERT

1 (9 ounce) bag small chocolate covered toffee candy bars, crumbled
30 caramels
⅓ cup amaretto liqueur
½ cup sour cream
1 cup whipping cream

☐ Set aside about ⅓ cup crumbled toffee bars. Spread remaining candy crumbs in sprayed 7 x 11-inch dish.

☐ Melt caramels with amaretto in saucepan. Cool to room temperature.

☐ Stir in sour cream and whipping cream; whip until thick. Pour into 9-inch dish and top with set aside candy crumbs. Cover and freeze. Cut into squares to serve. Serves 16.

WINTER WONDERLAND DESSERT

28 chocolate cream-filled chocolate sandwich cookies, divided
2¾ cups milk
3 (3.4 ounce) packages instant pistachio pudding mix
1 (8 ounce) carton frozen whipped topping, thawed

☐ Crush cookies and set aside ⅔ cup. Place remaining crushed cookies in 9 x 13-inch dish.

☐ Combine milk and pudding mix in bowl. Mix for about 2 minutes or until it thickens. Pour over crushed cookies.

☐ Spread whipped topping over pistachio pudding.

☐ Sprinkle set aside cookie crumbs over whipped topping and refrigerate overnight before serving. Serves 12.

COFFEE MALLOW

3 cups miniature marshmallows
½ cup hot, strong coffee
1 (8 ounce) carton whipping cream, whipped
½ teaspoon vanilla

☐ Combine marshmallows and coffee in large saucepan. Cook on low heat, stirring constantly until marshmallows melt.

☐ Cool mixture to room temperature. Fold in whipped cream and vanilla.

☐ Pour into individual dessert glasses. Refrigerate until ready to serve. Serves 4 to 6.

ALMOND-CAPPED PEACH SUNDAES

1 (1 pint) carton vanilla ice cream
¾ cup peach preserves, warmed
¼ cup chopped almonds, toasted
¼ cup flaked coconut

☐ Divide ice cream into 4 sherbet dishes. Top with preserves.

☐ Sprinkle with almonds and coconut. Serves 4.

CHOCOLATE-COCONUT MIST

2 (14 ounce) packages flaked coconut
2 tablespoons butter, melted
1⅓ cups semi-sweet chocolate chips, melted
3 quarts mint chocolate chip ice cream

☐ Combine coconut, butter and chocolate in bowl until mixture blends well.

☐ Shape ⅓ cupfuls into 2½-inch nests on baking sheet covered with wax paper. Refrigerate until firm.

☐ Just before serving top each nest with ½ cup ice cream. Serves 10.

COOKIES AND CREAM DESSERT

25 Oreo® cookies, crushed
½ gallon vanilla ice cream, softened
1 (15 ounce) can chocolate syrup
1 (12 ounce) carton frozen whipped topping, thawed

☐ Press crushed cookies in 9 x 13-inch baking dish. Spread ice cream over cookies.

☐ Pour syrup over ice cream and top with whipped topping. Freeze overnight.

☐ Slice into squares to serve. Serves 10.

FUDGY ICE CREAM DESSERT

19 ice cream sandwiches
1 (12 ounce) carton frozen whipped topping, thawed
1 (12 ounce) jar hot fudge ice cream topping
1 cup salted peanuts, divided

☐ Cut 1 ice cream sandwich in half. Place 1 whole and one-half sandwich along short side of 9 x 13-inch pan. Arrange 8 sandwiches in opposite direction in pan.

☐ Spread with half whipped topping. Spoon teaspoonfuls of fudge topping onto whipped topping. Sprinkle with ½ cup peanuts.

☐ Repeat layers with remaining ice cream sandwiches, whipped topping and peanuts (pan will be full). Cover and freeze. Serves 12.

TIP: To serve, take out of freezer 20 minutes before serving.

BANANA SPLIT FLOAT

2 ripe bananas, mashed
3 cups milk
1 (10 ounce) package frozen sweetened strawberries, thawed
1½ pints chocolate ice cream, divided

☐ Place bananas in blender and add milk, strawberries and ½ pint chocolate ice cream. Beat just until they blend well.

☐ Pour into tall, chilled glasses and top each with scoop of chocolate ice cream. Makes 1 quart.

INDEX

C

Cabbage

Cakes

Cakes, Cookies, Pies & Desserts

N

Nuts

P

S

Salads

Sandwiches

Cookbooks Published by Cookbook Resources, LLC
Bringing Family and Friends to the Table

The Best 1001 Short, Easy Recipes
1001 Slow Cooker Recipes
1001 Short, Easy, Inexpensive Recipes
1001 Fast Easy Recipes
1001 America's Favorite Recipes
1001 Easy Inexpensive Grilling Recipes
1,001 Easy Potluck Recipes
Easy Slow Cooker Cookbook
Busy Woman's Slow Cooker Recipes
Busy Woman's Quick & Easy Recipes
Easy Meals-in-Minutes
365 Easy Soups and Stews
365 Easy Chicken Recipes
365 Easy One-Dish Recipes
365 Easy Soup Recipes
365 Easy Vegetarian Recipes
365 Easy Casserole Recipes
365 Easy Pasta Recipes
365 Easy Slow Cooker Recipes
Super Simple Cupcake Recipes
Easy Garden Fresh Recipes & Homemade Preserves (Photos)
Easy Soups and Slow Cooker Recipes (Photos)
Leaving Home Cookbook and Survival Guide
Essential 3-4-5 Ingredient Recipes
Ultimate 4 Ingredient Cookbook
Easy Cooking with 5 Ingredients
The Best of Cooking with 3 Ingredients
Easy Diabetic Recipes
Ultimate 4 Ingredient Diabetic Cookbook
4-Ingredient Recipes for 30-Minute Meals
Cooking with Beer
The Washington Cookbook
The Pennsylvania Cookbook
The California Cookbook
Best-Loved Canadian Recipes
Best-Loved Recipes from the Pacific Northwest

Easy Homemade Preserves (Handbook with Photos)
Garden Fresh Recipes (Handbook with Photos)
Easy Slow Cooker Recipes (Handbook with Photos)
Cool Smoothies (Handbook with Photos)
Easy Cupcake Recipes (Handbook with Photos)
Easy Soup Recipes (Handbook with Photos)
Classic Tex-Mex and Texas Cooking
Best-Loved Southern Recipes
Classic Southwest Cooking
Miss Sadie's Southern Cooking
Classic Pennsylvania Dutch Cooking
The Quilters' Cookbook
Healthy Cooking with 4 Ingredients
Trophy Hunter's Wild Game Cookbook
Recipe Keeper
Simple Old-Fashioned Baking
Quick Fixes with Cake Mixes
Kitchen Keepsakes & More Kitchen Keepsakes
Cookbook 25 Years
Texas Longhorn Cookbook
The Authorized Texas Ranger Cookbook
Gifts for the Cookie Jar
All New Gifts for the Cookie Jar
The Big Bake Sale Cookbook
Easy One-Dish Meals
Easy Potluck Recipes
Easy Casseroles Cookbook
Easy Desserts
Sunday Night Suppers
Easy Church Suppers
365 Easy Meals
Gourmet Cooking with 5 Ingredients
Muffins In A Jar
A Little Taste of Texas
A Little Taste of Texas II
Ultimate Gifts for the Cookie Jar

cookbook resources® LLC

www.cookbookresources.com
Toll-Free 866-229-2665
Your Ultimate Source for Easy Cookbooks